SURVIVORS

IN THE

SHADOWS

SURVIVORS IN THE SHADOWS

THREATENED AND ENDANGERED MAMMALS OF THE AMERICAN WEST

BY GARY TURBAK
ILLUSTRATED BY LAWRENCE ORMSBY

NORTHLAND PUBLISHING

To Abby Fullerton and all the other young people like her
who really care about our wild and natural world.
                                    —G.T.

In memory of Betti Albrecht, who began and inspired this book.
                                    —L.O.

FRONTISPIECE: *Southern Sea Otter*

The artist would like to thank the following biologists and photographers for help in providing research to illustrate the animals in this book: George Andrejko, Arizona Game and Fish, page xiii; Alan Carey, pages i, 10, 23, 45, 67, 100, 104, 108, and 111; Tim Haugen, pages 18-19; Ken Jenkins, pages 34-35, 83, and 134-135; Bob Miles, page 37; Elaine Harding-Smith, pages 48-49; Mary Swanson, page 53; Tom Ulrich, pages 14, 28, and 80; Norbert Wu and Ken and Cat Sweeney, pages 67 and 70-71; and Norbert Wu, frontispiece (pages ii-iii).

FIRST EDITION
ISBN 0-87358-561-5
Library of Congress Catalog Card Number 93-4723

Book design by Carole Thickstun

Cataloging in Publication Data
Turbak, Gary.
    Survivors in the shadows : threatened and endangered mammals of the American west / by Gary Turbak ; illustrated by Lawrence Ormsby.—1st ed.
        p.   cm.
    Includes bibliographical references (p.   ) and index.
    ISBN 0-87358-561-5 : $19.95
    1. Mammals—West (U.S.) 2. Endangered species—West (U.S.) 3. Wildlife conservation—West (U.S.) I. Ormsby, Lawrence, 1946–. II. Title
QL719.W47T87   1993
599'.0042'0978—dc20   93-4723

Printed in Hong Kong by Sing Cheong

0421/7.5M/9-93

CONTENTS

Introduction vii

Western Mammals Listed as Threatened or Endangered by the Federal Government

Amargosa Vole 1
Bats 3
    Gray Bat 5
    Indiana Bat 6
    Ozark Big-Eared Bat 6
    Lesser Long-Nosed Bat 7
    Mexican Long-Nosed Bat 8
Black-Footed Ferret 9
Columbian White-Tailed Deer 14
Gray Wolf 16
Grizzly Bear 22
Guadalupe Fur Seal 25
Hualapai Mexican Vole 27
Jaguarundi 28
Kangaroo Rats 30
    Stephens' Kangaroo Rat 31
    Tipton Kangaroo Rat 32
    Giant Kangaroo Rat 32
    Fresno Kangaroo Rat 32
    Morro Bay Kangaroo Rat 32

Louisiana Black Bear 33
Mount Graham Red Squirrel 36
Ocelot 40
Point Arena Mountain Beaver 43
Red Wolf 45
Salt Marsh Harvest Mouse 49
San Joaquin Kit Fox 52
Sonoran Pronghorn 55
Southern Sea Otter 58
Steller Sea Lion 61
Utah Prairie Dog 63
Whales 67
    Humpback Whale 69
    Sperm Whale 73
    Right Whale 75
    Sei Whale 76
    Fin Whale 77
    Blue Whale 78
Woodland Caribou 80

Western Mammals Listed as Threatened or Endangered by the State Governments

Arizona 85
    Black-Tailed Prairie Dog 85
    Chihuahuan Pronghorn 87
    Meadow Jumping Mouse 87
    Mexican Long-Tongued Bat 88
    Mexican Gray Wolf 88
    Navajo Mexican Vole 89
    New Mexican Banner-Tailed Kangaroo Rat 90
    Southwestern River Otter 90
    Water Shrew 91
    Yuma Puma 92
    Jaguar 93
    Federally Listed Species in Arizona 93
California 94
    Wolverine 94
    San Joaquin Antelope Squirrel 96
    Sierra Nevada Red Fox 96
    California Bighorn Sheep 97
    Mohave Ground Squirrel 97
    Island Fox 98
    Peninsular Bighorn Sheep 98
    Federally Listed Species in California 99

Colorado 101
    Lynx 101
    River Otter 102
    Wolverine 103
    Federally Listed Species in Colorado 103
Idaho 104
    Fisher 104
    Idaho Ground Squirrel 106
    Wolverine 107
    Federally Listed Species in Idaho 107
Kansas 108
    Eastern Spotted Skunk 108
    Federally Listed Species in Kansas 110
Montana 110
    Federally Listed Species in Montana 110
Nebraska 111
    River Otter 111
    Swift Fox 113
    Southern Flying Squirrel 113
    Federally Listed Species in Nebraska 114
Nevada 114

New Mexico **115**
    Desert Bighorn Sheep **115**
    Arizona Shrew **117**
    White-Sided Jackrabbit **117**
    Colorado Chipmunk **118**
    Spotted Bat **119**
    Least Shrew **119**
    Southern Yellow Bat **120**
    Least Chipmunk **120**
    Montane Vole **121**
    Pine Marten **122**
    Southern Pocket Gopher **122**
    Meadow Jumping Mouse **123**
    Federally Listed Species in New Mexico **123**
North Dakota **124**
    Northern Swift Fox **124**
    Black Bear **126**
    Fisher **126**
    Mountain Lion **126**
    River Otter **127**
    Federally Listed Species in North Dakota **127**
Oklahoma **127**
    Federally Listed Species in Oklahoma **127**
Oregon **128**
    Kit Fox **128**
    Wolverine **130**
    Federally Listed Species in Oregon **130**
South Dakota **131**
    Cougar **131**
    Black Bear **134**
    River Otter **135**
    Swift Fox **135**
    Federally Listed Species in South Dakota **135**

Texas **136**
    Jaguar **136**
    Eastern Big-Eared Bat **138**
    Manatee **138**
    Palo Duro Mouse **139**
    Margay **139**
    Coatimundi **141**
    Coue's Rice Rat **142**
    Mexican Wolf **142**
    Texas Kangaroo Rat **142**
    Black Bear **143**
    Southern Yellow Bat **143**
    Spotted Bat **143**
    Pygmy Sperm Whale **144**
    Dwarf Sperm Whale **144**
    Goose-Beaked Whale **145**
    Gervais' Beaked Whale **145**
    Short-Finned Pilot Whale **145**
    Atlantic Spotted Dolphin **146**
    Rough-Toothed Dolphin **146**
    Killer Whale **146**
    False Killer Whale **147**
    Pygmy Killer Whale **148**
    Federally Listed Species in Texas **148**
Utah **148**
    Federally Listed Species in Utah **148**
Washington **149**
    Pygmy Rabbit **149**
    Federally Listed Species in Washington **150**
Wyoming **150**
    Federally Listed Species in Wyoming **150**

Epilogue 151

    The Gray Whale: One that Came Back **151**
    Conclusion **154**

For Further Reading 155

Index 157

INTRODUCTION

Early in the sixteenth century, nearly a hundred years before the Pilgrims landed at Plymouth Rock, Frenchman Jacques Cartier explored the wilds of the north Atlantic. On rocky islands well off the Canadian coast, he encountered a bounty of black and white fowl standing some thirty inches tall and showing no fear of humans. These were the great auks. With stubby, flipperlike wings and a clumsy penguinesque posture, they must have brought a smile to the sailors' faces.

And a boost to their appetites. These birds, wrote Cartier, are "obviously and appetizingly edible, as big as geese and so fat it is marvelous." Unwary and unable to fly, the great auks dumbly stood their ground as Cartier's crew clubbed to death enough of them to fill two longboats. That night the Frenchmen dined well.

Soon, great auks became a favorite food of New World sailors. In 1536, English explorer Robert Hore stopped at one of the islands and instructed his crew to stretch a spare sail from ship to shore. Across this canvas bridge the sailors herded scores of great auks, which were then butchered, salted, and stored in wooden casks. In addition, auk eggs graced many a sixteenth-century dining table, their feathers filled pillows, their fat aided cooking, and their spare parts ended up as fish bait.

Originally, the birds thrived south to Massachusetts, but as human numbers rose in the New World, the teeming great auk populations gradually diminished. For nearly three centuries the birds hung on, but in June of 1844 collectors killed the last pair on Eldey Island off the coast of Iceland. The great auk that day earned the dubious distinction of being the first North American wildlife species to become extinct. It would not be the last.

THE EVOLVING WILDLIFE ETHIC

Wildlife has played an important role in America's development. Deer and turkeys fed colonists through the winter. The profitable fur trade opened up the West. Market hunting became a thriving nineteenth-century industry. The transcontinental railroad was built on bison meat. Wherever pioneers went, they encountered new and different species, often in numbers that defied the imagination. The wildlife supply seemed inexhaustible.

But, of course, it was not. As the country lurched its way through the nineteenth century, America gradually began to question the precept of unlimited wildlife. One by one, once bountiful species began limping toward oblivion—pronghorn antelope, turkeys, white-tailed deer, elk, beaver, and many more. Slowly, the idea sank into the American psyche that protection must replace exploitation, and a U.S. conservation ethic was born.

At the urging of sport hunters, states began passing laws to prohibit spring waterfowl shooting, boat-mounted battery guns, plume collecting, and—eventually—all market hunting. Next came closed seasons for hunters and the revolutionary notion of daily bag limits, concepts embraced by the emerging conservationist/hunter/wildlife constituency. State bureaus emerged to implement these laws, and federal statutes and agencies looked after migratory species. Finally, wildlife had legal standing. Early in this century, a quiet Wisconsin biologist named Aldo Leopold fused the good intentions of a conservation ethic with the good sense of science, creating the institution of wildlife management.

Eventually, the nation's newfound concern for wildlife became codified in sweeping laws that went far beyond hunting restrictions. The Pittman-Robertson Act raises billions of dollars for wildlife by taxing hunting paraphernalia. The Duck Stamp Act preserves millions of acres of wetland habitat. The Lacey Act prohibits the sale or interstate shipment of illegally taken game. And—finally—the Endangered Species Act casts a blanket of protection over all living things.

THE

ENDANGERED

SPECIES

ACT

Of all the environmental legislation ever enacted—anywhere in the world—the Endangered Species Act (ESA) is arguably the farthest reaching, most benign, and least selfish. The U.S. Congress passed precursor legislation in 1966 and 1969, but it was the 1973 ESA that forged a new relationship between Americans and the troubled species with whom they share the land. In 1973, a forward-looking Congress drew a line in the sand of American resource use and said the pell-mell destruction of wild things must stop. Conservationists refer to the ESA as the crown jewel of environmental laws.

The ESA directs that imperiled animals and plants be divided into two groups. Species facing the immediate possibility of extinction are labeled *endangered* and those likely to become endangered are considered *threatened.* Currently about seven hundred native species (and more worldwide) are on the two lists, and authorities add another fifty or so every year. Nearly four thousand more "candidate" species await inclusion on the lists, and several have become extinct before they could be included.

Perhaps the most remarkable aspect of the ESA is that it requires the administrative agencies—the U.S. Fish and Wildlife Service and the National Marine Fisheries Service—to list as threatened or endangered all imperiled species, not just those with overwhelming economic or aesthetic value. Economics may be considered later, but only biological evidence is to be considered when deciding which species to list as threatened or endangered.

In 1977 this fight-for-the-little-guy approach met big-time politics and development head-on when the massive Tellico Dam was proposed for the Little Tennessee River in Tennessee. In the river—and only there—lived an obscure three-inch fish called the snail darter, which would likely become extinct if the dam were built. Eventually, it took a special act of Congress to push the dam through, but only after the snail darter had been given a new home elsewhere. In the ensuing years, the ESA has stopped timber sales, moved interstate highways, curtailed home building, and in many other ways proved that it has the power to achieve its lofty goals.

The ESA works like this: The two lead agencies are charged with the task of identifying species threatened and endangered. Placement on either roster affords the plant or animal special protection and consideration when it or its habitat is in danger. Next, the agencies are supposed to formulate a detailed recovery plan outlining their goals for that creature and the steps required to return the species to a healthy status. (Only about half of all listed species currently have recovery plans in place.) The recovery plan may include a mixture of techniques to manage the wildlife itself, restore habitat, and militate against further collapse of the species. The ultimate goal of the ESA is not to put imperiled species on the threatened or endangered lists, but rather to get them off. A few animals—the American alligator, bald eagle, and peregrine falcon, for example—have staged remarkable recoveries thanks to the ESA, but hundreds of others continue to need lots of help. Most benefits of the ESA are still in the pipeline.

Naturally, not everyone is thrilled with the ESA. The simple presence of an endangered species can radically alter massive human endeavors and cost a lot of people a lot of money. Occasionally, the cabinet-level Endangered Species Committee has been convened by the Secretary of the Interior to settle a particularly controversial matter. Because this committee, in essence, has the power to determine whether a species will live or die, it has been nicknamed the God Squad.

Proponents and critics alike complain that the ESA is too much like a fire department, rushing in after the fact to minimize the damage. How much better it would be, they say, to protect habitat and entire ecosystems in the first place than to have to pick up the pieces later. The trend toward ecosystem management has in fact already begun, and if it truly blossoms, a great deal of future endangered species agony may be averted.

Protection of imperiled species does not come cheap. It costs $60,000 just to get a species listed, and the price tag for full recovery of all listed species has been estimated at $4.6 billion. And this does not include the sometimes considerable costs of lost production and lost jobs when habitat is set aside for threatened and endangered species. In addition, landowners can be denied profits when the presence of a threatened or endangered species prevents them from doing as they please with their property. No, saving these creatures will not come cheaply.

W H Y   P R E S E R V E   E N D A N G E R E D   S P E C I E S ?

Economics is just one of the motors running the world. There are plenty of excellent reasons for doing everything we can to preserve the planet's rich biological diversity.

Much of civilization has been built on the backs of wild flora and fauna. Much of our food comes from three plants—wheat, corn, and rice—that were once wild grasses. One-fourth of the world's medicines either come directly from living things or consist of synthesized compounds mimicking those found in nature. And who knows which plant or animal may next prove valuable to humans?

For years, loggers in the Northwest considered the yew a trash tree that got in the way of their operations. They burned it to make room for more valuable timber species. Recently, however, scientists discovered that yew bark helps cure cancer, and suddenly the tree is a highly valued species. Might hibernating grizzly bears one day show researchers how to slow human metabolism? Or humpback whales help us unlock the secrets of inter-species communication? Might some obscure animal edging toward extinction carry a cure for AIDS?

A diversity of wild species also creates stability in natural ecosystems. To be sure, the loss of any one animal will not bring an ecosystem crashing down. But where do we draw the line? Which species are essential and which are not? And to whom? In nature, all things are connected. Everyone knows, for example, that bald eagles don't eat grain, but in a sense they do. Wheat that feeds the insects that feed the fish really feeds eagles, too, but not one binocular-toting human eagle-watcher in a thousand senses that chainlike relationship. Individual species serve as our miners' canaries. Their extinction sends a strong signal that something is wrong.

Wild species also have aesthetic value. People enjoy seeing—or just thinking they might see—a black-footed ferret, a blue whale, a gray wolf, or any of hundreds of other threatened or endangered species. It adds pleasure to human lives just to have these animals around. And there is growing documentation that wildlife is good for the economy, too. The mushrooming promotion of "watchable wildlife" testifies to the fact that millions of people spend money on gasoline, food, lodging, binoculars, cameras, and dozens of other items in their pursuit of just looking at wildlife. Quite simply, wild creatures enhance the quality of our lives in real, definable, measurable ways.

Native wild species also have a host of scientific, educational, and historical values. Researchers have a tough time studying creatures that no longer exist. Students at all levels learn about natural systems best when the components are alive and well, not frozen forever solely on the pages of some textbook. The departure of each species radically diminishes our nation's heritage. America simply would not be the same without its bison, bald eagles, California condors, and their bestial brethren.

Above all else, however, humans have a moral obligation to nurture and care for the creatures with whom we share the planet. Try as we might, we cannot justify every creature's existence by measuring its contribution to human welfare. Who are we to play God, to say that this species or that should no longer live? While much has been written about the purported rights of individual animals, the real issue is whether humans have an obligation to preserve entire species. The ESA says we do.

E X T I N C T I O N

I S

F O R E V E R

Extinction is one of the few environmental changes that will never be undone. Dirty rivers can be made clean. Vanishing forests can be replanted. Sources of air pollution can be eliminated. But when a species vanishes, it is gone forever. Two decades ago, species (worldwide) were blinking out at the rate of about one per day. Now, a species disappears each hour. In the United States alone, five hundred animal and plant species have been lost since the Pilgrims landed in 1620. Most of these have disappeared since 1966.

Until rather recently, people pushed species toward extinction mostly by killing them directly—for their skins or their oil or because they preyed on livestock. This is no longer true. Today, habitat destruction is the extinction method of choice. When subdivisions, malls, pastures, roads, mines, clearcuts, oil wells, and other accoutrements of human progress replace wildlife habitat, the animals suffer. Sometimes the wildlife can go elsewhere, but we're rapidly running out of elsewheres, and with increasing frequency species are forced to make a last, desperate stand on some seemingly inconsequential section of forest, ocean, or prairie. Without human help, the animals always lose.

Early in this century, conservationist Aldo Leopold saw the juggernaut of development and the weight of human presence fracturing the natural order. We are taking the wild world apart piece by piece, he said, and the first rule of intelligent tinkering is to save all the pieces. The ESA is the safety net catching those pieces.

THE

ANIMALS

IN

THIS

BOOK

This volume deals with the threatened and endangered mammals of the American West. Because humans are mammals, we feel a special kinship with other species in this class. These often are the creatures we most like to see when we go wildlife watching—and those we most want to see preserved. To fully describe the natural history of each of these animals and explain the plight that brings it to the rim of extinction would take many volumes. Instead, each brief chapter here provides a snapshot of the species in words and illustrations. (In many instances, entire species are considered threatened or endangered. In other cases, however, only a certain subspecies, or race, is listed. Differences among related subspecies, or races, can be great or small and usually are pointed out in the animal's description. This book uses the terms *subspecies* and *race* interchangeably.) This volume is designed in such a way that it could be read cover to cover in just a few sittings; but also, you are invited to put it on your coffee table, where you may browse at your leisure, looking in on whatever creature currently piques your interest.

The first portion of this book covers the West's thirty-six mammalian species listed as threatened or endangered by the federal government. These range from rats in California to grizzlies in Montana to whales in the Pacific. If even a few members of a threatened or endangered species of mammal spend time in one of the seventeen westernmost states (Hawaii and Alaska excluded) or in the waters off their coasts, that species is included here.

Many states have mimicked the federal law by enacting their own endangered species statutes and compiling their own lists. The second part of this book is devoted to the state-listed animals that do not already appear on the federal rosters. For each western state that maintains such an inventory (a few do not), a single species is arbitrarily highlighted, and other state-listed species are briefly described. An animal listed as threatened or endangered by one state may be rather common elsewhere.

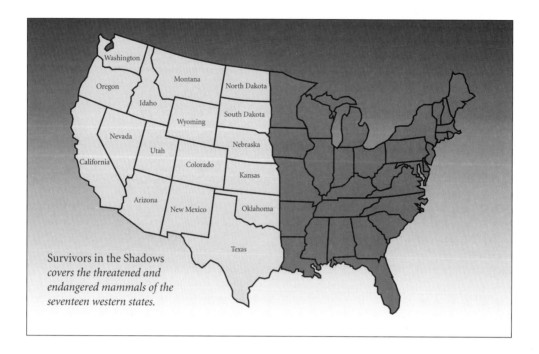

Survivors in the Shadows *covers the threatened and endangered mammals of the seventeen western states.*

Perhaps you will find a new wildlife friend here, a species you hardly knew before. Could that animal talk, it might ask for your help. And you can help: Become acquainted with threatened and endangered species in your state or region. Talk to wildlife authorities about them. Tell others what you learn. Volunteer your time in working with these species—or at the nearest wildlife refuge. Join a wildlife conservation group. Report violations of wildlife laws to authorities. In short, help take care of America's wildlife resource.

WESTERN MAMMALS

LISTED AS

THREATENED OR ENDANGERED

BY THE

FEDERAL GOVERNMENT

Hualapai Mexican Vole

AMARGOSA VOLE

Microtus californicus scirpensis
STATUS: ENDANGERED

This little creature is a study in contradictions and good-news-bad-news flip-flops. It also is one of the continent's most restricted mammals, living only in certain areas along three stretches of a single river in California. There are no population estimates, but authorities generally acknowledge that relatively few Amargosa voles exist.

In 1918, the bad news was that the Amargosa vole was thought to be extinct. This rodent, a subspecies of the more common California vole, had only been discovered in 1891, living in a single marshy region along the outflow of a spring near the Amargosa River near the town of Shoshone in Inyo County, California. Sometime during the next couple of decades, the vole disappeared from the marsh and—as far as anyone knew—from the face of the earth. For more than half a century, the fauna files spoke of the Amargosa vole in the past tense.

Then came the good news. In the 1970s, biologists discovered a few of the animals alive and well and hiding out—again in marshes—near the town of Tecopa, about eight miles from Shoshone and also along the Amargosa River. A few years later, more of the voles showed up a few miles downstream of Tecopa near the head of Amargosa Canyon. Meanwhile, Amargosas were found to exist also at the original discovery site near Shoshone. But that's all. These three small, isolated populations represent the sum total of Amargosa vole existence.

Voles are mouselike rodents that make their living by munching on green vegetation and staying out of the sight of hawks, owls, weasels, and other predators. As a group, they are stocky, hardy little creatures that range across the continent in all types of habitat and often in great numbers. Typically, they sport thick fur that almost hides their ears and makes their eyes appear small and beady. The characteristic that best distinguishes them from similar animals is their one- to three-inch furred tail (as opposed to the naked tail commonly associated with rats and mice). Typically, voles are tolerant of water, obsessed with grooming, and perpetually hungry. They nest both above and below ground and often create mazelike runways to get from A to B with speed and safety.

Beyond these generalizations, little is known about the Amargosa vole. It is colored with grays and browns and weighs a couple of ounces. When food quality and cover deteriorate on the surface, it spends much of its time in underground tunnels, even dining on subterranean plant fare. The tunnels probably also provide relief from the scorching sun in this part of California—not far from Death Valley.

The Amargosa vole's biggest contradiction is that it is a confirmed denizen of the desert that can exist *only* in a wet environment. Most wildlife species that inhabit the desert evolved organs and biological systems to help them cope with the shortage of water. But not this vole. Eons ago, large rivers flowed through this area, and the Amargosa vole chose for evermore a riparian lifestyle. So, in the midst of the Mohave Desert—probably the hottest and driest region of the country—the Amargosa vole can survive only on marshland that supports wet-ground plants such as bulrushes and saltgrass. Consequently, its range remains restricted to just those three sections of the Amargosa River.

As if that were not enough of a biological oxymoron, the biggest threat to this desert-dwelling rodent is—believe it or not—flooding. Much of the ancient river system in this area has retreated underground, but here and there (about ten linear miles total) the water returns to the surface to create at least occasional flows and enough year-round moisture to sustain the marsh terrain that sustains the vole. The rain that falls hereabouts, however, comes not in measured showers but in great seasonal torrents that spawn flash floods almost every year. The river's entire floodplain may remain inundated for several days. When this happens, the lowland-living voles head for higher ground, but some certainly drown, and all are put at risk of predator attack, starvation, extreme heat, or other calamity. Small portions of Amargosa valley terrain are high enough to escape most flooding yet low enough to support marshy vegetation. These precious areas constitute the core of Amargosa vole habitat and are the only places where these animals can live for more than just a few months in succession.

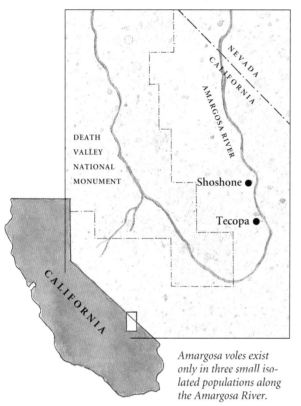

Amargosa voles exist only in three small isolated populations along the Amargosa River.

Another problem has been the presence of humans and their animals in the moist areas where the voles live. Some of the rodent's marshy homeland is maintained by springs, not river flow, but these are the very areas that attract people and livestock—both of which have a habit of altering wildlife habitat. For example, the spot where the vole was discovered in 1891 has been burned and converted to hog pasture. The spring that created this marsh has been diverted to provide water for a swimming pool and catfish farm. Most of the Amargosa River's original wetlands have been lost to human hands.

Once again, however, not all is as it seems. A railroad grading winds through much of the Amargosa's range, and it is this dike that creates most of the animal's best habitat by controlling flooding. In addition, much of the top vole habitat today gets its water from springs that have been drilled or enhanced by humans. On one hand, this endangered species suffers from some kinds of human disturbance. On the other, it remains rather dependent on human alterations to the land. The Amargosa vole is indeed an animal cloaked in irony.

BATS

See individual descriptions for scientific names
STATUS: ENDANGERED (ALL)

Note: The federal government classifies as endangered five species of bats that live—at least peripherally—in the West. The single description below covers the shared aspects of bat life, while the five entries that follow highlight individual differences.

First, a little review about these fascinating animals: Though it often requires some mental squinting to focus on this fact, bats are indeed mammals. They bear live young, nurture them with milk, and have generally hairy bodies. What sets bats apart from other mammals, of course, is their ability to fly. They are the only mammals to truly take leave of the earth. Contrary to popular belief, bats almost never get tangled in human hair; they are not blind (all have eyes, and many species actually can see quite well); they do not contract or transmit rabies more often than most other mammals; they are not rodents; and far from being dangerous, bats are among the best friends humans have in the wild world, primarily because of their appetite for insects.

Forty-three bat species exist in the United States, and there are approximately a thousand kinds worldwide. This means that one of every four mammalian species is a bat. Bats are nocturnal, leaving their roost—often in a cave, tunnel, tree, or old building—at night to feed and returning before dawn. Globally, they eat a variety of foods, but the five endangered species specialize either in insects or in pollen, nectar, and fruit.

Bats employ an extremely sophisticated technique called echolocation to navigate and to find prey. In flight, a bat emits a series of high-pitched sounds, about fifteen or so per second (in a frequency range above that detectable by human ears). These signals bounce off anything in the animal's path, and the bat listens for the returning sound, or echo. By analyzing this reflected signal, the bat can tell—instantly—the direction, distance, shape, size, texture, and speed of anything downrange.

Biologists believe that to pinpoint distance via echolocation, the bat must somehow "compute" the time that elapses between the sending and the receiving of the signal, then correlate that information with its "understanding" of the speed at which sound travels. And all this must be done in hundredths of a second while on the move. Because of the bat's need to hear returning echolocation signals, many species have greatly enlarged ears.

When an echo indicates the presence of something in a bat's path, the animal may boost its signals to hundreds per second for greater accuracy. Using echolocation, bats can pluck a mosquito from the air, pass through passageways barely bigger than their own bodies, and detect items as tiny as a human hair. Employing only sounds, bats can "see" just about everything except color. Human sonar and radar imitate this echolocation technique, but the bat's system—based on its extremely small size and infinitesimal energy requirement (after all, it can run on mosquitoes)—is much more efficient.

Echolocation only works, however, for distances under ten yards or so. In addition, certain insects have evolved the ability to hear the bat's signals—not unlike a fighter pilot knowing that an enemy has "locked on" to his plane with radar. Once they hear a bat signal, these insects may attempt to avoid death by diving for the ground or making other abrupt changes in their movements. At least one insect species has the ability to make sounds of its own and thereby partially jam the bat's echolocation system.

Insectivorous (insect-eating) bats—about 70 percent of all bat species—are the world's major consumer of nocturnal insects, with each bat devouring somewhere between one-fourth and one-half its weight in bugs every night. For some species, this can mean the downing of 3,000 or so airborne morsels before dawn. Feeding an entire colony requires tons of insects. The twenty million or so bats in a particular cave in Texas are believed to eat 250,000 pounds of insects each night.

Many bats are hibernators, spending the winter clustered together lethargically in a cave. Here, they survive by living off fat reserves. To slow the consumption of this limited supply of energy, their temperature may drop to just above freezing and their heart rate from about a thousand beats per minute (in flight) to only twenty-five. Three of five endangered bat species in the West (the gray, Indiana, and Ozark big-eared) are hibernators. Other northern hemisphere bat species (including the endangered lesser long-nosed bat and the Mexican long-nosed bat) migrate south like birds to escape winter.

Typically, hibernating bats mate in the fall, just before entering their long winter's nap. Throughout the winter, the female stores the male's sperm—live but as yet unused—within her body. In the spring, she ovulates, and the egg (or eggs) is fertilized. This method of reproduction accomplishes several important things. First, it permits mating to occur in the fall when food is still abundant and the bats are generally in good physical shape. Second, the delay in fertilization relieves the female of the burden of supporting a growing embryo during hibernation. And third, with sperm ready and waiting, gestation can begin as soon as the female is ready. This results in earlier births and more mature young when the crucial winter season rolls around again.

In spring, the pregnant females leave the hibernaculum (hibernating site) to form a nursery colony at some other place. A month or two later, the young—usually one per female—are born and nurse at the female's two chest nipples. When the adults depart the nursery cave to feed, they leave the youngsters clustered—often by the thousands—at the ceiling. The mothers locate their own offspring upon return by the unique sound of each baby's call. Bat youngsters are relatively well developed when born, and within a few weeks they're flying.

Bats have opted for a reproductive strategy that differs sharply from most other small mammals. Many rodents, for example, breed at young ages and produce large litters—sometimes several per year. The catch, however, is that most rodents live rather short lives. Bats, on the other hand, often don't mate until they're more than two years old, and then they produce only one or two offspring annually. Unlike rodents, though, bats have a relatively long life expectancy, with some individuals known to survive for thirty years.

Although some huge colonies remain in this country, many bat species have declined in recent years—certainly including most of those classified as endangered. Agricultural pesticides (transferred to the bats via the insects they eat), deforestation, pollution, and cave flooding all have taken a toll. But the greatest threat to bats today is human intrusion into roosting caves.

The presence of people in bat caves is always disturbing to the animals, but it is much worse in certain seasons. Humans entering a nursery cave can panic female bats into dropping their young—fatally—onto the cave floor or into water. And when people invade a hibernaculum, thousands of bats may awaken prematurely from their sleep and burn precious energy that is vital to their surviving the cold weeks still ahead. Scientists estimate that just one such awakening can cause the hibernating bats to expend ten to thirty days' worth of fat reserves. The result can be starvation.

Human intrusion into caves began in earnest during the last century, as spelunkers and seekers of minerals (such as saltpeter and onyx) headed underground in ever increasing numbers. More recently, some privately owned caves have been commercialized as tourist attractions, and others have been sealed shut as a safety precaution. Even some measures designed to protect bats have resulted in the animals' abandonment of caves. To keep people out of caves, authorities sometimes install bar gates at entrances. The spaces between the bars are too small to allow humans to enter, but supposedly are large enough to allow bats to pass through. On more than one occasion, however, conservationists learned too late that—for whatever reason—the bats would not fly through what seemed to human eyes to be a perfectly accessible gate.

Finally, there are the deliberate acts of violence perpetrated against bats. In various places vandals have swatted bats with clubs as they emerged in the evening, burned them from cave ceilings with torches, lit fires or exploded fireworks in caves, and in various other ways persecuted these harmless and often misunderstood creatures.

GRAY BAT

Myotis grisescens

The gray bat occupies limestone karst regions in the southeastern portion of the country, including parts of about a dozen states. It is included in this volume about mammals of the West because a few members of the species summer in northeastern Oklahoma.

The gray bat is relatively large (although it weighs less than half an ounce) and is covered with grayish brown fur that gives it a kind of woolly appearance. In the spring, gray bats may travel three hundred miles or more from their hibernacula to their summer ranges. Typically, a colony's summering ground consists of several roosting caves scattered along a few dozen miles of river or shoreline. Most feeding (for insects) occurs over or near water. Whenever possible, gray bats travel between roosting and feeding sites beneath a forest canopy—presumably to make themselves less vulnerable to predators such as owls.

At one time, the gray bat was among the most prosperous mammalian species on the continent—with a population of many millions. Certain individual hibernacula were known to contain 1.5 million of the animals. By 1982, however, the total gray bat population had declined to an estimated 1.6 million. There is no current overall population estimate, but authorities are confident that gray bat numbers have risen somewhat over the last dozen years—thanks mostly to protection of caves.

Most of the gray bat's problems center on its use of just a few major hibernacula. About 95 percent of all gray bats use only nine caves for hibernating, with about half the total population wintering in a single cave in Alabama. Even in the summer, gray bats—unlike some other species—rarely roost outside of caves, and their exacting subterranean requirements make many potential caves unsuitable. Gray bat acceptance of so few caves has made them especially vulnerable to human intrusion, and dozens of hibernacula and nursery caverns have been abandoned because humans entered the caves. This animal's future is dependent upon human ability and willingness to protect the caves they need.

INDIANA BAT

Myotis sodalis

Like the gray bat, the Indiana species exists primarily in the East, where it occupies portions of about twenty-five states. It is included here among western species because its range extends slightly into Oklahoma and Kansas. Most major hibernacula are in Indiana, Missouri, and Kentucky, where up to 85 percent of the population winters in only seven caves (with almost half using just two caves). Indiana bats hibernate in very dense clusters of up to three hundred individuals per square foot.

The Indiana species is a relatively small bat that makes its living plucking insects out of the air. Although it weighs only about a third of an ounce, its wings span ten inches. It has dark gray, dull fur. This species is named for the location, Wyandotte Cave in Indiana, where it was first described scientifically.

By 1983, the estimated population for this species was already down to about half a million, and that figure has since fallen appreciably—perhaps to 250,000. As with the gray bat, much of this decline is due to human disturbance of caves. In 1960, for example, two boys in Kentucky entered a cavern in a state park and tore masses of bats from the ceiling. They reportedly stoned, stomped, and drowned an estimated 10,000 of them.

Another incident nearly eliminated the hibernaculum for 140,000 Indiana bats. In 1986, two teenagers became trapped in an abandoned mine at Pilot Knob Hill in Missouri, the site of the bats' winter roost. Although the boys and the ensuing nineteen-hour rescue did not harm the animals directly, public pressure to seal up the mine threatened to eliminate a large percentage of all Indiana bats. In the end, however, the Pilot Knob Ore Company, owner of the mine, chose to donate the area to the U.S. Fish and Wildlife Service as a bat refuge.

Although loss of hibernacula is a big problem for the Indiana bat, its continuing decline may also be linked to summer habitat. During warm weather, Indiana bats often roost in hollow trees or beneath loose tree bark, and the lack of appropriate trees could limit their numbers as easily as a shortage of hibernacula. Also, there may be a problem with pesticides used in the highly agricultural areas where these bats spend the summer. This might explain why the Indiana species continues its fall, while the very similar gray bat—which lives in caves year round—is on the increase.

OZARK BIG-EARED BAT

Plecotus townsendii ingens

The plight of the Ozark big-eared bat is similar to that of the Indiana and gray species. Like the other two, this bat congregates in just a few areas for hibernating and raising young, making it vulnerable to disturbance. In addition, this subspecies of the Townsend's big-eared bat is often sought out by collectors because its extremely large ears give it an exotic appearance.

This race maintains colonies only in Oklahoma and Arkansas, although nonendangered "sister" subspecies of the Ozark bat exist throughout western North America. The Ozark bat has lost the use of some caves, but it appears that additional suitable sites continue to go unused, making the decline of this race something of a mystery. Actually, there has been some recent good news for this subspecies, as several new colonies have been discovered. The current population estimate is about 2,000—up from only 250 or so in 1979.

The Ozark big-eared bat is well named. Its ears protrude about an inch above its head—a rather great distance for so small an animal. The ears are so large that they actually connect in the center of the forehead, and they can be held erect or curled backward like the horns of a wild ram. This bat is brown ranging to reddish with a tan underside. Typically, this species occupies caves in all seasons, conducting short migrations between summer and winter caverns. It seems to prefer regions dominated by oak, hickory, beech, maple, and hemlock, and it feeds primarily on moths.

LESSER LONG-NOSED BAT

Leptonycteris curasoae yerbabuenae

This bat and the Mexican long-nosed bat are very different from the three other bats endangered in the West. As denizens of the arid Southwest, these two are at the northern edge of their range, which extends south into El Salvador (for the lesser long-nosed) and Guatemala (for the Mexican species). They are different, too, in the food they eat. Both are primarily vegetarians (although they eat some insects), specializing in the extraction of nectar and the collection of pollen from certain desert plants. The lengthy snouts that give these animals their names are adapted specifically for poking into flowers.

The lesser long-nosed bat (formerly called the Sanborn's long-nosed bat) is rather large as North American bats go, weighing up to an ounce and measuring three inches or so in length. Its wingspread is up to fifteen inches. It is gray to reddish brown. In this country, the lesser long-nosed bat exists only in south-central Arizona and in extreme southwestern New Mexico. As an occupant of desert scrub country, it roosts in mines and caves and feeds on several species of cactus and agave (century plant). Unlike the darting, erratic flight of the insectivorous bats, this species travels mostly in a direct line.

Lesser long-nosed bats can feed either perched on a plant or hovering before a flower like a hummingbird. In fact, in some places these bats are regular nighttime visitors to hummingbird feeders filled with sugar water. Hairlike protuberances on their three-inch tongues collect pollen and nectar. Later in the season, they also dine on whatever fruit is available. After a good night's feeding, their bellies may be so distended that the animals appear pregnant.

Researchers believe that the lesser long-nosed bat (along with similar species) plays a crucial role in the continued existence of desert plants such as agave and giant cacti. Over the eons, these plants and bats have evolved a classic symbiotic relationship. As the bats move from plant to plant feeding on pollen and nectar, they help ensure good pollination. The bats get a meal, the agave and cacti get pollinated, and everyone wins. To take advantage of their efficient nocturnal pollinators, the plants bloom only at night.

In September, lesser long-nosed bats depart the United States for Mexico, where they apparently remain active throughout the winter. They return to this country in April or May. In 1974, a survey of all known U.S. roosting sites turned up only 135 individuals, but more recent bat scholars question the thoroughness of that study. Today, there appear to be several summer colonies of lesser long-nosed bats in Arizona. Population tallies are hard to come by, but one survey of roosting sites in 1989 came up with an estimate of between 7,500 and 35,000 of the animals.

Once again, human disturbance is a major factor contributing to endangered status.

This is especially true in Mexico, where bats are often feared and destroyed because people mistakenly believe they feed on blood. (There are three species of vampire bats in Mexico that do just that, but other species are actually very beneficial to humans.) Consequently, bat colonies are frequently destroyed intentionally. In addition, some plants that produce food for these bats are being replaced by agricultural crops, and the agave is increasingly harvested for use in making liquor.

MEXICAN LONG-NOSED BAT

Leptonycteris nivalis

This sooty brown bat is closely related to the lesser long-nosed bat, and virtually everything mentioned above about that animal—except its range—applies to the Mexican long-nosed bat. The Mexican species appears to prefer elevations above 5,000 feet, which probably accounts for its rather short seasonal stay in this country, generally June through August.

This bat originally occurred in southwest Texas and perhaps part of New Mexico, but today only a single colony is known to exist in the United States—in Big Bend National Park in Texas (at an elevation of 7,500 feet). The Mexican populations of this species have not been well studied, but it is almost certain that few, if any, colonies there would be as well protected as those at Big Bend.

The park population, however, has fluctuated greatly over the years. In 1967, observers estimated nearly 11,000 bats there, but in 1970 none showed up from their winter stay in Mexico. In 1971, 8,000 appeared, and for several years thereafter the figure ranged between 200 and 6,600. In 1992 none of the animals appeared. No one is certain why such large fluctuations occur, but they could be caused by changing food availability either at Big Bend or in other parts of the bat's range. The bat's 1992 absence in the park might, for example, be linked to recent wet years and the resulting abundance of agave blossoms elsewhere.

BLACK-FOOTED FERRET

Mustela nigripes
STATUS: ENDANGERED

For much of September 7, 1991, excited biologists busied themselves with last-minute preparations on a remote stretch of prairie just north of Medicine Bow, Wyoming. Some moved cages into positions. Others readied cameras. A few conducted tests of radio tracking equipment. No one wanted anything to go wrong with the great experiment that was about to be launched. Finally, at 9:45 P.M., one of the scientists calmly opened the door of a cage containing two black-footed ferrets. Startled at first by their new freedom, the animals seemed reluctant to leave the nest box that had long been their home. In a few moments, however, the pair darted off into the Wyoming night. Over the next several weeks, forty-seven additional ferrets followed in their footsteps. Once again, the black-footed ferret was part of wild America.

The ferret saga on this continent actually began about 100,000 years ago, when this member of the weasel family came here from Asia via the Bering land bridge. As a small but capable predator, the black-footed ferret found a seemingly limitless prey base in the form of several billion prairie dogs that dotted the plains from southern Canada to Texas. The ferret occasionally pursued and caught rabbits, mice, and other small animals, but it was the ubiquitous prairie dog to which this predator hitched its star. As the prairie dog went, so went the ferret.

Long and lean, the black-footed ferret is perfectly adapted for entering the labyrinthine burrows that keep prairie dogs safe from most other predators. Though adult male prairie dogs often outweigh the two-pound-plus ferrets, the outcome of an encounter between the two is rarely in doubt. A quick bite to the neck, and the prairie dog dies. One prairie dog provides enough food, assuming nothing is wasted, to sustain a black-footed ferret for about a week. And since prairie dogs are prolific while ferrets are not, the two species can strike a balance that allows both to prosper.

Operating without a real home burrow, the black-footed ferret nomadically covers a hundred acres or so of prairie dog colony. At night it prowls the subterranean tunnels, visiting as many as four hundred burrows before dawn. Topside movement between burrow entrances is made quickly and with caution, for the ferret itself often falls prey to coyotes, bobcats, and raptors. The ferret sleeps wherever dawn may find it, rarely showing itself above ground during the day.

The black-footed ferret looks much like a mink but with the more tubular body of a weasel—designed over the centuries for easy access to burrows. Short legs and pointed nose uphold the weasel tradition. This species is brown to tan to yellowish on top, lighter on the sides and cream-colored on the belly. The five-inch tail is tipped with black. Although the ferret is active all winter, it does not turn white. A typical adult might measure eighteen inches in length (plus tail). The ferret's feet are, of course, black, but an even more prominent marking is the dark facial mask that gives the animal the look of a comic book crook. (Some biologists suspect that the mask evolved as a way to camouflage the ferret's countenance as it peeked from burrow entrances.) Ferrets breed in April and May,

giving birth about six weeks later to, on average, three or four young. By October the juveniles are on their own.

Despite the ferret's nocturnal nature, early Native Americans knew about the animal and admired its hunting prowess. But the European settlers who came to the West in great numbers during the nineteenth century scarcely noticed the ferret, and it was only in 1851 that John Audubon and John Bachman entered the animal in the scientific annals after examining a specimen sent to them from Wyoming.

The pioneers, however, were abundantly aware of the prairie dog, whose teeming colonies blanketed the plains. As the West got divided and redivided into countless small farms and ranches, the new owners came to the universal conclusion that these ubiquitous rodents were anathema to agriculture. Prairie dogs ate crops. Their burrow mounds impeded the smooth progress of machinery. And livestock occasionally stepped into burrow entrances and broke their legs. The consensus late in the last century was that the prairie dog had to go. So out came the traps, guns, and poisons, and the prairie dog war was on.

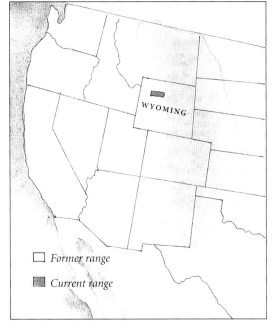

Former range

Current range

Simultaneously—and somewhat paradoxically—westerners waged war against the predators that killed prairie dogs, because these carnivors also killed calves and lambs. Part of this assault included the setting out of meat laced with strychnine or other poison, bait that sometimes found its way into ferret stomachs.

As a result of these offensives, the black-footed ferret—which was offensive to no one—suffered both a diminishing prey base and a direct, though unintended, attack.

The not-so-surprising result was a decrease in the ferret population. Biologists still argue about how numerous ferrets once were, but one calculation—made by multiplying known ferret densities by the total amount of good, prairie dog–occupied habitat—resulted in an estimate of 5.6 million ferrets in existence prior to the prairie dog wars of the late 1800s. Suffice it to say that at one time there were lots of ferrets.

For a long time, no one noticed—or probably cared about—the ferret decline. Even into the middle of this century biologists assumed that the animal was broadly (but sparsely) distributed throughout much of its former range, which included parts of a dozen states. But the diminution of the black-footed ferret was far greater than anyone suspected, and by the late 1950s sightings of this animal had become a rarity. Already pessimists spoke of extinction.

Then in August 1964 a farmer in Mellette County, South Dakota, discovered a few ferrets on his land, and biologists rushed to study the animals. (Heretofore, ferrets had never been looked at scientifically.) Over the next several years, scientists documented the existence of ninety black-footed ferrets dispersed over eight counties in the heart of that state's prairie dog country. As far as anyone knew, these animals were all that remained of the black-footed ferret species.

By 1971 the status quo was coming undone at this apparent last bastion of ferretdom. The discovery of additional ferrets had ceased, reproduction was not filling adjacent open habitat, and the relationship between biologists and landowners had soured. Gradually, biologists began capturing what ferrets they could find and moving them to research facilities in Maryland. In all, nine ferrets made that trip. Two females even bore young there, but the kits died almost immediately, and by 1979 all the captive ferrets were dead.

Meanwhile, back in South Dakota, there were no more ferrets to be found. Canada, Texas, and Oklahoma declared the animal extirpated. In 1974, the U.S. Fish and Wildlife Service established a black-footed ferret recovery team, but no one was sure there were any left to recover. As the ferretless months and years ticked by, it became increasingly apparent that this once common predator must indeed be extinct.

But no one bothered to tell all this to Lucille and John Hogg's dog, Shep. The Hoggs lived on a ranch near Meeteetse, Wyoming, and on September 26, 1981, Shep presented his owners with the body of a small, minklike animal that apparently had made a play for his food bowl. Unsure of what kind of animal it was, the Hoggs took the corpse to a local taxidermist, who promptly alerted authorities to the fact that a wild ferret—albeit a dead one—had been found. More than seven years had passed since anyone had seen a ferret in the wild.

Officials swarmed over the Hogg spread. When a hired hand at a nearby ranch reported seeing an animal that looked like a ferret, the search widened—and hit paydirt. Over the next few years, biologists documented a veritable treasure trove of black-footed ferrets there on the Wyoming prairie. In 1983, they put the population at 88, and just a year later the count went to 129 (including 25 litters of young)—even more ferrets than had existed in conservationists' wildest dreams.

But the sweet smell of success soon wafted away with the Wyoming wind. In June 1985, a graduate student doing a routine prairie dog study discovered a plague epizootic running rampant among the prairie dogs in the newfound ferret population. While the disease presented no direct threat to the ferrets, its decimation of prairie dog numbers could rob the predators of the food they require. Authorities at first tried dusting the prairie dog colonies with a pesticide to kill the fleas that carried the disease, but this proved futile.

About this time, ferrets began disappearing. From a high of 129 animals in 1984, the count plummeted to 58 in August of 1985, then to 31 in September, and to 16 in October. Only after most of the ferrets had perished did authorities discover the real killer—canine distemper, a disease to which ferrets are extremely susceptible. Somehow (the origin was never determined) distemper had entered the ferret ranks, and with the plague outbreak serving as camouflage, it silently ravaged the population.

With the black-footed ferret apparently aboard a fast train headed for oblivion, authorities launched an all-out effort to capture all the remaining ferrets they could find, with the hope of breeding them back to prosperity in captivity. By February 1987, every black-footed ferret known to exist in the wild had been rounded up. When several of the animals died of distemper contracted before their capture, only eighteen animals were left. There seemed little doubt that this fragile group constituted the entire worldwide supply of black-footed ferrets. Almost certainly, the ferret was at this point the rarest mammal on earth, and the scenario that followed may someday rank as one of the great miracles of wildlife management.

Over the next four years, biologists gently coaxed black-footed ferrets back from the brink of extinction. In ultra-secure, super-sterile facilities, scientists oversaw the natural rebuilding of a species. High technology (such as closed-circuit TV and DNA studies) blended with low-tech methods (such as using Siberian polecats as surrogate mothers for orphaned ferret kits) to gradually increase ferret numbers. Once again, these fascinating animals exceeded everyone's greatest hopes. By the fall of 1991, the captive ferret population had mushroomed to 325 individuals—enough to justify the return of some of them to the wild.

So, on September 7, 1991, that cage door swung open, and two black-footed ferrets came home to wild Wyoming. Many of the forty-nine ferrets released that fall were dead by spring (mostly due to predators), but scientists had expected as much. (Even in fully wild populations, up to 80 percent of the young of the year perish by spring.) More important was the fact that some of the survivors bred in the spring of 1992—an accomplishment that completely surprised ferret biologists. In July of that year, at least two females from the 1991 release had produced young (a total of six kits), and at least two of these juveniles (and their mothers) were still alive in November 1992. That fall, authorities released another ninety captive-reared young ferrets into the same area. As additional captive ferrets become available, they too will be put back into the wild—probably in Montana and South Dakota as well as Wyoming.

The black-footed ferret obviously has made great strides, but there is still a long way to go. The current recovery plan calls for the eventual establishment of ten separate populations, each with thirty or more breeding adults. Biologists hope by the year 2010 to have 1,500 of the animals in the wild. Just a few years ago, that goal would have sounded ludicrous, but people are beginning to realize that with black-footed ferrets anything is possible.

COLUMBIAN WHITE-TAILED DEER

Odocoileus virginianus leucurus
STATUS: ENDANGERED

White-tailed deer represent one of the great wildlife success stories of all time. Several million white-tails probably lived in America during colonial times, but a couple of centuries of exploitation and habitat loss drew their numbers down to about 300,000 (and falling) as the twentieth century dawned. Alarmed by the decline, America's sport hunters requested and paid for changes in management that first halted the free fall, then reversed the trend. Today, white-tailed deer are almost everywhere, with many becoming pests in back yards and gardens. The national population estimate stands at about fifteen million. There are, however, thirty-eight subspecies of white-tails in America, and not all of them participated in the great comeback. One that did not is the Columbian white-tailed deer. (The only other white-tailed deer race listed as endangered is the key deer in Florida.)

When Lewis and Clark journeyed across the West in the early 1800s, they encountered along the Columbia River white-tailed deer similar to—but somewhat smaller than—those they knew in the East. Later, settlers to the Northwest substantiated the abundant existence of what came to be called the Columbian white-tail. Originally, this deer ranged over a significant portion of western Oregon and Washington—possibly from Puget Sound nearly to the California border.

Like so many other animals, however, it had problems coping with the changes wrought by white settlers. As a lowland race, the Columbian white-tail fell into immediate competition with pioneers for rights to the lush river bottom areas. When farmers cleared trees to plant crops, the deer lost valuable cover. Where cattle grazed, the deer usually did not. Many Columbian white-tails naturally ended up on a pioneer's dinner table, and market shooters (an honorable profession in the nineteenth century) also killed their share. The deer's preference for riparian areas made it easy to find in the long, narrow strips of habitat along rivers.

In the early 1930s, some authorities believed this white-tail race had disappeared entirely from the Columbia River region and survived only in an isolated area in southwestern Oregon near the city of Roseburg. A few years later, however, a small population was "rediscovered" near the Columbia.

Today, there are two separate populations of Columbian white-tailed deer. One, numbering about 800 to 1,000 animals, exists on the islands and shoreline bottomland of the lower Columbia River, some in Oregon and some in Washington. Several different groups, each separated from the next by a river channel or patch of unfavorable habitat, make up this population. Part of this herd's territory (several islands and adjacent mainland near the mouth of the Columbia) has been made into a wildlife refuge. The other population—about 7,000 animals—lives as it has for some time in Douglas County in southwestern Oregon near Roseburg. The deer here also use lowland riparian habitats, but some of their range includes rolling oak woodlands.

Both these populations have increased greatly in recent years, thanks to good management and complete protection. Both have met the criteria established years ago for "downlisting" them from endangered status to simply threatened, and authorities have petitioned to have that change implemented. Removing this deer from the threatened species list will be tougher to achieve, however, because that will require permanently protected habitat, and much of their current habitat—especially in the Roseburg area—is privately owned.

Washington and Oregon have long since prohibited the sport hunting of Columbian white-tails, but poachers and cars still kill some animals. Coyotes probably take a few fawns. But the biggest threat facing this subspecies is still human competition for choice habitat. Ongoing logging and brush removal methodically reduce the amount of cover available to the deer in terrain that is often heavily populated with people. Native trees and shrubs—Sitka spruce, cottonwood, dogwood, alder, and willow—now occur only in patches. And the Roseburg population is especially pressured by new residential developments along river corridors.

Biologically and behaviorally, Columbian white-tails are not very different from other races. Like their kin, they exhibit an especially appealing form of grace and beauty. Regardless of how many times people have seen deer, they still stop and look at white-tails. There just seems to be a message of freedom and adventure inherent in a white-tail bounding over the countryside.

White-tails are not herding animals, preferring instead to spend their lives alone or in groups of only two or three. Winter conditions, however, sometimes force them into larger aggregations. The annual rut occurs in November, with does giving birth to one or two fawns the following spring. Primarily nocturnal, white-tails usually spend their daytime hours resting, although they become active early in the evening and remain so after first light (the two best times for people to see them).

There are genetic differences between Columbians and other white-tails, but as far as nonscientists are concerned, this deer's most distinctive characteristic is a somewhat diminished size. An adult doe Columbian white-tail might weigh 85 or 90 pounds and a buck 125 pounds—appreciably less than other white-tails. Also, the buck's antlers generally are smaller than those of most other subspecies. And unlike most deer, Columbian white-tails are grazers, not browsers, preferring grasses and forbs to the herbaceous, woody fare most deer eat.

GRAY WOLF

Canis lupus
STATUS: ENDANGERED

It is perhaps the most primeval sound in all of nature: the howl of a wild wolf. Lonely, eerie, haunting, surreal. A cry from the distant past. The sound begins deep within the belly of the beast, rises to falsetto clarity, then trails off into silence. But soon there is another. And another. The wolf's howl is at the same time a call, a query, an announcement and a challenge. It supercedes all other sounds and seems still to own the air even after its maker has quit. No living thing can ignore it.

People and wolves are much alike—social, predatory, competitive, aggressive, the leaders of their respective branches of evolution. Perhaps that is why the howl has for millennia summoned uncounted humans to the front lines of a war against wolves. Maybe that explains why the very word *wolf* inspires images of evil, death, destruction, and searing green eyes glowing in the night. Since long before anyone bothered to record such things, people and wolves have been locked in conflict, a battle that cannot be explained solely by the facts.

The gray wolf—also called the timber wolf in some places—once ranged from Alaska to Mexico and from Maine to California (and across portions of Europe and Asia). It thrived in any habitat that supported populations of ungulates such as deer, moose, bison, and elk. In this country, only the most arid deserts of the Southwest were devoid of wolves.

Physical characteristics can vary with geography, but generally the gray wolf stands about thirty inches tall at the shoulders, with adult males weighing about ninety-five pounds and females perhaps fifteen pounds less. Their color can range from pure white to jet black, but most animals, true to their name, are shades of gray. Wolves can trot tirelessly for hours and hit thirty-five miles an hour when they need to. When hunting is poor, they can go many days without food.

Wolves are among the most social—and most hierarchical—mammals on earth. The literal top dog is called (by humans, anyway) the alpha male, and all others in the pack are subservient to him. There is also an alpha female to which all other females are subordinate. From this pair down, a defined pecking order lets each wolf know who ranks above and who lies below. Social standing is frequently reinforced via a complex system of body language and mock fighting—but rarely with real aggression.

On the hunt, the alpha male makes most of the decisions, takes the lead in the attack, and has first crack at eating the prey. The rest of the pack members dine in the order of their social standing, and if the food runs out before all the bellies are full, the lowest in rank go hungry. Pack size varies considerably, but eight or ten might be about average. Usually only the alpha pair are allowed to reproduce.

They mate in late winter, and nine weeks later from four to seven pups are born, usually in a burrow. Rearing the youngsters can be a truly communal affair. For two weeks or so, the female may forgo hunting entirely to stay with her offspring, during which time the pack carries food to her—either in their mouths or in their bellies for regurgitation at the nursery burrow. When the pups are a couple of months old, the adults often move them to a rendezvous site (usually a meadow with timber and water nearby) where they can play above ground while the pack hunts. Sometimes a member of the pack—not necessarily their mother—stays behind as a sort of baby-sitter.

One reason wolves form packs is to facilitate the killing of large prey such as moose and elk. Typically, wolves follow their sensitive noses to their prey, then assess the animal for potential weaknesses (such as youth, old age, injury, or illness). If the prey appears healthy and vigorous, the predators may well choose not to strike, as flailing hooves and antlers can be formidable weapons. If the wolves detect a vulnerability, however, the assault is on.

In human terms, wolves making a living is not a pretty sight, but nature does not make such judgments. Typically, there is no plan of attack, but rather an all-out pell-mell attempt to sink wolf teeth into prey flesh. The beginning of the end usually occurs when one of the wolves secures a grip on the victim's throat or muzzle. Others may tear at the animal's hamstrings. Still others may rip open its abdomen. Before long, the prey goes down, and death quickly follows.

On the prairies of the American West, millions of bison (and to a lesser extent other hoofed animals) once kept a large population of wolves well fed. That situation changed quickly, however, during a couple bloody decades late in the last century, when human shooters wantonly slaughtered bison and in the process changed forever the course of events. With the bison gone, the adaptable wolves quickly turned their attention to cattle and sheep and almost overnight became significant slayers of livestock.

Nineteenth-century settlers in the West needed little urging to attack wolves with a vengeance, as fear and hatred of wolves had long been part of their culture. When Europeans first arrived on this continent, they brought with them a loathing of wolves imbedded in their traditions. As early as 1630, American wolves had a bounty on their head, and by the time of the Civil War the animals had largely been eliminated from the East.

In the West, the newest wolf war was waged with an arsenal of traps, bullets, and especially poisons. Every dead cow, sheep, or bison on the prairie became—with the addition of a little strychnine—a potential wolf assassin. In some places, government veterinarians infected captive wolves with mange and turned them loose to transmit the disease to wild wolves. In 1914, annual wolf bounties topped $1 million, which was an awful lot of money in those days. In 1915, when the livestock industry convinced the federal government to hire a virtual army of wolf killers, the outcome of the wolf war was inevitable.

While it is easy to understand a rancher's dislike for wolves on economic grounds, the hatred that fueled the fires of wolf persecution went much deeper than that. For centuries the belief that wolves kill people had been handed down from generation to generation, first in Europe and later in this country. Classic children's literature, for example, is rife with evil wolves. Had fact-gathering then been what it is today, these people would have known that wolves virtually never attack humans.

Bears sometimes attack people. Cougars occasionally attack people. Domestic dogs often attack people. But wild wolves, for all intents and purposes, simply do not. In all of North American history, there has been no documented instance of a wild wolf killing a human, and there have been only a handful of cases in which wolves assaulted people at all (in no instance was a person seriously injured). The story in Europe, going back many additional centuries, is much the same. Still, the ill-founded image of human-killing wolves persists even today. A U.S. senator from Montana recently remarked that if wolves are returned to Yellowstone National Park, "there'll be a dead child within a year." The truth is that lightning bolts, bee stings, and miscellaneous objects falling from the sky are all more of a threat to human safety than wolves.

Whatever the impetus for the great western wolf war, the animal was no match for people and their killing tools. Soon, the few wolves remaining in the West existed only in pockets of wilderness such as Yellowstone National Park, and even there the persecution squads sought them out and killed them. Government hunters ran out of wolves to kill in Yellowstone in the 1920s, and not long after that the howl of the wolf disappeared entirely from the American West.

That did not mean, however, that the species itself was in any great danger, as wolves continued to do well in several places. Today, Alaska is home to 6,000 or 7,000 of the animals and Canada about 55,000. Another 1,600 or so exist in the woods of northern Minnesota, and small populations live in Michigan and Wisconsin. In 1978, the gray wolf (including the Mexican wolf subspecies native to the American Southwest) was declared endangered in the lower forty-eight states—except in Minnesota, where it is considered threatened. The West, however, remained entirely wolfless until recently.

Throughout the 1970s, reports surfaced of wolves prowling the woods of northwestern Montana, but these animals (obviously immigrants from Canada) remained shadowy and mysterious. In the early 1980s, however, biologists documented the animal's increasing presence, and today they believe Montana is home to about fifty wolves. Idaho has about a dozen, and eastern Washington a few. Four litters of pups were produced in Montana in one recent year, and officials believe some reproduction may be occurring in the Idaho population. After half a century of absence, the wolf has returned to the West.

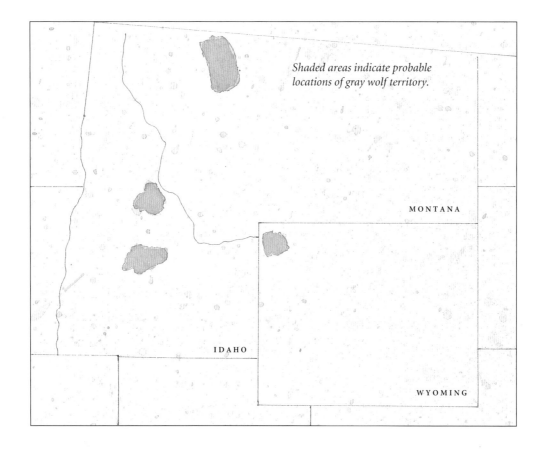

Shaded areas indicate probable locations of gray wolf territory.

The gray wolf recovery plan calls for the eventual establishment of three separate populations of ten breeding pairs each—in northwestern Montana, central Idaho, and Yellowstone. Much of the current controversy over wolves involves their proposed reintroduction to the Yellowstone ecosystem. Conservationists have long wanted wolves (probably from Canada) released in the Yellowstone area. Livestock interests, backed by most federal legislators from the affected states (Wyoming, Idaho, and Montana), have opposed the return of the animals to the park. Wildlife authorities are currently preparing an elaborate environmental impact statement covering all aspects of wolf presence in the park and a host of Yellowstone wolf management options. In the meantime, however, the wolves themselves have scrambled the issue.

In August 1992 a professional film maker on a stakeout at a bison carcass in Yellowstone captured footage of a wolflike animal feeding on the carrion. And in September of that year a hunter just south of the park shot and killed a 95-pound canine. Intensive forensic study determined this animal to be a purebred wolf and a descendant of a Montana pack. With wolves just a couple of hundred miles away in northwestern Montana, it would certainly be possible for the animals to recolonize Yellowstone on their own.

The idea that wolves may have naturally returned to Yellowstone has thrown all factions into something of a tizzy. Some wolf proponents would be thrilled to have wolves return naturally to Yellowstone. Others believe that a planned reintroduction would get more animals there faster and work better. (The two situations are not necessarily mutually exclusive, but officials might be less eager to launch a reintroduction project if a few wolves have already repatriated themselves to the park area.)

The prospect of having wolves in the Yellowstone ecosystem does not please any wolf opponents, but some could accept animals that get there on their own. Others would much prefer an introduced population (if wolves must be there at all), because those animals could be labeled "experimental" and therefore susceptible to management options such as the killing of individuals that prey on livestock. Naturally occurring wolves, on the other hand, are fully protected by the Endangered Species Act. This distinction has put some wolf opponents in the curious position of supporting the quick reintroduction of wolves to Yellowstone.

The Yellowstone wolf situation changes almost daily, so watch your newspapers for the latest chapter in this saga. And the next time you visit Yellowstone, listen at night for that ancient howl.

GRIZZLY BEAR

Ursus arctos horribilis
STATUS: THREATENED

With the possible exception of the wolves, no threatened or endangered species is as controversial as the grizzly. In fact, the big bear may be the most loved, hated, admired and despised animal in all of North America. The grizzly is, in many ways, the greatest wildlife species on the continent.

Once, grizzlies roamed from Mexico to the Arctic Ocean and from the Pacific eastward across the Great Plains. There may have been 100,000 of them—10,000 in California alone.

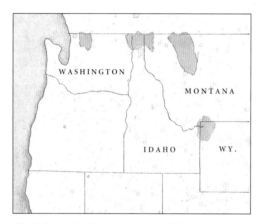

Shaded areas indicate current grizzly bear range.

Then came the pioneers and their livestock. When "griz" dined on mutton or beef—or killed a human—out came the guns, traps, poisons, and fear. "The only good grizzly is a dead grizzly," became the western watchword. Scientists named the beast *Ursus arctos horribilis,* settlers set out to eliminate it, and the great bear retreated. Texas lost its last grizzly about 1890, California 1922, Oregon 1931, Arizona 1935, and on and on. Meanwhile, human creations like logging, ranching, mining, energy exploration, subdivisions, ski resorts, and golf courses have whittled away at grizzly habitat.

Today, the great bear clings to a mere 2 percent of its former range—in five separate and isolated populations in Montana, Wyoming, Idaho, and Washington. (A very few grizzlies also may remain in the wilds of Colorado. A hunter killed one there in 1979, and there have been recent unconfirmed reports of grizzly presence in the state.) The big bruins are difficult to count, but the best guessers put the overall figure (for the lower forty-eight states) at about 1,000 grizzlies— that's all that remain of yesteryear's tens of thousands. The two largest populations in the lower forty-eight states are around Yellowstone National Park (perhaps 250 bears) and in northern Montana along the Continental Divide (maybe 600 or 700 bears). As a species, however, grizzlies are in no danger of extinction, thanks to the 25,000 or so in Canada and 40,000 more in Alaska.

To help with the lower–forty-eight tally, biologists have taken to shooting the bears with cameras. Deep in the western wilds, researchers attach 35 mm cameras to trees and set some fetid bait (part of a road-killed deer, for example) nearby. The grizzly follows its nose to the spot, where its body heat triggers an infrared sensor that trips the shutter. Previously tagged bears are easy to identify, and many others have distinctive markings. The result is some sense of how many bears are out there. And some surprising pictures. One photo-shy Montana grizzly chomped one of the cameras to death—the last frames on the film showing nothing but fangs.

For the most part, fear and loathing of the great bear have passed into history, although savvy westerners still exercise caution in grizzly country. A male grizzly weighs about five hundred pounds (with some hitting half a ton) and can loom eight feet tall when standing on its hind legs. A grizzly can kill a cow with one blow, outrun a horse, outswim an Olympian, and drag a dead elk uphill. And unlike black bears, with their relatively mild disposition and consistent behavior, grizzlies are impulsive, petulant, unpredictable, and very dangerous. One may run from humans like a rabbit, and the next attack with the power of a freight train.

Although the bears prefer vast chunks of wilderness, human presence does not deter them from using an area, which means the two species often collide. Roads are the biggest problem. Roads bring people to hunt, fish, camp, watch birds, cut firewood, build homes, and poach wildlife. Some grizzlies will go elsewhere (as long as there is an elsewhere), while others will stay and likely get into trouble by killing a calf, raiding trash cans, threatening people, or in some other way making life uncomfortable for the two-legged newcomers. As opportunistic omnivores, grizzlies eat everything from grass to maggots to elk—and when people are around, garbage, road-killed deer, honey, dog food (and the dog), or just about anything else.

Not long ago, biologists found a grizzly chasing calves on a ranch near Kiowa, Montana, on the Blackfeet Indian Reservation. They trapped the four hundred pound male and shipped him thirty air miles into the remote Bob Marshall Wilderness. A couple of months later, the bear was back on the reservation killing sheep. After another move and a stint of good behavior, he killed a cow. Again, authorities shipped him to a new area and monitored his behavior—even frightening him away from livestock with firecrackers. Before long, the bad news bear killed yet another cow, and officials reluctantly ended his life with a bullet.

Illegal grizzly killers take their toll, too. With bear body parts in high demand (the gall bladder alone may bring $4,000 on the Asian aphrodisiac market), profit poachers annually kill an unknown number of the animals. So do grizzly haters, who may simply let the carcass lie. And every year, hunters mistakenly shoot grizzlies. One Arkansas hunter in Montana shot a grizzly he thought was a black bear. Discovering his error, he buried the carcass (with help from his guide and colleagues) and built a campfire on the spot. The secret didn't keep, however, and all were later convicted.

Another reason for the bear's predicament is its plodding reproductive rate, one of the lowest among terrestrial mammals. When she gives birth for the first time, a female grizzly is, on

average, already five and a half years old. The cubs—usually two—remain with their mother for two years, during which time she does not breed. Ergo, by her tenth birthday a female grizzly will have produced only four young. Two of these are likely to have died, and one of the two survivors will probably be a male (and somewhat superfluous in the polygynous grizzly society). Even a fully successful grizzly female will add only three or four females to the population in her lifetime.

Grizzlies are solitary, reclusive, nocturnal wanderers, sometimes operating across a home range of up to fifteen hundred square miles. They have no natural enemies other than their own kind, and they do not defend their territory, but rather choose to avoid each other—except during the summer season of breeding.

After mating, the female grizzly's anatomy takes advantage of a biological trick called delayed implantation, in which the fertilized eggs almost immediately cease development and remain in a sort of suspended animation for several months. In autumn, the eggs (usually two) attach to the female's uterine wall and begin growing again. In mid-winter, while she hibernates in a den on some remote high-country hillside, a pair of one-pound cubs are born.

The great bear's name comes from its pelage, a thick mat of long, light-tipped hairs that give the coat a grizzled look. Overall, though, grizzlies may be any color from buff to jet black. Since so-called black bears also come in many colors, grizzlies must be identified by other characteristics—a concave or dish-shaped face, a large hump behind the front shoulders, and long claws that extend well past the toes.

The bear's senses are a mixed bag—poor eyesight, human-level hearing, and an extraordinary sense of smell. Grizzlies have been known to follow the odor of a rotting carcass for more than two miles. An old Indian legend says that when a leaf fell in the forest, the eagle saw it fall, the coyote heard it fall, and the grizzly smelled it fall. It is this championship nose that often draws grizzlies toward human garbage, livestock, and—too frequently—a deadly confrontation.

Human-bear conflicts and attacks occur several times each year, mostly in Yellowstone and Glacier National Parks. Occasionally, a grizzly takes a human life—and often pays with its own. Though bear attacks receive plenty of press coverage, they actually are rare, especially considering that millions of people visit the two parks annually. Even for someone living in the grizzly-occupied West, the chances of getting hit by lightning are greater than the chances of suffering a grizzly attack.

Another kind of grizzly confrontation goes on almost daily in the West. Lots of people want to make a living—or a profit—in grizzly habitat by grazing cattle, cutting trees, pumping natural gas out of the ground, or using the land in a dozen other ways. They don't like the grizzly much, because the law says they must give the bear consideration as they ply their trades. Other people—those the first group refers to derogatorily as "environmentalists"—want to save the bear. They see the grizzly as a great living symbol of wildlife, the West, wilderness, and human dedication to other species. In the press and in the courts the two factions go at each other, sometimes with bearlike fury. The outcome—the grizzly's future—remains uncertain.

For now, however, the great silver-tipped bear still stalks the western woods. It still rolls huge boulders aside to feast on the insects below, follows its nose to distant carrion, chases ground squirrels across alpine meadows, and—occasionally—passes through the vision of some watching human. It surely is a sight that person will not soon forget.

GUADALUPE FUR SEAL

Arctocephalus townsendi
STATUS: THREATENED

The Guadalupe fur seal is another animal that nearly slipped through the cracks. More than once, it was thought to be extinct, but on each occasion a few seals eventually showed up to prove the doomsday theorists wrong. It is, however, a severely restricted species, confined mostly to the area around a single Pacific island (Guadalupe), 150 miles west of Baja California. Recently, Mexican authorities counted 3,259 of the animals at Guadalupe, almost certainly the highest total in many decades.

Like so many of their marine mammal kin, Guadalupe fur seals suffered from human exploitation. Once, these medium-sized seals occupied the rugged coasts and islands from San Francisco south past the tip of Baja California. No one was counting, of course, but there must have been tens of thousands of them. Then late in the seventeenth century came the flotilla of folks bent on harvesting the sea—an international armada with ships from Russia and Britain as well as the United States. Methodically and relentlessly, with no notion of husbanding a precious resource, the crews killed Guadalupe seals wherever they found them. It must have been quite an enterprise, for even today remnants of the rock slaughter sheds can be seen on Guadalupe Island.

Most Guadalupe fur seals disappeared in the early 1800s, and by the time the twentieth century rolled around, they already were thought to be extinct. Scientists belatedly identified the species from a couple of scavenged skulls, but no one expected ever to see a live Guadalupe fur seal again. In 1928, however, a fisherman presented the San Diego Zoo with a pair of the animals (both bulls, unfortunately). They came, he said, from a group of about sixty that still existed around Guadalupe Island. Scientists were thrilled, but the fisherman—angry about what he considered to be inadequate payment for his services—was not. Reportedly, he returned to the island and slaughtered every seal he could find.

Guadalupe Island is the epicenter of Guadalupe fur seal existence.

Again, many authorities considered the seals extinct. Rumors of Guadalupe fur seals were circulated from time to time, but it was only in 1949—when one of the animals showed up on San Nicolas Island (one of the Channel Islands southwest of Los Angeles)—that the species' demise could be disproved. Five years later, an expedition to Guadalupe Island found a group of fourteen seals. Fully protected by both the United States and Mexico, this small colony has steadily grown to the few thousand that exist today.

Although Guadalupe Island (now a wildlife sanctuary) remains the epicenter of this seal's existence, more and more of the animals are appearing elsewhere. Several dozen sightings have occurred on California's Channel Islands, and additional Mexican islands also have reported the seal's presence. From 1981 to 1990, a Guadalupe fur seal bull regularly mixed with sea lions on San Nicolas Island, and in 1988 a second bull established his territory there.

So far, not much is known about this animal's biology or behavior. Males may stretch six feet from tip to tip and weigh up to three hundred pounds. Females are smaller. Both genders are dark brown or black with a gray cast to the head and shoulders. The head appears somewhat large and the snout long and pointed. Guadalupe fur seals apparently eat squid, lanternfish, mollusks, and probably other species of sea creatures. In late spring, bulls stake out territories on the traditional birthing-mating grounds on remote rocky coasts. Females arrive early in June. In less than two weeks, they give birth to the single pup they have been carrying, come into estrus, and breed again. Pregnant females may remain in the rookery vicinity most of the year, but other members of the colony spend much of their time at sea.

With the future of this species apparently linked forever to a seventeen-square-mile rocky spit of an island off the Mexican coast, it is not easy to be optimistic about Guadalupe fur seals. But these animals seem to have a knack for hanging on to life. And with populations slowly rising, this species is actually more prosperous today than at any time in over a century.

HUALAPAI MEXICAN VOLE

Microtus mexicanus hualpaiensis
STATUS: ENDANGERED

The Hualapai is one of a dozen Mexican vole subspecies that exist throughout a broad swath of Mexico and the southwestern United States. It is a stocky, blunt-nosed, short-legged, mouselike rodent with black, beady eyes and small ears hidden by long, dark, cinnamon-brown fur. Adults are about five inches in length (including an inch or so of tail) and weigh about an ounce. Voles seem to have a penchant for neatness and spend much of their time grooming and keeping their digs clean. They spend most of the remaining hours filling their bellies or the larders many of them maintain.

This species is extremely rare. Researchers first identified it in 1938 in the Hualapai Mountains of Mohave County in northwestern Arizona, but only fifteen individuals have ever been captured. Over the years, biologists discovered four populations in this region, but a 1990 survey found Hualapai activity in only one of those places, Pine Peak Canyon. In two of the others, vole habitat has been diminished by flooding, livestock, and human recreational use of the land. (Mining, road construction, and the introduction of non-native elk and squirrels to the Hualapai Mountains also have added to vole woes.) To make matters worse, two of the four sites—including the only one with recent vole activity—are privately owned. Fortunately for the Hualapai, the other two population sites lie on Bureau of Land Management holdings.

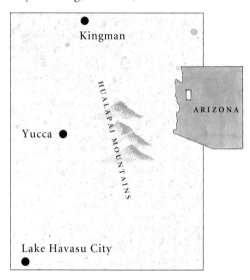

Many gaps exist in our understanding of this species, but Hualapai Mexican voles appear to prefer woodlands interspersed with grass and sedge habitat. Most occurrences have been between 5,500 and 8,000 feet of elevation in the neighborhood of moist springs or seeps. Biologists believe that in generations past, when the Hualapai Mountains contained more grassy, moist habitats than today, this vole was more numerous and widespread. In a very real sense, better habitat breeds more voles, as abundant green vegetation actually causes the birth rate to rise.

These animals appear to be somewhat colonial, with burrows and above-ground runway systems designed for quick escape by all. Probable predators include owls, skunks, snakes, and foxes. The Hualapai's diet features a variety of green forbs, grasses, and other plant material. Like others of its kind, this species can be active day or night and apparently year round as well. Litter size is likely only two or three young. With so little knowledge about this creature, authorities find it currently impossible even to formulate a recovery plan, and with so few Hualapai voles in existence, learning more about them will be difficult. The Hualapai Mexican vole is easily one of the most endangered mammals in America.

JAGUARUNDI

Felis yagouaroundi
STATUS: ENDANGERED

This cat is *extremely* rare in the United States—if it even exists here at all any more. The last confirmed presence of a jaguarundi in this country occurred in Cameron County, Texas, on April 21, 1986, when a car struck and killed one of the animals. Since that time, nothing—and there wasn't much U.S. jaguarundi activity before then, either. A few of these cats may still be hiding out in the south Texas brush, but biologists haven't been able to find them.

Actually, two jaguarundi subspecies are listed as endangered in the United States—*Felis yagouaroundi cacomitli* in Texas and *Felis yagouaroundi tolteca* in Arizona—but inclusion of the Arizona race is truly wishful thinking. On March 17, 1938, an adult jaguarundi was supposedly identified near the Huachuca Mountains in Santa Cruz County in extreme southern Arizona. Since then, this species has appeared on various lists of Arizona wildlife, but no one really believes any jaguarundis still exist in the state. And maybe there never were any. The 1938 sighting was made at a rather long distance, which leads some biologists to suspect that the observers were mistaken.

The Texas situation is different. Jaguarundis definitely have occupied parts of Texas, especially the mesquite thickets, chaparral, and thorny brushlands of the lower Rio Grande region. Several museum specimens are known to have come from Texas; two of the animals were trapped in Willacy County in 1969. The 1986 incident constitutes the last documented jaguarundi presence in the state. Although biologists today have been unable to locate any more jaguarundis in Texas, they do not rule out the possible existence of a small population in the Rio Grande Valley near the state's southern tip. Texas is at the northern edge of this animal's range, however.

Both U.S. jaguarundi races—along with two additional subspecies—range into Mexico and Central and South America. Authorities suspect that any actual jaguarundi sightings in Arizona and Texas may in fact be itinerant animals from Mexico. Most such reports, however, are probably cases of mistaken identity. With only a fleeting glimpse—often in poor light—almost anyone might mistake a dog, house cat, or other animal for a jaguarundi. Also, unnamed individuals have released at least one captive jaguarundi into the lower Rio Grande Valley of Texas, possibly accounting for some reported sightings.

Although thoroughly feline, the jaguarundi in some ways appears to be otherwise. Its long, slender body and short legs give it the look of a marten. Its flattened head and aquatic abilities seem to be borrowed from the otter. Its quick, nervous movements are weasel-like. And its largely diurnal lifestyle makes it different from most other cats.

Jaguarundis come in red (actually reddish brown) and gray color phases, which once led folks to believe there were two separate but otherwise identical species out there. We now know that it's one animal with two possible coats. Surprisingly, red and gray kittens can exist in the same litter.

Even more than the rest of the cat clan, the jaguarundi keeps its affairs a secret. Combine this animal's preference for dense, impenetrable cover with its extreme wariness, and you have a cat that is difficult to spot, tougher to capture, and almost impossible to study. Consequently, biologists still know relatively little about this animal.

An adult jaguarundi weighs fifteen to eighteen pounds, making it somewhat larger than a house cat but appreciably smaller than a bobcat. As a predator, its diet includes rabbits, rats, mice, birds, frogs, turtles, and probably several other small prey species. Although primarily a ground dweller, it climbs well and does some of its hunting in trees. It also is a good swimmer. The jaguarundi seems to prefer lowland habitats of thick forest or overgrown fields. Since young have been found at all times of year, this cat (like some others) appears not to adhere to a specific breeding season. An average litter contains two to four young.

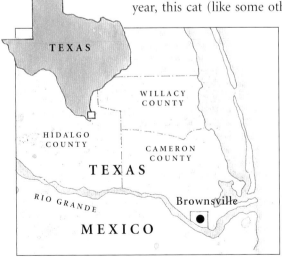

The jaguarundi is one feline that has not been persecuted for its fur, but it is killed fairly frequently in Central and South America for dining on domestic poultry. Habitat destruction causes some problems there, as well. In the United States, the absence of acceptably seclusive habitat will probably always hold jaguarundi numbers to a minimum.

KANGAROO RATS

See individual descriptions for scientific names
STATUS: ENDANGERED (ALL)

Note: The federal government classifies five kangaroo rat species or subspecies as endangered. All exist exclusively in California. The single description below covers the shared aspects of kangaroo rat life, while the five brief entries that follow highlight individual differences.

The appellation, of course, is odd—and extremely appropriate. Kangaroo rats are named for the Australian animal so well known for its large hind legs and its ability to leap over large objects in a single bound. Ditto these rats, but on a much smaller scale.

In all, there are twenty-one species of kangaroo rats in the American West. Typically, they measure from four to eight inches in body length and sport long tails. Their weights range from little more than an ounce to more than six ounces. Coloration varies from pale yellow to dark brown—invariably with a white underside. Most have a white band across the flank. Even to people who normally dislike rats and mice, these animals are quite attractive, looking very little like the sewer-dwelling relatives whose name they share, and very much like squirrels or gerbils or hamsters.

With so many species (and several subspecies), it can be difficult for nonscientists to tell one kangaroo rat from another, but three characteristics make it easy to distinguish this clan from other rodents. First, kangaroo rats appear to have disproportionately big heads. This is because their skulls contain hollow chambers near their ears that serve to amplify the low-frequency sounds (rustling of a snake or the rushing of air over a raptor's wings) that often signal danger. Second, they have very large hind legs. It is these appendages, of course, that give the rat its unusual form of locomotion. And finally, kangaroo rats have tails longer than their bodies, usually with a tuft of hair at the end. They use the tail for balance when sitting up and as a sort of rudder during leaps.

These three attributes permit kangaroo rats to occupy open terrain that many other rodents would find too dangerous. Their predators include coyotes, foxes, weasels, owls, house cats, and other carnivores. At the first hint of danger (audible or otherwise), the kangaroo rat springs into the air, traveling up to six lateral feet in a single leap. If a change of course seems warranted, the rat swings its long tail in mid-air and realigns itself for a second leap in a new direction. When required, the rat can execute successive, rapid-fire leaps that make it ricochet around like an energized rubber ball. With luck, a few such bounds will leave the predator behind and bewildered. However, scurrying—not bouncing—is the normal method of locomotion for an unpanicked kangaroo rat.

When not foraging for food, kangaroo rats generally while away the hours out of predatory view in a burrow. Some species excavate a labyrinthine system of tunnels, even to the extent of creating a pile of tailings more than a foot high and covering several square yards. Each night, the kangaroo rat goes topside in search of sustenance—seeds, fruit, leaves, stems, buds, and insects. What it does not eat on the spot gets jammed into cheek pouches for transport to an underground pantry or a topside cache. More than fifteen pounds of edibles have been found in such kangaroo rat storerooms. The rats use their small front feet to push food into the front-loading pouches, and when it's time to unload, a swipe of the foot along the outside of the pouch causes the contents to come out.

Efficient kidneys and trips above ground only during the cooler, more humid night have essentially eliminated the kangaroo rat's need for free water. Apparently, these animals get all the moisture they need in the food they eat. For reasons not well understood, kangaroo rats do, however, require frequent baths—in dust. When captive kangaroo rats are denied access to bathing dust, they develop sores and matted fur.

Although these animals do not hibernate, at least some species remain in their burrows for most or all of the rainy winter, subsisting on food stored the previous fall. The hot, dry summer often brings another period of inactivity. Like many rodents, kangaroo rats can breed year round, although fewer litters are born in the winter. Three litters per year is probably the maximum for most females, with from one to six young produced each time.

Kangaroo rats advertise their presence for mating and territorial purposes and warn of nearby predators by drumming their large hind feet rhythmically on the ground. Biologists suspect that some of these rats can recognize each other by their foot-drumming signatures. The powerful hind feet also serve as weapons and as excavation tools during burrow construction.

For all five endangered kangaroo rats, the story is essentially the same. They existed amid natural vegetation in one part of California or another until European settlers arrived. As people cleared the land for agriculture, replaced native plant species with crops, put livestock on the land, and built cities, kangaroo rat habitat disappeared—and much of what remained got chopped into smaller and smaller chunks. This trend continues even today.

Not all the news is bad, however. Some populations of endangered kangaroo rat species exist on public land, where they can be protected. In other cases, public agencies and private conservation groups are working to acquire new habitat and restore previous areas to the conditions the rats require. Rat relocations have taken place, complete with human-provided food caches as a sort of "habitat warming" gift. And one county even charged the buyers of new homes in kangaroo rat habitat $1,950 each, money earmarked for the creation of a rat sanctuary.

STEPHENS' KANGAROO RAT

Dipodomys stephensi

This species is native to the Perris, San Jacinto, San Luis Rey, and Temecula valleys in Riverside, San Bernardino, and San Diego counties, California. The Stephens' kangaroo rat prefers sparse, coastal sage scrub or slightly disturbed annual grasslands mixed with other habitats on flat or gently rolling terrain. More than half of this historic range is no longer suitable for the rat, and much of what remains is privately owned and therefore subject to degradation. Populations are scattered and isolated like the habitat.

TIPTON KANGAROO RAT

Dipodomys nitratoides nitratoides

Natural habitat for this rat generally includes sparsely covered terrain vegetated with iodinebush, saltbush, red sage, or sea blite. The Tipton kangaroo rat once ranged over nearly two million acres of the southern San Joaquin Valley, but today it exists on a small fraction of that land—with only a few thousand acres secure in public ownership. Biologists believe that about 1 percent of the original population remains.

GIANT KANGAROO RAT

Dipodomys ingens

As the name suggests, this is the largest of all kangaroo rats. An adult may reach a weight of six-plus ounces and a length of more than a foot (including six or seven inches of tail). This species also has an extra toe (five in all) on its hind feet. Its original habitat included a few million acres of annual grassland in six southern California counties, but the giant kangaroo rat exists today in just a few areas at the southern edge of that range. Because these plots tend to be separated from one another, individual rat populations are subject to extirpation from flood, fire, and pesticides (aimed at the common California ground squirrel). Giant kangaroo rats live in colonies, with each individual maintaining its own territory.

FRESNO KANGAROO RAT

Dipodomys nitratoides exilis

This species once existed on nearly a million acres of alkaline sink shrublands and arid grassland in the San Joaquin Valley, but suitable habitat has over the years been reduced to about six thousand acres, fewer than a thousand of which are currently occupied by the rat. Early in this century, the Fresno kangaroo rat was thought to be extinct but was "rediscovered" in the 1930s. This species appears to have the most restrictive habitat requirements of all kangaroo rats. In addition to human-caused problems, periodic droughts and competition with other kangaroo rat species plague this animal. The Fresno kangaroo rat is the smallest member of its genus.

MORRO BAY KANGAROO RAT

Dipodomys heermanni morroensis

Way back in 1922, a biologist estimated that the range of the Morro Bay kangaroo rat consisted of no more than sixteen square miles (and possibly as little as four square miles) near the town of Morro Bay in San Luis Obispo County, California. Today, that range has shrunk to just a few hundred acres broken into four isolated pieces. In 1989, biologists estimated a total population of only fifty animals. This subspecies requires sandy soil for easy digging and coastal scrub habitat, including such vegetation as lupine, mock heather, coyote bush, and California sagebrush.

LOUISIANA BLACK BEAR

Ursus americanus luteolus
STATUS: THREATENED

Historically, black bears dwelled in North America from Alaska to Mexico and from Newfoundland to California. Only the arid zones of the southwestern United States were without these bruins. Bears have largely disappeared from the plains states and some other areas, but tens of thousands still roam the woods in many additional regions.

Scientists have identified sixteen subspecies of black bears. The one that used to live in large numbers in Louisiana, Mississippi, and Texas is called the Louisiana black bear, and it is no longer numerous. But the situation is more complicated than that, as there is significant scientific uncertainty concerning the designation of this animal as a separate subspecies. No obvious characteristics distinguish the Louisiana black bear from certain relatives elsewhere. Examination of skulls suggests that the subspecies distinction is warranted, but genetic analyses of blood and hair samples do not. Further clouding the issue is the fact that in the 1960s authorities moved 163 Minnesota bears to Louisiana in an attempt to bolster a sagging population. No one knows whether these northern animals bred with local Louisiana black bears, but if they did, the gene pool has been rather muddied.

Unanswered questions notwithstanding, federal officials in 1992 listed the Louisiana black bear as a threatened subspecies. Since this race cannot be identified strictly by biology, it is instead defined by geography. Simply put, the Louisiana black bear is any black bear living in east Texas, in the lower two-thirds of Mississippi, or anywhere in Louisiana. By that standard, this race has an estimated population of 225 to 350 animals. Few, if any, of these live in Texas. Mississippi may have 25 to 50 bears scattered statewide in the Mississippi, Pearl, and Pascagoula river drainages. The remainder exist in Louisiana, primarily in the Tensas and Atchafalaya basins.

Unlike black bear subspecies in some regions (which can vary greatly in color), the Louisiana race is almost exclusively coal black, but often has a white blaze on the chest. A large male might weigh between three and four hundred pounds and stand three feet tall at the shoulder. Females are smaller. These animals have an incredibly acute sense of smell, which allows them to follow their noses to the next meal.

Black bears are most active at night, but some daytime movements do occur. Normally a bear will loaf away the lighted hours in a simple daybed scratched in the forest floor. When night falls, it sets off to fill its seemingly bottomless pit of a stomach. Like black bears everywhere, the Louisiana race is best known for its iron gut. As the quintessential omnivore, bears will eat anything that even resembles food—berries, tree bark, acorns, wheat, insects, corn, grass, fruit, roots, and a long menu of other items. Human garbage seems to be high on their list of delicacies, and of course honey is the preferred dessert. Sometimes they catch and eat small animals like ground squirrels, but black bears are not great predators. Most of the meat in their diet comes from carrion.

Food consumption is especially great in the fall as the bruins prepare for denning. Even in the deep South, black bears may spend most or all of the colder months in a "den," usually a brush pile or hollow tree. Some Louisiana black bears apparently go through winter the same way their northern relatives do, in a state of suspended animation.

Although these bears might not eat, drink, urinate, or defecate for months, they cannot truly be said to hibernate because their body temperature, respiration, and heart rate remain almost normal. Many southern bears, however, remain semi-active during the winter, denning intermittently for short periods.

It is during winter denning that the cubs are born. Mating takes place in early summer, but the embryos do not attach to the uterine wall until later (a phenomenon called delayed implantation). Consequently, gestation gets stretched to more than seven months, and the young appear in January or February. The cubs—usually two—emerge from the den with their mother and remain under her care until the summer of the following year, at which time she sends them off on their own so she can breed again. Young black bears become sexually mature at the age of three or four.

Although settlers killed a lot of Louisiana black bears for food, hides, and oil (rendered from the fat), the main reason for this animal's continuing plight is loss of habitat. Two centuries of forest clearing and wetland draining have left bear habitat in short supply. The twenty-five million acres of hardwood bottomland that once existed in the Mississippi River valley have been reduced to just five million acres, and in the Tensas basin barely 15 percent of original hardwood stands remain.

Today, Louisiana black bears confine their movements to the remaining hardwood and floodplain forests, places where their encounters with people are likely to be infrequent. Black bears are adaptable creatures that can, unlike some species, tolerate human presence—up to a point. They do, however, need sufficient sites for denning, bedding, food gathering, and escape. With the total population so low, restoration of this race will not be easy and will require great quantities of cooperation from both public and private resource managers.

MT. GRAHAM RED SQUIRREL

Tamiasciurus hudsonicus grahamensis
STATUS: ENDANGERED

A few years ago, this small rodent became one of the most political animals in America, sparking an intra-science feud, spawning lawsuits, and eventually becoming the focus of a federal statute. In the squirrel's name, a radical environmental group promised violence, and someone anonymously threatened one player in the controversy with death. Then–Secretary of the Interior Manuel Lujan was even led to proclaim that if you've seen one red squirrel, you've seen them all. Not bad for a shy rodent on a secluded mountain top.

This subspecies' story actually began about eleven thousand years ago, when massive geologic changes left some red squirrels isolated on a mountainous, wooded "sky island" in what would later be called southeastern Arizona. Surrounded by desert and with their nearest kin a couple of hundred miles away, this sequestered population had no way to mix with others of their kind or to expand their range. As the ensuing millennia came and went, these animals adapted themselves exclusively to the spruce-fir zone above 8,000 feet. They also became more and more genetically separated from their relatives. The most obvious changes were a shorter body and longer tail, but scientists recently have found additional, more subtle differences.

With European settlement of America, the squirrel's insular alpine habitat became known as Mount Graham, part of the Pinaleno Mountains. In 1894, taxonomists declared this isolated animal a separate subspecies of red squirrel—one of twenty-five races on the continent. (Interestingly, Mount Graham—at a latitude of about 32 degrees—constitutes the southernmost region suitable both for this squirrel and for the spruce-fir forest.)

No one knows how many Mount Graham red squirrels once existed, but early residents of the region described them as "common" and "abundant." As humans became more frequent visitors to the mountain, however, the squirrel's habitat began to shrink—mostly because of logging. This squirrel thrives only in stands of mature conifers, the kind of vegetation that also attracts timber harvesters. Additional habitat losses can be attributed to road building, home construction, recreational development, and fires.

By the 1920s, the Mount Graham red squirrel was already in decline, and by the 1950s it was no longer abundant anywhere. A decade later, at least one biologist believed (incorrectly) that it had vanished entirely. In the 1970s, the squirrel did indeed disappear from one of Mount Graham's peaks—possibly because of a fire in the area—and its habitat elsewhere on the mountain continued to shrink. Competition from the Abert's squirrel, introduced into the area in the 1940s by the Arizona Game and Fish Department, also may have contributed to the decline of the Mount Graham red squirrel. Today, habitat suitable for this subspecies totals fewer than twelve thousand acres, only about half of what originally existed.

The significantly diminished squirrel population continued to live in relative political obscurity until the mid-1980s, when the University of Arizona proposed the construction of a $200 million astronomical observatory atop Mount Graham. Conservationists argued that the project could destroy the rare squirrel (which had been listed as endangered in 1987), and the battle was joined. Hearings and meetings seemed to occur almost daily.

Some agencies waffled; others stood their ground. Countless hours of testimony were recorded. Reams of documents were generated. Astronomers fought with biologists over the project. The radical environmental group Earth First! suggested that any telescopes in the squirrel's range might somehow get broken. Someone mailed a death threat to a biologist who supported the observatory.

Seeking to extricate itself from this morass, the University of Arizona in 1988 petitioned the state's congressional delegation in Washington to execute an end run around the environmental roadblocks. This resulted in the passage of a federal statute exempting the project from further environmental review. Specifically, the act directed the Forest Service (the agency with final jurisdiction) to grant the university a permit to construct at least three—and possibly as many as seven—telescopes on the peak.

The legislation did, however, require several actions to help mitigate the project's negative effects on the squirrel. These included the prohibition of some recreational activities in areas above 10,000 feet elevation, the construction of a new and less intrusive road to the observatory, closures of several other roads on the mountain, the reforestation of some areas of squirrel habitat, and further studies of this subspecies. Several conservation organizations sued to prevent construction of the observatory, but the courts said the project could go forward. To date, two of seven possible telescopes have been built, and authorities say that so far the squirrel has not suffered. No one knows, of course, what effect future development will have.

Inextricably tied to conifer forests, the Mount Graham red squirrel's population rises and falls with seed cone production. When cones have been scarce, the total number of squirrels in the subspecies has dipped below 150. Following good cone years, the tally has risen to nearly 400, as more females breed and more bear two litters. Authorities believe the squirrel's present habitat can support no more than about 650 of the animals. The current best estimate of this subspecies' population is between 290 and 374 individuals.

Actually, that figure is more than an estimate. Thanks to a couple of specific behavior patterns, the Mount Graham red squirrel is one of just a few rodents in the world to have been more or less completely censused. These squirrels subsist by doing what squirrels do best—hoarding food. As seed cones mature each year, each squirrel gathers as many as it can into a central storehouse called a midden—a pile of cones and cone parts cached for winter use (the animal does not hibernate). If no other foods were available, a squirrel would likely need about 170 cones per day to survive, which means each animal must harvest the seeds from nine to fourteen mature trees. Consequently, midden storage is no slight or haphazard practice. These cone granaries often are handed down from one generation to the next and can grow to a foot in depth and more than a dozen feet in diameter.

In addition, these animals are highly territorial and protective of their middens. Each squirrel's territory normally has just one midden, and each midden belongs to just one squirrel. This provides biologists with a relatively easy way to count a population without even laying eyes on the animals themselves. The number of active middens should roughly equal the number of squirrels present. It's not always necessary to tally middens throughout the squirrel's entire range; an accurate midden count on a known portion of squirrel habitat can be extrapolated into a population figure for the entire area. As a result, authorities are rather confident of their Mount Graham red squirrel census statistics.

Mature trees do more for this squirrel than just provide seed cones. The closed canopy of an old-growth forest also keeps the ground below cool and moist. This, in turn, prevents the cones from opening before the squirrels need the seeds. It also promotes the growth of mushrooms, a major squirrel food in the summer. Finally, the interlocking branches of mature trees create squirrel escape routes, and rotting cavities offer good nesting sites.

Although general red squirrel biology and ecology are rather well understood, biologists do not know a great deal specifically about the Mount Graham subspecies. In many aspects, they can only assume that this race mimics the others: The red squirrel is a small, bushy-tailed arboreal rodent weighing about half a pound and measuring thirteen inches in length including five inches of tail. A scolding bark and drumming hind feet often announce its presence. Breeding takes place during the early spring (with a second mating season occurring later in some cases), with a resulting litter of three to five young. Nests can be in a tree cavity, a downed log, or (rarely) in open but sheltered branches. Besides cone seeds and mushrooms, these squirrels consume twig bark, berries, pollen, buds, and even occasional animal items such as bird eggs,

The entire Mount Graham red squirrel population (between 290 and 374 animals) lives on the "sky island" of Mount Graham in southeast Arizona.

38

avian fledglings, mice, and carrion. Coloration of the Mount Graham race ranges from gray to brown, with hints of rust or yellow on the back.

To protect the few remaining Mount Graham red squirrels, commercial logging, firewood cutting, and Christmas tree gathering are prohibited in the animal's habitat. Even campground firewood collecting is restricted. No hunting of red squirrels in this region is allowed. Authorities closely monitor midden numbers and squirrel populations. The biggest unknown factor remains the construction of the observatory and the effectiveness of the mitigating requirements.

Though it is almost certain that this race will never again be particularly abundant, biologists are optimistic that with proper care and restoration of habitat, the Mountain Graham red squirrel can be around for a long time to come. Computer models indicate that as forest succession on the mountain proceeds, more squirrel habitat will be created. But even if all goes well, say the computers, two centuries of forest maturation will increase the terrain's carrying capacity to only about 1,000 squirrels. These isolated animals will never live far from extinction.

OCELOT

Felis pardalis
STATUS: ENDANGERED

The ocelot's story is a familiar one: A beautiful and little understood cat at the northern edge of its range in the southern United States is shot and trapped without limit and now exists in very low numbers in this country (but is more prosperous farther south). With just a little tinkering, this description also fits the jaguar, jaguarundi, and margay—all on one endangered list or another. In a familiar scenario, ocelots were for decades simultaneously sought for their fur and persecuted as a predator. Now they are rare in the United States.

The ocelot is a beautiful cat, and that has been part of its problem. Until more or less banned by international agreement in recent years, there existed a thriving commerce in ocelot skins, which were fashioned into coats for the would-be chic. It took about a dozen ocelot pelts to make each coat, which at one time sold for $40,000 apiece. As recently as two decades ago, tens of thousands of ocelot skins were being traded on international fur markets, but recent laws (in many countries) have slowed that traffic to a trickle. The fur industry's enchantment with ocelot hides is understandable. Ocelot pelage ranges from creamy buff to reddish gray and is decorated throughout with irregular black blotches, spots, stripes, and rosettes. This is an extremely attractive animal, with no two individuals colored exactly alike.

When worn by its original owner, the ocelot's coat covers a lithe feline weighing twenty-five pounds or so—about the same size as a bobcat. The ocelot measures perhaps forty-five inches from end to end, but almost half that is tail. Its head is small, its eyes large, and its ears short. Like most wild felines, an ocelot on the move is a picture of grace, agility, stealth, and alertness. Because of its captivating beauty and relatively small size, the ocelot has long been employed as an exotic house pet. This is, however, a universally bad idea, since the cat has an odor that is offensive to people and claws that can injure humans and virtually destroy furniture. Not to mention the fact that wild animals belong in the wild.

Historically, the ocelot's range in the United States included most of Texas, a significant portion of south-central Arizona, and small fringes of Oklahoma, Arkansas, and Louisiana (where they border Texas). Ocelots have not maintained a significant presence in Arizona for quite some time, however. The last documented existence of this cat in that state occurred in 1964, when hunters killed one in the Huachuca Mountains. It is possible that ocelots have been in Arizona since then, but there have been no confirmed sightings. (Actually, authorities suspect that a few ocelots have been killed in Arizona since 1980, but the cat's protected status makes people very reluctant to report any ocelots that are shot or trapped, even unintentionally.) Not much good ocelot habitat exists in Arizona today, and the current consensus is that any ocelots in that state are almost certainly wanderers from Mexico or possibly captive cats that have been released.

Texas, however, still maintains one or two small populations of these cats. Biologists believe that a breeding population of 80 to 120 ocelots exists in the dense thorn-shrub plant communities in the southern part of the state. Four counties constitute the core of this ocelot range, but at least occasional sightings occur over a thirteen-county area. In addition, there may be a small population in south-central Texas. Studies of the DNA makeup of Texas ocelots suggest, however, that geographic isolation is gradually reducing their genetic diversity. The lack of diversity can result in the proliferation of undesirable traits and increased susceptibility to disease.

Fortunately, overall ocelot prosperity is not limited to their existence in the United States, as the cats range along both Mexican coasts and into South America as far as Argentina. To cover that much territory, an animal must be rather flexible, and the ocelot is. This cat exists in habitats ranging from tropical rain forests to savanna to shrubland—

41

as long as there is dense cover of some kind. Ocelots are mostly solitary, with each cat covering its one- to three-square-mile territory every few days.

The ocelot eats whatever prey is most abundant locally—mice, rats, rabbits, birds, lizards, monkeys, domestic poultry, snakes, insects, and a host of other creatures. It hunts primarily at night, often walking briskly to flush prey, then capturing its victim in a quick, pell-mell rush. Like other cats, the ocelot also knows how to stalk and set ambushes. In addition, it swims well and climbs trees with ease. Sometimes a mated pair will hunt as a team.

Wherever ocelots exist, a major threat to their prosperity is the loss of habitat, as more land is cleared for farming, grazing, and housing developments. Soil fertile enough to grow the dense cover ocelots require also is capable of producing excellent crops, and each year in Texas more ocelot habitat gives way to fields of vegetables, sugar cane, cotton, and sorghum. Additional ocelot acres become urbanized.

Consequently, authorities are not optimistic about the ocelot's future in Texas. Habitat restoration programs are creaking into motion, but decades will likely pass before they produce tangible results. In the meantime, the ocelot in the United States could disappear. The existence of healthy populations in Central and South America means, however, that this stunning and adaptable cat should be around for some time to come.

Pt. Arena Mountain Beaver

Aplodontia rufa nigra
STATUS: ENDANGERED

Introductions are definitely in order here, since this animal is easily one of the most restricted, least known of all the creatures on the threatened and endangered species lists. And its name is of little help. For starters, the Point Arena mountain beaver is not a beaver and is not even closely related to beavers. It does not have a flat tail, does not build dams, and does not live in streams. So forget the beaver part. In addition, this animal does not necessarily live in the mountains. In fact, it very much prefers wet, lowland areas (although it does exist at some rather high elevations). The only redeeming aspect of this species' name is that it truly is associated with a place called Point Arena (in California). So much for what the Point Arena mountain beaver is *not*. Now let's look at what it *is*.

The *Aplodontia* family consists of a single genus and species, making it a sort of evolutionary cul de sac. Scientists believe the seven subspecies of *Aplodontia* to be the oldest group of living rodents—as though nature started down one route toward rodentdom, then backtracked to take off in another direction. This left the mountain beaver as the sole resident of a dead-end street that has remained an obscure line on the mammalian map. This animal has survived essentially unchanged for eons.

Mountain beavers exist only in North America and only in the Pacific Northwest and California, although in past millennia their range included much more of the West. One subspecies or another lives in scattered pockets of habitat in western British Columbia, Washington, Oregon, and California. In some places they are rather common, but their quiet, woodsy lifestyle generally keeps contact with humans to a minimum (although they do occasionally get into trouble by digging in gardens or damaging young trees).

However, the *nigra* race—the Point Arena subspecies—is anything but common or wide ranging. It exists only in California, only in Mendocino County, and only on about twenty-five square miles of coastal woodlands. Biologists first collected specimens of this race (in 1914) near the town of Point Arena, and the name stuck. The current population estimate for the entire subspecies is about 150 animals scattered among ten sites.

But what is a mountain beaver, anyway? Well, it has variously been said to look like a muskrat without a tail, a big pocket gopher, or something that moved here from Australia. In more prosaic terms, this rodent is cylindrical, stout, and compact. An average adult weighs from four to six pounds and measures a foot or more in length. Its head is heavy and blunt with long whiskers, and its ears and eyes are small—the latter appearing somewhat beady. Mountain beaver legs are short with prominently clawed feet. The animal's tail is just a rounded stump barely an inch or so long. Its fur is coarse and dark.

The Point Arena mountain beaver exists only in cool, moist, wooded habitat with a mild climate and little seasonal temperature fluctuation. All populations are found in sheltered gulches or on steep, north-facing slopes. Vegetation in these areas can include cow parsnip, thimbleberry, poison oak, wood rose, red alder, ferns, firs, and pines. A thick understory of food plants and deep, firm soil for good digging are the basic mountain beaver housing requirements. This primitive animal likely survives only on the West Coast because these conditions have generally been present there without interruption for a long time.

As might be expected for a species that prefers rather moist areas, the mountain beaver handles water with ease. It swims well, crosses creeks with little concern, and doesn't even mind flooded tunnels. This animal is a notorious burrower, sometimes creating a network of subterranean passages that altogether may include a hundred yards of tunnel with a dozen or more entrances (most just beneath the surface). Its home range, however, is rather small, usually a small fraction of an acre.

Although these animals live in colonies of a sort, there are few interactions among individuals outside of the short spring breeding season. For a rodent, the Point Arena mountain beaver has a painfully slow reproductive rate. Females begin breeding only in their second year and produce just one litter of two or three young per annum. By fall, the young are nearly full grown and depart in search of their own territories.

The mountain beaver makes its living—mostly at night but with some daytime activity, too— consuming the abundance of green plants that define its habitat. The rather low nutritional value of its food requires the consumption of huge quantities, and this hardworking animal (maybe that's why it's called a beaver) often harvests surpluses for storage in either above-ground haystacks or in a subterranean pantry. Compounding its diet problems is a rather inefficient digestive tract that causes many nutrients to pass unused through the animal's system—a condition the mountain beaver often corrects by consuming its own droppings. Likewise, its primitive kidneys cannot concentrate urine, which requires the animal to drink frequently—another reason for living in moist areas.

Grazing, highway construction, home building, pet attacks, stream impoundment, erosion, the introduction of exotic plant species, and the proposed construction of a microwave tower all pose a threat to one group or another of Point Arena mountain beavers. Several of the ten colonies live on private land, which usually means a less secure future. And, of course, the highly localized nature of this subspecies makes it susceptible to inbreeding and natural disasters such as fire, flood, and earthquake. Only late in 1991 was the Point Arena mountain beaver added to the endangered species list.

Red Wolf

Canis rufus
STATUS: ENDANGERED

Although it certainly isn't out of the woods just yet, the red wolf has taken some big steps back from the brink of extinction. From a low of only seventeen animals in the 1970s, this species has clawed its way up the tally ladder to a current census of about two hundred—and climbing. Where the red wolf goes from here will depend to a great extent on how thoroughly the American public comes to understand this shy beast.

The red wolf is an in-between species, smaller than the gray wolf but larger than the coyote. Males weigh sixty to eighty pounds and females about twenty pounds less. Although some Texas populations of *Canis rufus* once had a decidedly reddish cast to their coats, coloration in this species can range from black to gray to yellowish and does include a rusty red in some individuals.

These animals generally lack the rather aggressive nature of their two relatives. They usually do not run in large packs like gray wolves, and they have none of the brazen character that makes coyotes so resilient and adaptable. The red wolf rarely kills a large animal such as a deer or sheep. Given a choice, red wolves would like nothing better than to spend a quiet lifetime secluded in a southern forest living off rabbits, squirrels, muskrats, nutria, raccoons, fish, and even some plants.

This nocturnal predator originally ranged across the South from Texas to North Carolina and north as far as Pennsylvania and Illinois, but as soon as European settlers arrived here, that domain began to shrink. Although the red wolf caused few people any harm, it was still a rather large predator and therefore had to go. The same war that decimated the ranks of gray wolves, grizzly bears, cougars, kit foxes, and other carnivores took many red wolf lives. In addition, this species suffered from the loss of its preferred wooded, bottomland habitat. As the pioneers cleared forests and drained swamps, the red wolf silently slipped closer toward oblivion.

By the 1960s, this species existed only in a five-county region on the Louisiana-Texas border. So few of the animals remained that many of the survivors had begun interbreeding with coyotes. Knowing that the red wolf would be swallowed up genetically if they stood by and did nothing, wildlife authorities decided to capture every red wolf they could find in the hope that captive breeding might restore the species.

In the mid-1970s, biologists live-trapped more than four hundred large wild canines from this last red wolf stronghold, but close examination revealed coyote or coyote–red wolf hybrid characteristics in most of these animals. Only forty-three of the captives appeared to be true red wolves, but to be absolutely certain of their genetic heritage, biologists began breeding them and scrutinizing their offspring. In the end, only seventeen of the forty-three apparent red wolves produced offspring that were completely devoid of coyote characteristics. With all individuals remaining in the wild considered to be coyote-red wolf hybrids, these seventeen animals became the Adams and Eves that authorities hoped would rescue a dying species.

At the Point Defiance Zoo in Tacoma, Washington, officials began the delicate process of rebuilding a wild species with captive breeding. The project has since broadened to include thirty-one facilities in more than a dozen states. Late in the 1970s, authorities experimented with relocation techniques by turning a few red wolves loose on Bulls Island, South Carolina, a 5,000-acre tract that is part of the Cape Romain National Wildlife Refuge. The attempt proved that reintroductions could indeed work, but that much larger tracts are required for breeding populations of red wolves. So the search began for a mainland site of sufficient size.

In 1987, authorities released the first wolves into the Alligator River National Wildlife Refuge in North Carolina, a 150,000-acre peninsula of swamp, marsh, and forest—exactly the kind of habitat red wolves like. This site has since become the showplace of red wolf restoration. Today, about thirty wolves roam this refuge, most having been born there of releasee parents. The only problem is that the Alligator River Refuge cannot hold many more of the red wolves that biologists eventually plan to return to the wild.

In addition to permanent releases, mating pairs of red wolves are regularly turned loose on three islands off the South Carolina, Florida, and Mississippi coasts. On these island laboratories, the adults get a taste of life in the wild away from humans while producing young that know no other kind of existence. Later, the entire family can be captured and rereleased at a permanent location. This stint of wild but controlled living increases the wolves' chances for a long life while reducing the likelihood that they will develop behavior patterns that could cause problems.

In 1992, red wolves reached another milestone in their remarkable comeback when biologists turned twelve of the animals loose in Great Smoky Mountains National Park on the Tennessee–North Carolina border. This marked the first time that a major predator had been reintroduced to a national park. With two red wolf populations now in the wild, authorities have begun looking for a third release site. (The recovery plan calls for three separate populations totaling 220; another 330 will remain in captivity.) National Forest land in the southern Appalachians is one possibility, but it may be a few years before any wolves are turned loose there.

Appropriate release sites can be hard to find, since an ideal reintroduction locale should contain at least 150,000 acres and relatively few people. But more important than land may be the public attitude toward this animal. Although red wolves are incredibly shy predators that typically flee from encounters with humans, the notion persists that people are somehow in danger when wolves are about. The often obscured truth is that wolves—especially red wolves—simply do not attack people. In addition, red wolves suffer unjustly from the livestock-killing, game-destroying reputations of their coyote and gray wolf relatives. Although red wolves certainly are capable of dispatching deer, sheep, and other ungulates, they almost never do.

Still, the fear and hatred of wolves can run deep. In the early 1980s, the U.S. Fish and Wildlife Service considered releasing red wolves into the Land Between the Lakes area (owned by the federal government) of western Kentucky and Tennessee. The proposal foundered, however, when local residents—led by livestock interests—raised a great outcry against the wolves.

When the Alligator River land in North Carolina became available for red wolf releases in 1984, authorities feared a similar public reaction. This time, however, officials devoted considerable effort to educating the public about the true nature of red wolves, and the local populace responded with a thorough acceptance of the project—support that continues today. People living near future release sites may need the same kind of convincing.

Public relations is not the red wolf's only problem. Roads through their brushy habitat make attractive travel corridors, and two of the animals have been hit by cars. An alligator killed one. Another choked on a raccoon kidney and died. One died from injuries sustained in a fight with another wolf. And a female perished as a result of birthing complications. Even though red wolves are at the top of their food chain and have no predators, their life expectancy in the wild is only a few years.

Finally, there is the taxonomic cloud that has long hung over the red wolf's head. This animal was not described scientifically until the late date of 1851, and ever since then biologists have speculated about whether it might in fact be a cross between the coyote and the gray wolf and not really a separate species at all. This theory received a big scientific boost recently when researchers took an extensive look at the DNA of these three species. Virtually every sample of red wolf DNA examined by the scientists matched that of either coyotes or gray wolves. This could mean that red wolves are indeed relatively recent wolf-coyote hybrids. Or, it could indicate that at some point in the distant past red wolves crossbred with the other two species. In either case, the genetic similarities raise questions in some minds about the need to preserve red wolves as an endangered species.

Another school of thought suggests that *Canis rufus* may in fact be *the* progenitor wolf. This theory says that in the beginning there was only the red wolf and that it evolved in North America. Some of these animals then migrated to Asia and Europe across the Bering land bridge, only to return millennia later as gray wolves. According to this hypothesis, the gray wolves, which had evolved into a much larger and more assertive animal, proceeded to force their red wolf "parents" southward onto the range where European settlers found them a few centuries ago.

Most people today, however, are probably more interested in the red wolf's future than in its past. When they look at a red wolf, they see a flesh-and-blood animal scrambling to stay alive, not a series of DNA squiggles on a microscope slide. Most large predators have taken a great beating at the hands of humankind, and only recently has society begun to redress those mistakes. With continuing human help, the red wolf could turn one of our classic blunders into a great success.

SALT MARSH HARVEST MOUSE

Reithrodontomys raviventris
STATUS: ENDANGERED

Ten to fifteen thousand years ago, this species' predecessors established themselves along California's central coast in what would later be called the San Francisco Bay region. As the saline sea invaded shallow valleys, it probably isolated some of the mice on islands that contained little or no fresh water. Forced to adapt to a salty environment or perish,

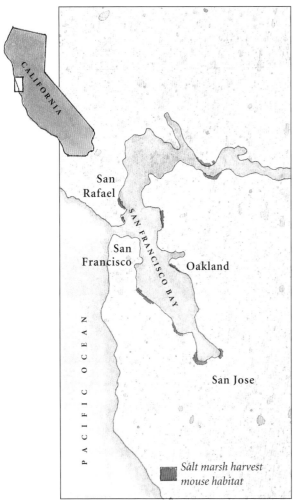

Salt marsh harvest mouse habitat

these diminutive rodents quickly (at least in evolutionary terms) learned to cope with high levels of salt. Eventually, the saline wetlands of coastal California became their habitat of preference, and for uncounted generations, salt marsh harvest mice have prospered in an environment that remains hostile to most other creatures.

Except humans. For well over a century now, people have been flocking to the coast of California, and little by little the habitat of the salt marsh harvest mouse has been altered. Today, this species clings to a tenuous existence on relatively tiny plots of ground. No good counts are available, but it is unlikely that more than a few thousand of these mice remain.

The salt marsh harvest mouse weighs less than half an ounce and is under three inches in length (plus another three inches of tail). The upper part of its body comes in various shades of buff and brown. The belly ranges from white to cinnamon. Living as it does in close proximity to water, this species swims well and floats on the surface like a cork. Despite a breeding season that can last most of the year, the salt marsh harvest mouse actually has a rather low reproductive rate. One or two litters per year is typical, with only three or four young produced each time. The animal's diet consists mostly of seeds and green vegetation. Individuals in some populations drink sea water directly, while others prefer water that is less heavily salted. Highly efficient kidneys permit the ingestion of so much salt.

Never very widespread, the salt marsh harvest mouse has in recent decades become confined to smaller and smaller portions of the San Francisco Bay complex (the bay plus its tributaries). About 150 years ago, this region contained nearly 300 square miles of tidal marshland and was home to a menagerie of wildlife, including sea otters, countless shore birds, and hundreds of thousands of ducks. Then came the gold rush, the settlers, and the city of San Francisco. As early as 1850, the pioneers were filling coastal wetlands to provide room for the growing metropolis. Nearby, farmers turned additional acres of marsh into agriculturally productive land, and dikes created ponds for the creation of salt by evaporation. Upstream mining operations dumped cubic miles of soil into the ecosystem.

Today, barely a fifth of the original marshland exists—and much of what remains has been (from the mouse's point of view) adversely modified. Some marshy habitats are little more than narrow strips along dikes. Others have undergone significant changes in vegetation. Outflows from sewage treatment plants affect some by freshening the water and altering the vegetation. And as the backfilling, draining, and diking persist, the mouse continues to suffer.

The salt marsh harvest mouse lacks the frenetic, darting demeanor of many of its kin, moving instead at a much more relaxed pace. Cool morning temperatures sometimes put the animal in an extremely sluggish state. Researchers have easily picked up torpid mice and put them in a pocket—only to have the animals revive fully after ten minutes or so of warming. This species does not dig burrows; it chooses instead to create an above-ground grassy home, modify an old bird nest, or even get along with no nest at all. Lack of escape cover—especially at high tide—makes the salt marsh harvest mouse vulnerable to predation from snakes, hawks, owls, and other meat eaters.

Consequently, salt marsh harvest mice continue to survive only in the densest marshlands—commonly those dominated by pickleweed. These animals are so reliant on thick cover that even a roadway thirty feet wide presents a formidable barrier to their movements. As the remaining supply of dense cover is further divided into smaller and smaller tracts, mouse populations become increasingly isolated and therefore subject to genetic drift and annihilation from natural catastrophe or human activity.

The continued existence of this little animal hinges on the protection and enhancement of existing marshes in the San Francisco Bay area. Privately owned habitat is always in danger of alteration, and some significant battles already have been fought between developers and conservationists. Other marshes, under the management of state or federal wildlife agencies, are more secure. It is likely to be some time, however, before this mouse is safe from the threat of extinction.

SAN JOAQUIN KIT FOX

Vulpes macrotis mutica
STATUS: ENDANGERED

Long ago, a group of diminutive foxes (eight subspecies in all) opted for life in the desert. Perhaps the coyotes and wolves were fewer there. Or maybe the digging was easier, for kit foxes depend heavily on taking sanctuary in underground burrows. Whatever the reason, these little animals carved out a niche for themselves hunting rodents, rabbits, and other small prey in regions the rains mostly avoided. One of these creatures came to dwell exclusively in a river valley of what would later be called California. When humans got around to labeling all things biological and geological, they gave both the fox and the valley the name San Joaquin.

The first thing you notice about kit foxes is their small stature. In fact, their title comes from their modest proportions, probably by way of some early human name giver who thought them the immature offspring of another species. Kit foxes appear to be about the same size as a house cat, but even this is deceiving, for the average adult kit fox tips the scales at a petite five pounds—only about half the weight of a well-fed domestic tabby. Standing erect, their front shoulders are just a foot off the ground. Though only someone with a caliper and a scale could tell the difference, the San Joaquin subspecies is the largest of the kits, which as a group are the smallest foxes in North America.

This creature's small size and delicate features contribute to its attractive appearance. Its summer coat is buff to gray, changing in winter to rusty sides and grizzled gray on the back. Its belly remains a striking white year round. The bushy foot-long tail culminates in a distinctive spot of black, which matches the ebony accents on the sides of its face. Perhaps the most diagnostic kit fox feature, however, is a set of ears that appear disproportionately large. (One possible reason for the big ears is that sound serves these hunters better than smell in dry air that does not hold scents well.)

Historically, the San Joaquin kit fox ranged from San Joaquin and Stanislaus counties in the north to Kern County in the south. Early trappers estimated a density of one fox per square mile (a figure that biologists say still applies to good habitat), which could have put the animal's population in the neighborhood of twelve thousand individuals. At any rate, the San Joaquin kit fox was fairly common when humans began settling the valley in large numbers.

Though people felt no particular malice toward the kit fox, they nonetheless did much to eliminate it. The prevailing philosophy of the day held that predators were by nature bad, and so they were eliminated at every opportunity. If a trap or poison bait set for a coyote or wolf killed a kit fox instead, that was okay, too. Schoolboys with rifles—and everyone else for that matter—shot the foxes on sight, and the kit's unsuspicious and trusting nature made it an easy target. When irrigation water became available and farming boomed, kit fox habitat went under the plow, and their numbers dwindled further. Urbanization and oil production in the valley consumed additional habitat.

The most recent population estimate for this species is about seven thousand animals, with half of the foxes in just two counties (Kern and San Luis Obispo). The recent long-term drought did not help that figure any, but the dry spell broke in 1992, and biologists are hopeful that kit fox numbers will rise as more moist conditions give a boost to prey numbers.

Like all others of their kind, the San Joaquin kit fox is a highly nocturnal predator that spends most of its daylight hours resting safely in a subterranean burrow, which it either excavates itself or appropriates from some other digging creature. Kit foxes (and their close relatives the swift foxes) are the only canines to use burrows throughout the year, not just while raising pups. Biologists believe that a shortage of appropriate dens may be a significant factor limiting kit fox use of an area.

53

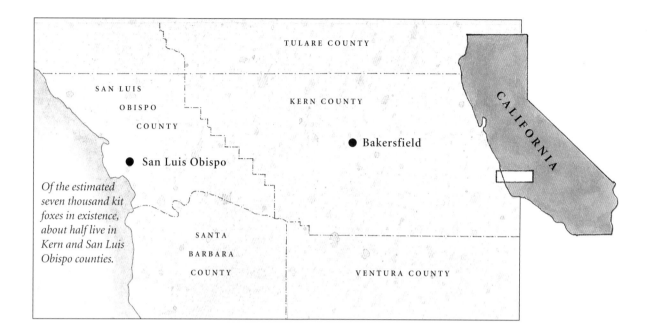

TULARE COUNTY

SAN LUIS

OBISPO

COUNTY

KERN COUNTY

● Bakersfield

● San Luis Obispo

Of the estimated seven thousand kit foxes in existence, about half live in Kern and San Luis Obispo counties.

SANTA

BARBARA

COUNTY

VENTURA COUNTY

CALIFORNIA

Authorities have been encouraged, though, by research indicating that the animals can and will use artificial dens such as culverts, well casings, and abandoned pipelines.

The kit fox follows a rather predictable routine, leaving its den to hunt after dark and returning just before dawn. Because of this highly nocturnal schedule, few people—even residents of kit fox country—ever lay eyes on this little predator. Mice, kangaroo rats, rabbits, and other small animals make up the bulk of its diet, and it appears that the fox also gets all the moisture it needs from the bodies of its prey. When given the opportunity, the kit fox will drink, but apparently water is optional—an extremely helpful adaptation for an animal destined to live in arid terrain.

Since the war against predators ended a few decades ago, kit fox fortunes have improved somewhat, although habitat loss often replaces premature death as a limiting factor. Some San Joaquin kit foxes are still mistaken for other species and shot, and trappers still take some by accident. Others are hit by vehicles on highways, where they go to make a meal out of road-killed jackrabbits and other carrion. Poisons intended only for rodents also take some fox lives when the predators ingest the toxin-filled prey.

Another threat is the coyote, a much larger cousin of the kit fox. Since these two species feed on many of the same animals, they compete directly for a limited prey base, a situation that may lead the coyote to eliminate the fox whenever it gets the chance. In fact, the kit fox's penchant for hiding out in a burrow may have evolved as a way to stay away from coyotes most of the time. Fox tunnels typically measure no more than ten inches in diameter, too small to admit a coyote or other larger predator.

With the available habitat continually shrinking, kit fox numbers are not likely to make any great gains in the near future. With help, however, perhaps this diminutive desert denizen can hold off against further losses and continue to grace the California night for a long time to come. (For additional information about kit foxes and their close relatives, the swift foxes, please refer to the Oregon and North Dakota sections of this book, pages 128 and 124.)

SONORAN PRONGHORN

Antilocapra americana sonoriensis
STATUS: ENDANGERED

The Sonoran pronghorn (named for the Mexican state of Sonora) has chosen a tough life for itself. In fact, it's hard to imagine any animal—let alone a large one like the pronghorn—surviving in some of the Sonoran's habitat, which is to say the desert. This is a true-blue desert animal, and that is what makes it unique.

A couple of centuries ago, pronghorns roamed the American West in numbers too great to count. Some estimates of their abundance run as high as forty million animals, making this species nearly as abundant as bison. Lewis and Clark and the pioneers who followed them west spoke of great teeming herds that made the entire prairie appear to be alive. From Oregon to Iowa and from Canada to Mexico, pronghorns carpeted the plains.

Scientists later determined that the great pronghorn masses were actually composed of five subspecies, each differing from the next in rather minor ways, as is often the case with subspecies. A lay person passing through a herd containing all five races (not that such a collection ever existed) would likely have been unable to distinguish one from the other. Consequently, it is impossible to know how many Sonorans once existed. Certainly, there were many more pronghorns in the regions where these animals now live, but just how many of them were Sonorans and how many were other subspecies is anyone's guess.

Because this animal is uniquely American, Europeans had never seen such a creature before and consequently had only mixed luck in naming it the pronghorn antelope. The "prong" part fits well, referring to the forward-jutting point that emerges about halfway up the male's prominent horn. They even got the "horn" part right, as this headgear is truly a horn and not an antler such as elk and deer wear. But calling this creature an antelope is incorrect, although it's easy to understand how that happened. Despite its resemblance to the Old World antelopes, the pronghorn is actually the last living member of a distinctly American family of herbivores that existed here five million years ago.

As they did with the bison, the European newcomers to this country devastated the great pronghorn herds. Some were shot for food and used efficiently. Thousands of others were killed only for their tenderloins, with the rest of the meat left on the prairie to rot. Still others were slaughtered for wolf bait, their corpses laced with poison and scattered around the West like land mines ready to destroy any meat eater that found them. When farmers turned huge tracts of prairie into cropland, millions of pronghorns had to move on, and many more surrendered their territory to the ubiquitous sheep and cattle that came to populate the western range.

As the agriculture industry fenced the West, pronghorns found themselves locked out of some prime territory. For eons, there had been no obstructions on the prairie, and these animals had never learned to jump—there simply was nothing to jump over. So fences gave them fits. If the bottom strand of a barbwire fence was a foot or so off the ground, the pronghorns sometimes learned to slide under the obstruction. But woven wire (often used for sheep) and barbed wire strung close to the ground thwarted their movements, even though the fence was just a few feet high and certainly jumpable if the pronghorns had only known how.

A century of human settlement saw pronghorn numbers plummet from many millions to about twelve thousand. But just as these animals appeared to be slipping down the slope toward certain extinction, three things came to their rescue: the emerging conservation ethic, the new science of wildlife management, and sport hunters. Hunters asked for and got new laws that stopped the wanton slaughter and unregulated shooting of pronghorns. Refuges provided some sanctuary. And wildlife scientists learned how to build pronghorn herds. Thus aided by humans, pronghorns ceased their decline and reversed course. As fast as their ranks had shrunk, they now grew. Today, more than a million of the animals roam the prairie, with populations in every western state.

No one knows for sure, but historians believe that the downturn in the far less numerous Sonoran pronghorn mimicked that of the species as a whole. Originally distributed throughout southern Arizona and into Mexico, the Sonoran's range and numbers shrank considerably during the years of Arizona settlement. Overhunting was long thought to be the major cause, but forty years of protection has not led to a major recovery. Consequently, authorities now point the finger of blame also at habitat loss due to overgrazing and the dewatering of some major rivers. Despite public ownership of most Sonoran pronghorn range, the land has been slow to recover—testimony to its fragile nature.

For the Sonoran pronghorn, it was isolation—not human inspiration or perspiration—that probably saved the day. Only in 1945 did researchers even identify the Sonoran as a distinct subspecies, distinguished from the others by its lighter color, smaller size, and slightly different cranial measurements. That Sonorans survived at all is likely due to the fact that they dwell in some of the most inhospitable habitat on the continent. Because few people passed through the harsh deserts of southern Arizona, small populations of Sonorans were able to hang on there.

Luckily, these survivors chose for the most part to live on public lands—the Cabeza Prieta National Wildlife Refuge, the Organ Pipe Cactus National Monument, and an Air Force gunnery range. A 1992 survey located 125 Sonorans in Arizona, leading authorities to speculate that the U.S. population (allowing for unseen animals) may total about 250. Approximately that many more are believed to exist in Mexico. These numbers represent an increase from counts and estimates of a few years ago.

That these animals can live where they do seems something of a miracle. Their preferred habitat consists mostly of flat, sandy, rocky desert. Creosote, paloverde, and cactus are the primary vegetation. Rainfall is scant, sporadic, and in some places in some years nonexistent. Arriving moisture quickly soaks into the ground. Daytime temperatures sometimes reach 120 degrees Fahrenheit. There are no towns, no ranches, no mining—just desert and a few hardy Sonoran pronghorns. These animals are so adapted to their harsh environment that they may have evolved a waterless lifestyle. Biologists aren't ready to say for sure, but Sonorans just could be getting by without ever drinking water. With surface water a real rarity, they appear to get most—and possibly all—of their moisture from the vegetation they eat and by licking droplets of dew.

Most of what is known (or assumed) about Sonorans has been extrapolated from studies on *Antilocapra americana americana,* the pronghorn subspecies commonly seen on western prairies. Aside from biological and behavioral differences linked to the Sonoran's unique habitat, the endangered race differs little from its kin, except to be about 10 percent smaller.

Pronghorns of all subspecies are well equipped for life in open country. They long ago gave up all hope of hiding, and have instead evolved a striking white-on-brown color pattern that makes them stand out on the generally bland prairie. White stripes grace the pronghorn neck, and its rear and belly are mostly white as well. When alarmed, the animal flares its white rump hairs, creating a warning signal that can be seen for a mile.

Huge, wide-set eyes (larger even than those of a horse or cow) defend against predators by spotting them early. Conventional wisdom says that pronghorn vision is about equal to a human looking through eight-power binoculars. Once danger has been seen, the amazing pronghorn legs and lungs take over, whisking the animal gracefully away faster than any other mammal in the western hemisphere. Stories (reliable and otherwise) of pronghorn speed abound, but the animals have been known to hit fifty miles an hour and can cruise at thirty miles an hour for several miles. Coyotes and eagles are the primary pronghorn enemies, with most predation occurring in the spring when newborn fawns are vulnerable.

An adult male pronghorn (*americana* race) might stand 38 inches tall at the shoulder and weigh 120 pounds; does are somewhat smaller. Both genders grow horns, but female headgear is short and without the prominent prong of the male. Horns fall off in early winter and grow back the following summer. The bucks also sport a black cheek patch the females lack. In spring and summer, pronghorns eat whatever grass and forbs they can find (and crops like alfalfa and wheat if they're available), but they primarily are grazers of brushy shrubs. In late summer and early fall, bucks spar (mostly nonviolently) for breeding rights, with the winners assembling female harems of twenty or so individuals. Fawns—usually twins—are born in the spring.

The future of the Sonoran pronghorn is an open question. With so few of the animals in existence, they certainly must be considered one of America's most imperiled species. On the other hand, their habitat remains relatively secure, and their numbers have been slowly increasing. Authorities have selected two sites for possible relocations to start new herds, and it also has been suggested that the Phoenix Zoo propagate Sonorans in captivity for eventual return to the wild. Currently, however, there are no definite plans for either project. In the meantime, these desert dwellers will likely continue eking a living from some of the harshest, most inhospitable habitat on earth.

SOUTHERN SEA OTTER

Enhydra lutris nereis
STATUS: THREATENED

Everyone knows the sea otter. Television news crews and wildlife film makers have nearly made a cliche of the shot that begins with a panoramic view of the ocean, then narrows to an appealing, almost quizzical-faced animal floating on its back in a bed of kelp. Before the viewer's eyes, the sea otter grasps a clam in its forepaws and smashes it against the flat rock lying on its chest. Deftly, the otter removes the tasty innards from the shell and gobbles them down. Then it smoothly rolls over and slips beneath the surface for another trip to the undersea pantry. Cut to commercial.

Sea otters are indeed the darlings of the deep. Pelagic teddy bears, they've been called. Kids giggle at their sometimes clownlike antics. Adults marvel at their aquatic skills. And everyone admires their lush fur and streamlined beauty—everyone except some commercial fishermen, who believe the otters are eating them out of ship and sustenance. But that's getting ahead of the otter's remarkable story.

The civilized world came to know the sea otter by way of a Russian shipwreck in 1741 on the Commander Islands, which lie between the Aleutians and the Kamchatka Peninsula in the Bering Sea. The expedition's leader, Vitus Bering, perished in the ordeal, but his men survived, in part by eating the strange, docile, sea-going animals they took to calling beavers. After several months of maroonment, the crew managed to build a boat and sail back to Siberia, taking with them the plush pelts of these animals. Folks quickly renamed this newly discovered animal the sea otter, and furriers' hearts beat fast at the sight of such lustrous skins. The sailors said there were thousands more otters where these had come from, and suddenly the rush was on.

For the next 170 years, ships sailed the Pacific rim in search of sea otter pelts. Originally, otters occupied coastal waters from Baja California north to Alaska, around the Aleutian Island arc, and southwest nearly to Japan. No one knows, of course, how many otters there were or how many were killed, but both numbers had lots of zeros. Perhaps a million otters gave their lives for fur coats, but that is only a guess.

In a sequence of events that seems so predictable now—and so surprising back then—otter numbers eventually began to dwindle. By 1900, vessels that formerly brought back thousands of pelts were returning with only dozens. Then in the early years of this century, the flow of otter skins stopped entirely, despite a price tag of $1,000 or more per pelt. The otters were simply gone. Though no one knew for sure, many people believed that the last otter had been killed, that the animal had finally been pushed into the abyss of extinction.

In 1911, the United States, Japan, Russia, and Britain signed a treaty prohibiting the hunting of sea otters, but no one knew if any otters were left to protect. For twenty-five years, the extinction theory held. Finally, in 1936, someone discovered a small colony of the animals living near Amchitka Island southwest of Alaska. From there south, however, a great otter void remained.

Then, on March 19, 1938, rancher Howard Sharpe strolled onto the front porch of his home perched above the rugged coast just south of Carmel, California. As he peered

58

casually through a powerful telescope at nothing in particular, some slight movement caught his eye. Soon he found himself looking at an animal he had never see before, a creature bobbing calmly on its back amid a bed of kelp. And not just one. The closer he looked, the more he saw, and before long his estimate rose to three hundred animals. But what were they? Seals? Sea lions? Some strange form of walrus? Only later, after Sharpe succeeded in coaxing biologists to his porch, could the truth be known. Incredibly, the pelt takers had overlooked a small colony of sea otters, which in anonymity had grown to considerable size.

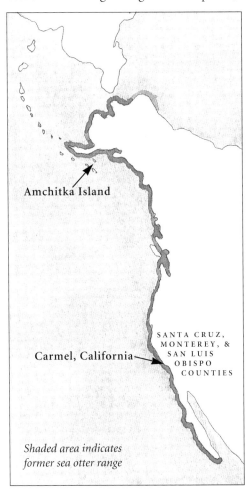

Amchitka Island

Carmel, California

SANTA CRUZ, MONTEREY, & SAN LUIS OBISPO COUNTIES

Shaded area indicates former sea otter range

takers had overlooked a small colony of sea otters, which in anonymity had grown to considerable size.

Much has happened to sea otters since their return from apparent extinction in the 1930s. Scientists now say there are actually three subspecies of otters—two sharing the animal's northern range and a southern sea otter (also called the California sea otter) officially known as *Enhydra lutris nereis.* Differences among the three are slight, however, limited mostly to minor variations of cranial measurements. With protection, natural range expansion, and planned relocations, the two northern species have reclaimed sizeable chunks of their former range and increased their numbers substantially. Today, these populations likely contain between 100,000 and 200,000 otters.

The southern sea otter has not been as prosperous, and it is this race that is listed as threatened. Since 1938, the California otter population has grown only to about 2,000 animals, which now occupy approximately 220 miles of shoreline off Santa Cruz, Monterey, and San Luis Obispo counties. A few years ago, authorities attempted to start a new southern sea otter population by relocating about 140 of the animals to San Nicolas Island, one of the Channel Islands southwest of Los Angeles. This experiment has been far from successful, however, as only a dozen or so relocated otters remain at San Nicolas. Some returned to their original range, and a few were known to be killed, but most just disappeared.

Despite their relatively low numbers, southern sea otters have become a nuisance—and even a threat—to some people. Lots of fishermen make a living pulling shellfish from the continental shelf off the California coast, and many of them see otters as an impediment to their continued employment. To keep its blubberless body warm, an otter requires a huge caloric intake—up to 25 percent of its own weight in food each day. Much of this sustenance comes in the form of sea life that human fishermen also value—crabs, clams, and mussels, for example—and what otters eat, fishermen can't catch. Abalone fishermen have been especially hard hit by otter appetites. (Otters also feed on a host of sea species that have no commercial value.)

The authorities who manage all these resources have attempted to effect some compromises, but they have not worked well. For a time, a boundary to the otter's range was supposed to exist in the neighborhood of San Luis Obispo (thereby protecting the shellfish industry to the south). Otters that strayed south of this line were supposed to be captured and returned to the main part of their range, but these animals are difficult to catch and often don't stay where they're put, and this program is now defunct. Many abalone fishermen in sea otter territory have simply given up trying to compete with these animals and have either gone out of business or chosen to pursue other types of fish.

For most people, however, the sea otter remains a joy to behold. It is the largest member of the Mustelidae family, a clan that includes weasels, mink, badgers, and skunks. Unlike most of its kin, the otter is not at all shy about performing its daily chores in full view of anyone who cares to watch. In some places—such as Cannery Row wharf in Monterey Bay—they can be seen almost any day diving for food or consuming the catch in their patented tool-assisted backfloat style.

Southern sea otter males average sixty pounds (females about forty) and can be nearly five feet long. Their front feet possess significant prehensile qualities, and their rear toes are webbed for underwater propulsion. The horizontally flattened tail serves as a rudder. Although sea otters are graceful, powerful swimmers, they become awkward on land and seldom venture more than a few yards from the water. Their fur is among the thickest, most luxuriant in the world. Someone has estimated (or counted?) that an otter pelt contains a billion hairs, and the animals spend a lot of time grooming this dense coat, which must be kept clean to prevent matting and the hypothermia that would likely result. Sea otter color ranges from black to reddish brown, with head, throat, and chest often shaded with gray or creamy white. Prominent facial whiskers lend the animal a comical look.

Beds of kelp are the sea otter's favorite habitat. Although capable of diving to 250 feet, they do most of their foraging in shallower water. Otters can stay submerged four or five minutes, but a minute or two is a more likely average. If a female is tending a pup, she leaves the youngster bobbing like a cork on the surface while she dives for food. Otters are so adapted to life in the sea that they even breed and give birth in the water.

Compared to populations in other areas, the southern sea otter has had a slow recovery on the California coast, perhaps due to the proximity of so many people. Occasionally, someone still shoots an otter, but accidental entanglement in fishing nets is a much bigger problem. Some young otters also get hit by boats. The biggest potential threat to southern sea otters, however, is an oil spill. A hundred million barrels of oil pass through southern sea otter territory each year, and a major spill could foul the fur of a large portion of this population. Otters with only 25 percent of their fur contaminated with oil would likely get cold and die from hypothermia.

Barring such a catastrophe, however, the southern sea otter is likely to continue doing what it does best—fishing the ocean floor and entertaining people. For most folks, the otter represents the best opportunity to see a threatened or endangered mammal in the wild.

STELLER SEA LION

Eumetopias jubatus
STATUS: THREATENED

In 1741, Vitus Bering, the Danish navigator turned Russian explorer, led an expedition into the previously uncharted waters around the mass of land and islands we now call Alaska. Sailing with him was a German surgeon and naturalist named George Wilhelm Steller. While shipwrecked on one of those islands, Steller made detailed notes concerning the abundant native wildlife, and one of these species—a large seal-like animal—eventually was named in his honor. (Bering's name, of course, became attached to several geographical features in the region.)

Steller (the man) did not have to look very hard to spot his namesake. The sea lion he discovered is huge. Bulls grow to ten feet in length and weigh up to a ton—about the same as a bison. Females are considerably smaller. The Steller species is much larger than any other sea lions or the closely related fur seals.

In familiar pinniped form, the Steller sea lion has a long head and neck, large and expressive eyes, and small, pointed ears. Whitish whiskers sprout from its upper lip, and a short, glossy coat covers its body. A layer of blubber wards off the aquatic cold. Flippers provide propulsion in the water and act as primitive legs while the animal is on land. Coloration ranges from nearly black to reddish and yellowish brown.

Eons ago, a portion of mammaldom opted for life in the sea. Some species—whales and their kin—severed entirely their ties with the land. Others, such as the Steller sea lion, made only a partial transition, maintaining forever some vital links with terra firma. Though sea lions spend most of their time in the water, they regularly clamber up the rocky shoreline of remote islands to rest or to reproduce. Much of what we know about these animals comes from observations made at such haul-out (resting) sites and rookeries (birthing and breeding places). The sea lion's lifestyle while in the water remains something of a mystery.

Steller sea lions inhabit secluded shorelines and island coasts from Japan around the northern Pacific rim and south down the western U.S. coast to California. Their centers of abundance are in the Gulf of Alaska and around the Aleutian Islands, although more than fifty different rookeries (and many more haul-out sites) have been identified. Relatively few Steller sea lions—perhaps only four thousand or so—exist along the western U.S. coast, which is why they're classified as threatened. California has three small rookeries, Oregon two, and Washington none. All three states have haul-out sites.

Steller sea lions are great travelers, conducting extensive annual migrations that even today are not fully understood. But they are in a sense homebodies, too. Each spring, the bulls arrive at traditional rookeries to establish—via roaring, hissing, biting, and other forms of aggression—coastline territories onto which they hope to attract harems. In a few weeks, the cows arrive, many pregnant with a single pup. The forty-five-pound youngster is born a few days later, and just a couple of weeks after that, the female comes into estrus and mating follows.

Once breeding has occurred, the embryo develops for a few weeks, then falls dormant. Several months later it attaches to the uterine wall and starts growing again (delayed implantation), with parturition eventually occurring nearly a full year after conception. Once the breeding season has ended, the bulls—which have not eaten for perhaps sixty days—abandon the rookery for the sustenance and serenity of the sea. The cows and pups remain for a couple more months, but eventually they too return to the ocean. The following spring the cycle repeats.

Like most other wild creatures, the Steller sea lion's primary activity is finding and consuming food, which in this case means walleye pollack, herring, capelin, salmon, cod, flounder, skates, octopus, crabs, mussels, and other sea life. Most feeding occurs crepuscularly (at dawn or dusk) or at night, and up to fifty of the animals sometimes dine as a group. Though clumsy on land, the Steller sea lion is a master of the aquatic environment—diving, turning, and looping around like an ace fighter pilot. Feeding forays may take them 60 miles from shore and down to depths of 600 feet.

Native northern peoples hunted the Steller sea lion with the spears and other primitive weapons in their arsenals. An animal this large provided a lot of food for the family table—not to mention the valuable hide and the oil rendered from sea lion blubber. Aboriginal harvests, however, likely made only the smallest of dents in sea lion populations. Nineteenth- and early twentieth-century killing—of pups for their fur and of adults for their oil and because they feed on fish—eliminated tens of thousands of the animals.

Still, lots of Steller sea lions remained. Although the animals are virtually impossible to count while at sea, they can be censused easily while at their rookeries. In the 1950s, biologists began keeping track of Steller numbers by flying over rookeries during the birthing and breeding season. These annual tallying trips have revealed a curious—and alarming—trend. In 1960, wildlife authorities estimated Steller sea lion numbers for the Aleutian Islands and Gulf of Alaska (where most of these animals live) at 140,000, and in the 1970s, officials said the worldwide population was between 245,000 and 290,000. By 1985, however, the Alaska figure had fallen to 68,000, and four years later it was down to 25,000—a decline of 82 percent in just three decades. Meanwhile, the global figure appears to have plummeted from about a quarter million to something in the neighborhood of 40,000 to 66,000 animals.

And no one really knows why. Native peoples still kill a few Steller sea lions. Some get caught in fishing nets, poachers shoot some, and fishermen intentionally kill some because they believe the animals eat too many fish. Sharks and killer whales take a few. Additional fingers of blame point to diseases, pollution, and climatic changes, but all these things combined appear incapable of causing such a precipitous drop in Steller sea lion numbers. The current best hypothesis holds that the sea lions are suffering from a general lack of food. Prey species, the theory goes, have undergone population declines of their own (possibly from overharvest by commercial fisheries), and when the prey disappears, so do the predators. No one can predict when—or if—the Steller decline might end, but under the best of conditions it will take a long time for the species to recover.

UTAH PRAIRIE DOG

Cynomys parvidens
STATUS: THREATENED

Morning in the prairie dog colony. With the sun already well above the horizon, the first prairie dog head pops into view in a burrow entrance. A moment later, that animal is above ground, stretching away the effects of a long night's sleep. Soon it is joined by dozens more of the rodents. For the next several hours, these short-legged animals will forage, loaf, inspect their territories, greet friends, banish strangers, and keep watch for predators. By late afternoon, they will tire of it all and one by one slip quietly back into the burrows. Tomorrow, they'll do it all again.

Prairie dogs exist only in North America, where they are thought to have evolved during the Pleistocene period, ten thousand to one million years ago. Early French explorers christened the ubiquitous rodents "little dogs" because of their barking sound. Part of that name stuck, although prairie dogs are in no way related to canines.

Centuries ago, prairie dogs attached themselves to the coattails of the bison, elk, pronghorn antelope, and other ungulates that grazed the western plains. The herds of hoofed animals chewed the tall prairie grass down to a modest height, which allowed prairie dogs to prosper, because the shorter vegetation made it easier to spot predators. Periodically, the wandering grazers returned to trim the grass, thereby maintaining the prairie dog heyday. There's even some reason to believe that the rodents returned the favor by grazing on the grass themselves, keeping it in a perpetual state of new growth and therefore more nutritious.

Utah Prairie Dog Habitat

At any rate, prairie dogs became one of the continent's most successful wild creatures. They existed in a great swath from Alberta to Mexico, including at least a dozen states in the West. In 1804, the Lewis and Clark expedition noted that the animals "appear here in infinite numbers." Naturalist Ernest Thompson Seton estimated a total prairie dog population of five billion at the beginning of the twentieth century. The largest colony, in Texas, is said to have covered 25,000 square miles and contained possibly 400 million animals.

Above all else, prairie dogs are social creatures. Colonies of Utah prairie dogs are divided into neighborhoods called clans, each of which is a loose family group controlled by a dominant male. About two-thirds of all adults of this species are female,

63

primarily due to conflicts between juvenile males and adult males. Clan boundaries can be anything from vegetation patches to rocks to demarcations only the prairie dogs can see. An animal entering another clan's territory will likely be run off, while two members of the same clan often greet each other with a kiss (yes, even biologists call it that).

The United States is home to four species of prairie dogs, and one more lives in Mexico. The Utah prairie dog is by far the least populous in this country and the one with the smallest range—just a portion of southwest Utah. Early in this century, an estimated ninety-five thousand members of this species lived on the prairie, but then came a range war, with prairie dogs the declared enemy. Ranchers got tired of feeding the ubiquitous rodents, damaging machinery on the prominent burrow mounds, and having livestock step in holes. So they brought out the poisons, and prairie dog numbers (not just in the Utah species) began to fall. Drought, overgrazing, habitat destruction, and plague epizootics also played a part in the great prairie dog decline.

By 1972, biologists were estimating a total population of only 3,300 Utah prairie dogs in just thirty-seven colonies, and experts predicted that the species would be extinct by the year 2000. In 1973, however, authorities declared the animal endangered, and soon thereafter populations began to increase. In 1984, this species' status was upgraded to threatened. The most recent census suggests a spring population of about 7,000 adults. This tally swells to about 21,000 when the young are born, then falls rapidly during the summer as many juveniles die of natural causes. By the following spring, the count typically is again well under 10,000 animals.

One factor in this animal's substantial comeback has been an extensive relocation program. Between 1972 and 1992 (when funding for the program was cut), authorities moved more than 15,000 Utah prairie dogs from private land to public tracts. This satisfied much of the ranchers' need to reduce the size of problem colonies while simultaneously putting more of the threatened animals fully under public agency control.

The mass relocation of so many highly social animals proved to be a difficult task, at least at first. Authorities dug five-foot starter holes for the prairie dogs, built fences to keep them from straying, and in some cases removed predators. Early in the program, however, little thought went into the selection of which animals to release when. Consequently, some new colonies failed to take root, and many of the relocatees died. Eventually, though, biologists learned to release the males in the spring and others in the fall. The excavation-minded males spent the summer improving the starter burrows, and by autumn the beginning of a new colony existed. Hibernation followed, and in the spring the survivors formed new clans.

Burrows play a big role in prairie dog life. Mating, birthing, nursing, and often death take place there. The burrows provide sanctuary from most enemies, and the animals spend the entire winter underground. With short, muscular front legs and sturdy claws, a prairie dog typically excavates fifteen feet of passageways that descend from three to six feet beneath the surface. Often, a shelf of sorts is placed just inside an entrance, so that the occupant can listen to above-ground activity while staying out of harm's way. Prairie dogs often pile the dirt from all this digging in large mounds around an entrance. The mounds make good lookout posts and help keep water out of the tunnels. Without the maze of subterranean tunnels, there would likely be no such thing as a prairie dog.

In late August or early September, adult male Utah prairie dogs decide they have had enough for one year and retire to their burrows for hibernation. The females follow suit a few weeks later, and the juveniles do the same in a couple of months. Although some individuals emerge prematurely—and briefly—during the winter, most of these rodents

remain underground until late February
or early March.

All prairie dogs are rather similar
in appearance, with most differences being behavioral and
genetic. The Utah species is
one of three sporting a white-
tipped tail (the other two species
have black tips). Most individuals
are cinnamon to clay-colored with
dark brown around the eyes. They
typically measure about a foot in
length, including a two-inch tail.
These animals consume a variety of
vegetation (up to two pounds per
animal per week) and appear to get
most or all of their moisture from
the plants they eat.

A big part of prairie dog
life involves the avoidance of
predators. Black-footed
ferrets (themselves an
endangered species), with
their ability to enter any
burrow, are the quintes-
sential prairie dog predators, but they are extremely rare in the wild today.
More common enemies
include coyotes, bobcats,
badgers, hawks, and
eagles. As social creatures,
prairie dogs maintain a
warning system in which the
first individual to spot a
predator alerts the others
with a bark or rigid posture
or both. When the enemy
gets too close, the entire
colony dives into
the burrow shel-
ters. With the
danger passed,
they emerge again
and often display a
"jump-yip" behavior—
throwing their front feet
high in the air while emitting a

shrill yip. Biologists aren't sure, but this may be a kind of "all clear" signal.

Today, the biggest threat to this species is habitat loss and the degradation of habitat quality. Overgrazing by livestock, for example, can cause a shift in vegetation—away from grasses and toward shrubby plants—that reduces the suitability of the habitat for prairie dogs. With 60 percent of all Utah prairie dogs residing on private land, there is always the possibility that any given colony of the animals could be jeopardized by agricultural activities or even housing developments.

Although much money and effort are expended to help this threatened species recover, ranchers are permitted to shoot or trap an annual quota of Utah prairie dogs. Many colonies exist in alfalfa-growing country in valley areas, and prairie dogs love alfalfa. Crop losses and damage to farm equipment can be extensive (estimated at $1.5 million annually), and some farmers have been forced to abandon entirely fields taken over by the animals. The ranchers' annual kill (for which they must have permits) can go as high as 6,000 animals, but recently has been much lower (1,543 in 1992, for example). Mostly juveniles are killed, and biologists believe that the majority of these animals would not have made it through the winter anyway.

For more information about prairie dogs, please refer to the Arizona section of this book, page 85.

WHALES

See individual descriptions for scientific names
STATUS: ENDANGERED (ALL)

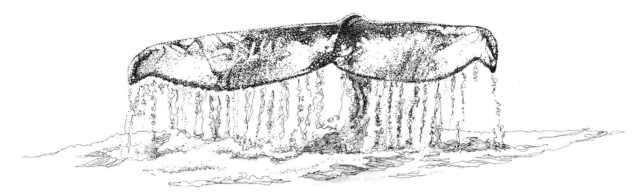

Six species of whales on the endangered list live at least part of the time in the Pacific waters off the coasts of California, Washington, and Oregon. These are the humpback, blue, sei, fin, right, and sperm whales. Accounts of these species follow, but the animals are so fascinating that an overview of the whale lifestyle is in order.

Whales are indeed special animals. Long ago, this branch of mammaldom opted for an eternity of life in the sea, gradually becoming more like the fishes than the mammal kin they left behind on land. Over the eons, they became graceful, powerful swimmers and complete masters of their environment. Genitalia, teats, and ears lie recessed within the whale body to decrease drag while swimming. The caudal fin (or tail or fluke) provides propulsion as the whale moves it up and down, pectoral fins aid in steering, and a dorsal fin increases stability. The whale's hair has disappeared, and a layer of blubber now provides both warmth and buoyancy. Whales give birth to live young and nurse them with milk. For hundreds of years, these air-breathing animals that live with the fishes have been a source of mystery and intrigue for humans.

Whales belong to the order Cetacea, which includes dolphins and porpoises, and are thus referred to as cetaceans. They are the largest animals on earth—and the largest ever to exist on this planet. Living whales are further divided into those having teeth (such as the sperm whale) and those with baleen (including the other five on the endangered list). Baleen is the horny, proteinaceous material that hangs in overlapping plates from the whale's upper jaw. Covered with hairlike bristles, the baleen strains out and holds food as huge quantities of water pass through the whale's mouth.

Four of the baleen whales (fin, sei, humpback, and blue) also are members of the rorqual family, which means they have long longitudinal grooves on the underside of their throats. The grooves expand to temporarily hold the water that brings the food. The other baleen whale, the right, is in a different family.

As mammals, whales must come to the surface periodically to expel the air that has filled their lungs for many minutes and replace it with a fresh supply. This is done through the nostril (called a blowhole) atop the whale's head, and the blow—the expelled air mixed with water—typically rises several feet in the air. Toothed whales have one blowhole, and baleen whales have two.

67

The shape and height of a whale's blow is so diagnostic that many species can be identified from this characteristic alone—tall and narrow from blue and fin whales, forward-pointing from the sperm whale, and twin plumes from the right whale, for example. Whales can stay submerged for long periods partly because of their ability to almost totally exchange the air in their lungs each time they take a breath. Humans and other mammals typically replace only a small portion of the lung's air with each breath.

Because of their huge size and the need to maintain a mammalian body temperature, whales must consume tremendous quantities of food—up to three million calories per day. Baleen whales feed mostly on krill, an umbrella term for a variety of shrimplike crustaceans, but they also consume some small fish and mollusks. Typically, a baleen whale fills its mouth with water, closes the opening, then uses its tongue to force the water out over the baleen, which strains out the food. The sperm whale dines on larger fare, mostly squid and fish. Surprisingly, baleen whales often eat little or nothing for half a year, then cram in food for a few months—up to four tons per day in the case of the blue whale—before starting a new fast.

Many whale species migrate annually between warm but relatively food-poor tropical waters and the colder, nutrient-rich waters near the Arctic and the Antarctic. The trip to the tropics is necessary because the largely blubberless calves would likely perish if born anywhere other than in warm water.

Because water is difficult to see through but a great medium for conducting sound, hearing is the dominant sense in whales, and most species are rather vocal—although whales have no vocal cords. Some species also use echolocation for finding food and for navigation.

A continuing whale mystery is the stranding phenomenon, in which one or even dozens of whales choose to beach themselves. Often the result is death; on many occasions humans have pushed or towed beached whales to sea only to have them return to land and die. Scientists are still sorting this one out, but the possible causes include ear infections, internal parasites, and even water-borne noise pollution that disrupts the animals' navigational techniques.

For the past millennium, humans have hunted whales for their meat, blubber, oil, and baleen. Valued for its combination of strength and flexibility, baleen—also called whalebone—was used in making buggy whips, umbrella ribs, corset stays, and the like. Before the discovery of petroleum, whale oil was a common lamp fuel and lubricant. For several centuries, while ships and harpoon weaponry lingered in a rather primitive state, whaling had little impact on most species. Beginning in the seventeenth century, however, and continuing until recently, commercial whale hunting had a disastrous effect. With relentless dedication, whalers from Europe and America—and in more modern times, Japan and the former Soviet Union—pursued each whale species in turn. When the most highly prized species became so diminished that hunting it was no longer profitable, whalers turned their attention to the next most lucrative kind of whale.

In the 1930s, whalers began to realize that the killing of too many whales would eventually mean the death of the industry itself, and so some rudimentary restrictions were instituted. But these proved nearly impossible to enforce and were of little help. World War II pretty much halted all whaling, but the end of that conflict saw whalers again ready at their harpoons. In 1946, the International Whaling Commission was established, with the dual task of maintaining healthy whale stocks *and* a healthy whaling industry. For nearly three decades, the needs of the industry superseded those of the animals. By the early 1970s, however, whale numbers had become so depressed—and the complaints of conservationists so loud—that the IWC adopted a new attitude about the leviathans of the deep. Protection of whales began to take precedence, and in 1982 the IWC called for an end to commercial killing of all large whales, which became effective in 1986.

The thirty-eight nations of the IWC have largely gone along with this moratorium, although a few—Norway, Japan, Iceland, and the Soviet Union—were dragged kicking and screaming into compliance. Japan and Norway still hunt minke whales for "research" (research that is often done with a knife and fork), and Japan turned to killing dolphins to replace the lost whale meat. In 1992, Iceland withdrew from the IWC (claiming, however, that it had no immediate plans to resume whaling), and in 1993 Norway resumed commercial whaling. Conservationists fear that if the coalition crumbles, whales may again be in for tough times. Since virtually all whaling occurs in international waters, legal avenues to halt the practice are few. The United States may, however, institute retaliatory economic sanctions against whaling nations.

HUMPBACK WHALE

Megaptera novaeangliae

Deep underwater the sounds seem to come from everywhere—rhythmic, repetitive, musical, and haunting. It is the song of the humpback whale, a melodic mystery that has intrigued mariners for centuries and still perplexes whale scientists.

By whale standards, the humpback is stocky, topping out at fifty feet or so while tipping the scales at about forty tons. It is distinguished by long flippers (pectoral fins), a hump in front of the dorsal fin, and in many individuals a series of bumps farther back along the spine (hence the name). Humpbacks are mostly dark gray with white on their undersides. *(Humpback whale illustrated on following pages 70-71.)* They are rorqual whales, which means they have deep grooves running from chin to belly to facilitate the great flow of water and nourishment that constitutes humpback dining.

Though it might be stretching things a bit to call them playful, humpbacks do exhibit a good measure of exuberance. They seem to take particular delight in breaching—hurling themselves completely out of the water and landing on their backs amid a tremendous spray of water. Some researchers think breaching may help knock loose the barnacles that plague humpbacks, but others believe there is more high jinks than hygiene in the showy maneuver. The whales also seem to enjoy smacking the surface with tail or flippers.

Humpbacks are found in all the world's oceans; they typically summer in cool waters, then migrate great distances to tropical climes for the winter. The population associated with the western United States spends the warm months near Alaska, then journeys a few thousand miles to Baja California. Their migrations follow traditional routes taught by one generation to the next. Remarkably, some humpbacks neither sleep nor eat during migrations that may last several months.

With gestation lasting a full year, humpbacks can both breed and deliver their young in the more hospitable tropical regions. Researchers once thought that females bred one winter, delivered a calf the next and mated again the following season. Now it is known that at least some female humpbacks give birth and breed again during the same warm-water respite. At birth, a calf weighs two to three thousand pounds and measures twelve to fifteen feet in length; the youngster will quadruple its weight and double its length in less than two months.

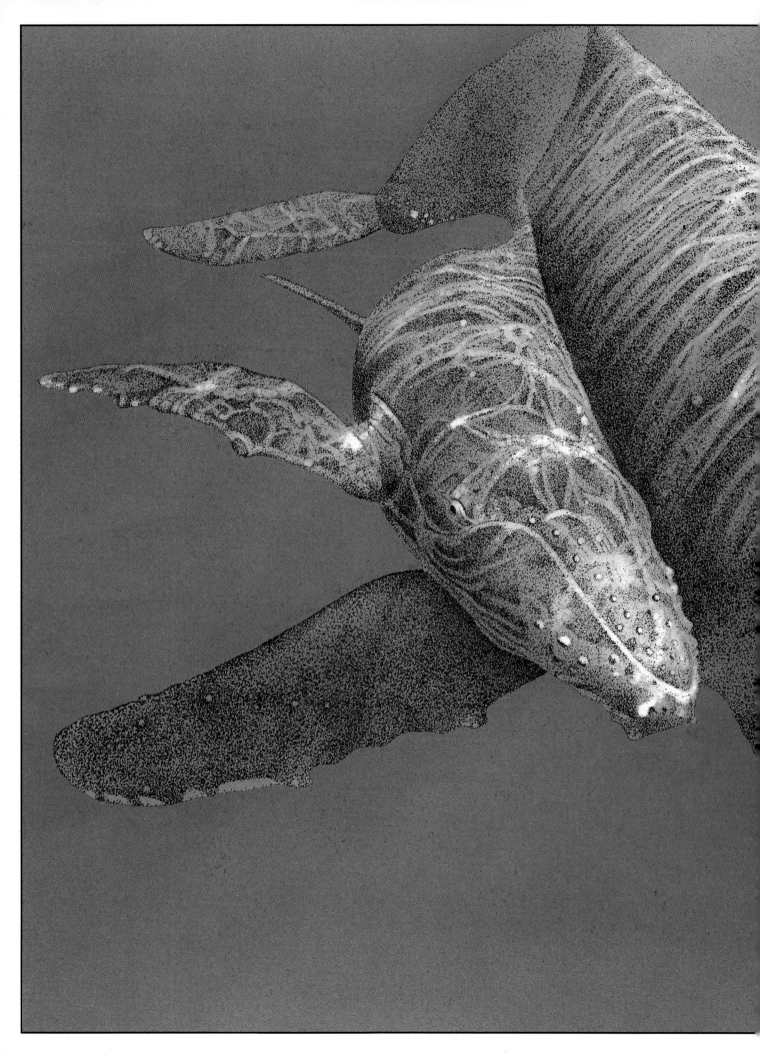

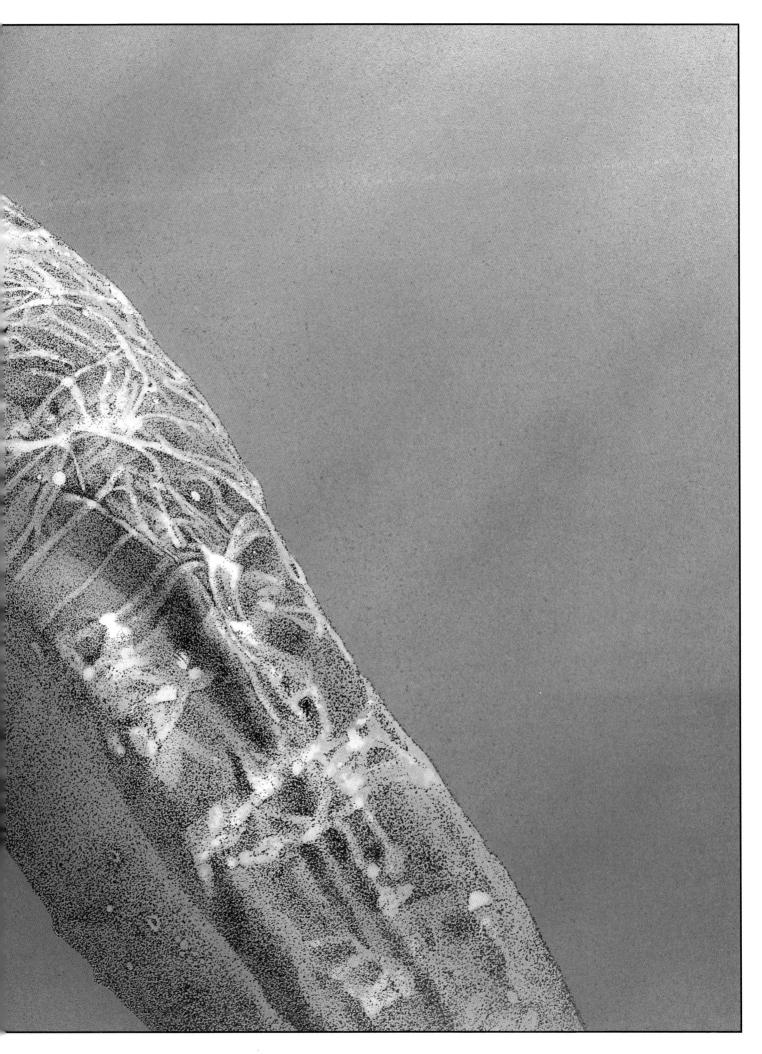

Humpbacks are opportunistic feeders, gobbling up whatever is available—crustaceans, herring, cod, or anything else that is edible (and probably a lot of stuff that isn't). One humpback was even found to have half a dozen cormorants in its stomach. Mostly, however, these whales dine on krill. Their normal feeding technique begins with an open-mouthed lunge at a school of fish or krill and the ensuing intake of huge quantities of water, food, and debris—up to five hundred gallons per mouthful.

At least occasionally, however, humpbacks employ a more sophisticated snacking system. Beginning beneath a school of fish, the whale slowly spirals toward the surface around its quarry, releasing air bubbles as it goes. The bubble barrier apparently concentrates the fish in a small area, where the humpback, mouth agape, eventually gorges itself—which is no small task. A large and hungry humpback whale can put away four thousand pounds of food a day.

Only sharks and killer whales are the humpback's natural enemies, preying primarily on calves. Because humpbacks are rather slow swimmers, however, they long ago became the quarry of many coastal hunting cultures, including American Indians. Later, whalers from many nations killed uncounted thousands of humpbacks, not because they were prized in any great way, but rather because they were easy to take in their shallow tropical wintering areas. Also, humpbacks often follow boats instead of fleeing them and remain docile even when they or their offspring are attacked.

As recently as the 1960s, a dozen nations still killed humpbacks—up to sixty thousand annually. In 1966, the International Whaling Commission granted the humpback complete protection. Whales are difficult to census, but authorities estimate a worldwide population of perhaps ten thousand—down from hundreds of thousands before the heyday of whaling ships. Probably fewer than two thousand of these inhabit the Pacific. When unhunted, humpback life expectancy might approach fifty years.

The aspect of humpback behavior that most intrigues scientists is the animal's penchant for singing. Literally. Melodically. Mysteriously. What the ethereal cry of the loon is to northern lakes, the songs of the humpback are to the ocean. The whales possess a remarkable repertoire of groans, whistles, clicks, creaks, and moans—and the ability to link these sounds into repeated units, phrases, and themes constituting compositions lasting up to half an hour. A couple of decades ago, their eerie music highlighted a popular human song by Judy Collins called "Farewell to Tarwathie" (from the album *Whales and Nightingales* by Elektra Records).

All humpbacks in a given population sing the same song, and each population's tune differs significantly from that of other regions. Even more amazing, however, is the fact that any given song is constantly evolving. The current rendition is never the same as last year's—or the one yet to come.

Researchers study humpback singing by recording the sounds, then charting pitch, timing, and other harmonic structures with a spectrograph. Recently, they discovered repeating patterns that appeared to mimic the human poetic device called rhyme. Could it be that humpbacks are broadcasting ditties—or sonnets—into the deep? More likely, say scientists, the whales use the rhyme to help them remember what must come next in a long, complex performance (the same way the phrase "Jack and Jill" helps us to remember the next line, "went up the hill").

No one knows how humpbacks sing. They have no vocal cords, so the sound necessarily comes from another source—perhaps air being moved from one internal chamber to another. Whatever the origin, it has plenty of power. In the acoustically excellent medium of water, even humans can hear the singing fifteen miles away. Researchers speculate that humpbacks may hear their brethren hundreds of miles distant. Only males sing (as they hang head down in the water) and only during breeding season, leading researchers to speculate that the sound is somehow related to mating rituals. Sometimes a male may sing for twenty-four hours straight.

Lots of questions about humpback singing remain unanswered. How do all the males in a far-flung population learn precisely the same song? How do they incorporate changes more or less simultaneously? Does their apparent ability to use rhyme indicate a level of intelligence previously believed impossible in animals? What does the singing signify? Will we ever learn to interpret it?

The answers lie in the ocean's depths.

Sperm Whale

Physeter catodon

Thar she blows! This is the quintessential whale. The whaler's whale. The whale's whale. The image that most often comes to mind at mention of the word *whale*. This is Moby Dick, the sperm whale.

This animal's name accents the ignorance that once clouded humankind's understanding of these mammoth sea mammals. Located in this whale's huge head is a reservoir filled with oil. Whalers long ago assumed this liquid to be the animal's seminal fluid and named the creature accordingly—and incorrectly. Apparently, no one had ever examined a female of this species, since the fluid's presence in both genders should have alerted someone to the fact that it contained no sperm.

Misnomer notwithstanding, there is no mistaking the sperm whale. Its massive, block-shaped head—comprising about a third of its body length—identifies this animal for even the most unschooled whale watcher. Another uniquely sperm characteristic is the blow—offset to the left and angled forward about forty-five degrees. Even the wrinkled, prunelike texture of this animal's skin is diagnostic. In color, this whale ranges from nearly black to slate gray, with varying white patterns on its underside. An adult male sperm whale may weigh sixty tons and be sixty-five feet long (females are much smaller). This species is quite gregarious, traveling in pods of twenty to eighty in all the world's oceans. Most sperm whales spend their entire lives in tropical and temperate waters, but mature males make annual treks to polar regions.

Although hunted earlier than many others, sperm whales escaped severe persecution for quite some time. As toothed whales, their mouths contained no baleen, and their purplish black, greasy meat was generally considered inedible (although the Japanese have long eaten sperm whales). Add to this the sperm whale's penchant for ramming ships just because someone stuck a harpoon in it, and you have a whale that humans mostly ignored.

This all changed about 1750, however, with the invention of a smokeless lamp that burned the sperm whale's special oil. Suddenly sperm whale stock shot up, and many a sea captain put this species on his hit list. A writer named Melville even wrote a book about the great sperm whale industry.

Sperm whales were hunted intensively until the mid-nineteenth century, when three factors converged to prevent its destruction. First, sperm whale numbers had been sufficiently depleted to cause whalers to lose some interest in this species. Second, new regions containing other species became available to whalers in the north Pacific. And third, the discovery of petroleum in Pennsylvania made whale oil for lighting obsolete.

Sperm whaling continued at a slow pace until the 1950s, when the depletion of other species sent the ships again in search of sperms. Throughout the 1960s and into the 1970s, whalers harvested 20,000 sperm whales annually. In 1986, sperm whales (along with all others) finally received full protection. Estimates of original sperm whale numbers range from 700,000 to 2 million. About half a million remain today, making the sperm one of the least imperiled large whales.

At the heart of the sperm whale's original popularity lies a large (is there anything about whales that isn't large?) organ called the spermaceti, a cavity four or five feet deep and ten feet long. Filling this reservoir are ten barrels or so of clear or straw-colored fluid. Scientists still quarrel over the whale's use of this liquid. One school says the oil somehow regulates the whale's buoyancy during its notoriously deep dives. This theory holds that the animal somehow cools the liquid (perhaps by circulating sea water through its nasal passages) to make it more dense, allowing the whale to dive deeper. Another school, however, believes the oil aids the whale in making its characteristic clicking sounds. So little is known about sperm whales that it's possible that both camps are right and the stuff serves two functions.

Aside from spermaceti oil, several attributes set sperm whales apart. For starters, this animal has the largest brain in the world—nearly twenty pounds. This does not mean, however, that it is the most intelligent creature around. Brain size is usually couched in terms of body weight, and because the sperm whale is such a big bruiser, its ratio of brawn to brain remains a rather low five thousand to one (compared to about sixty to one for humans). The sperm also has the thickest skin in the world—up to fourteen inches.

This whale also is the greatest mammalian diver, capable of reaching unbelievable depths and staying submerged for well over an hour. Several sperms have become entangled in cables lying on the ocean floor three thousand feet beneath the surface. And in 1969, whalers from South Africa located two sperm whales that dived and remained submerged for eighty-two minutes. When the pair surfaced, they were shot. The stomach of one whale contained two small sharks known to dwell only on the ocean bottom—where the whale was killed the bottom lay 10,476 feet down. No other mammal even comes close to that record.

The sperm whale typically feeds on the ocean floor, apparently by swimming along with its mouth open and raking in everything in its path. These treasures have included rocks, a coconut, fishing equipment, and even a boot (minus its owner). Though the animal has from forty to sixty teeth in its lower jaw, it does not appear to use these for grasping or chewing prey, which typically is swallowed whole and unmarked by teeth. When the whale's mouth is closed, the teeth fit into sockets in the upper jaw, which has no teeth worthy of the name.

The sperm whale eats a variety of sea life—including shark, lingcod, ray, salmon, octopus, barracuda, and albacore—but its favorite food is squid, which it consumes in great quantity. Squids each have two horny beaks—not unlike the upper and lower parts of bird beaks—as part of their jaw structures; their toughness often causes them to remain intact in whale stomachs. As many as thirty thousand squid beaks have been found in a sperm whale's stomach. Most of these creatures probably weighed only a couple of pounds apiece, but even giant squid are not off limits. One researcher found a 34-foot, 400-pound squid in the belly of a bull sperm whale. A 10-foot shark also was discovered intact inside a sperm whale. Each day, each adult sperm whale polishes off about 1,800 pounds of groceries. Virtually everything it eats gets swallowed whole.

Another sperm whale attribute that still puzzles scientists is the animal's almost constant, loud, pulsating clicking, which under water sounds much like a pounding hammer. Click patterns vary diagnostically among individuals, but whaleologists still aren't sure if these sounds are intelligent communications among friends or echolocations designed to find food. Current thinking is that the sound may serve both functions. Speculation also continues concerning the origin of the sound, with the prevailing theory suggesting that the free oil and cells saturated with oil in the animal's spermaceti somehow function as a reverberation chamber.

Finally, sperm whales—especially the males—are known for their pugnacious personalities. The bulls often engage in battles, leaving their heads profusely scarred (although some of this scarring may come from the hooks of squid objecting to being eaten). In whaling days, sailors sometimes found themselves in a small boat attached by rope to a harpooned sperm whale, which proceeded to drag them like a toy across the ocean. Apparently, this happened often enough for whalers to coin a name for the experience—Nantucket sleigh ride.

On occasion, sperm whales even sank ships—and not just fictional ones like the *Pequod.* In 1820, for example, the 238-ton *Essex* encountered a large sperm whale in the Pacific, but even before a harpoon could be fired, the whale attacked. Swimming along at about three knots, the whale rammed the ship broadside with its head. The vessel trembled, and the crew fell on their faces, but the whale was not done. After backing off, it charged again, this time completely caving in the bow. Within ten minutes, the ship sank.

RIGHT WHALE

Balaena glacialis

Right whale indeed! If ever a creature deserved to be renamed, it is this mastodon of the deep. Sadly, whalers long ago gave this whale its name simply because it was the "right" one to kill, which they did with singular dedication. Truly, this lumbering giant was a whaler's delight. Each massive (60 tons or so) right whale produced up to 150 gallons of oil and 1,000 pounds of whalebone (baleen). Moreover, this species had the uncommon good sense to bob like a cork on the surface when dead, instead of sinking as other species did (a problem whalers remedied by injecting the corpses with air). As a bonus, the right whale hung out near coastlines, seldom got hostile when attacked, and typically plodded along at only about three miles an hour. So easy was the right whale to catch, that most stocks were largely depleted even before the advent of diesel engines, exploding harpoons, and factory ships.

This species is generally brown or black and measures about fifty feet in length, one-fourth of which is head. The absence of a dorsal fin and a V-shaped blow (from twin nostrils) help identify the right whale at a distance. Like many other whales, the right is migratory, traveling to warm equatorial waters for breeding and birthing in winter, while spending the summer months at higher latitudes. Females bear a calf every third year, and their natural life expectancy appears to be about fifty or seventy-five years. This seems to be a peaceable species, with many accounts of right whales treating humans gently when others of their kind might have done otherwise.

This species' most diagnostic attribute is the cluster of callosities that appear on each animal's face and head. Looking much like giant warts, these growths are actually made of keratin, the same stuff contained in human hair and fingernails. Several inches thick and up to a yard in diameter, these patches lie in more or less symmetrical patterns about the whale's head. The callosities attract whale lice (not insects but tiny crustaceans), which often give the spots a pink or yellow hue. These parasites, in turn, attract gulls, which sometimes land on surfaced whales to feed on the lice.

The largest callosity typically appears on the tip of the upper jaw and is called the "bonnet" (because someone once thought it resembled the ladies' headgear). The size, shape, configuration, and color of these patches are unique to each right whale and often can be used to identify individuals. Callosities appear even on the youngest calves, so they are part of evolved right whale genetics and not acquired after birth. Their function remains a mystery, but various observers have guessed that they might be used to deflect water from the blowhole or to scrape against an opponent.

Right whales are skimmers, which means they feed by swimming along with their huge jaws wide open. A few hundred highly bristled baleen plates in that mammoth opening strain out the krill. When not busy screening supper from the ocean, right whales know how to have a good time. Although it seems to defy the laws of physics, this lumbering behemoth somehow gets up enough momentum to breach—coming completely out of the water, then falling on its side in a thunderous splash. When the wind is brisk, this species also goes sailing. Keeping its head and midsection submerged, the whale raises its giant flukes above the surface, where they act as a sail to propel the leviathan through the sea. Calves also appear to enjoy entangling themselves in ribbons of kelp.

Basques began harpooning right whales in the eleventh century, and the pace of the harvest quickened as whaling became a global industry. By 1700, European whalers had virtually eliminated rights from their waters, and over the next century and a half American whalers did the same. In 1937, the International Whaling Commission granted the right whale full protection, but still it swims on the edge of extinction, neither disappearing entirely nor staging much of a comeback. Perhaps four thousand right whales exist worldwide, but not many live in the eastern Pacific. Only a few of these animals likely travel between the Aleutians and equatorial waters, making sightings off the Washington, Oregon, and California coasts extremely rare. The right is the whale most in danger of extinction—and definitely the *wrong* one to have been hunted so extensively.

SEI WHALE

Balaenoptera borealis

The sei is kind of an in-between whale, not the largest, deepest diving, longest migrating, most colorful, or most imperiled of the six large cetaceans on the federal endangered species list. Pronounced "say," this animal's name results from the anglicization of the Norwegian word *(seje)* for pollack. Great schools of these fish—along with the whales—used to arrive off the coast of Norway about the same time each year, and so the Norwegians named the whale for its piscatorial companions.

Early whalers largely ignored this species, often believing them to be immature blue or fin whales. Even after the sei became well known, it got little respect from the sea captains, primarily because its thin blubber layer makes it less profitable to hunt. However, as the relentless whaling industry virtually eliminated in turn each of the more desirable species, the sei finally rose to the top of the heap. In the 1960s, whalers began killing this species in large numbers, and since then the estimated pre-exploitation population of 200,000 or so seis has dwindled to perhaps 50,000—with only about 14,000 in the northern hemisphere.

Sei whales are dark blue or gray on top with irregular oblong light splotches, which may be scars from the former presence of a certain parasitic worm or from shark attacks. The sei also sports a large, light, distinctive anchor-shaped patch on its underside. An adult sei might stretch fifty feet and weigh thirty tons, which is medium-sized in the world of whales. Capable of swimming at thirty miles an hour, the sei is one of the fastest of all whales.

This species is also a skimmer, straining delicacies from the water as it swims along. The sei's three hundred–plus baleen plates are covered with extremely fine, matted bristles that resemble wool—or even silk—in their softness. More delicate than that of many other whales, this baleen testifies to the diminutive size of the creatures on which the sei feeds. Among the most prominent of these are tiny crustaceans called copepods, which often assemble in great rafts. Because seis do much of their feeding near the surface, they often are accompanied by many sea birds, which dine on the same fare.

Sei whales are found in many of the globe's waters, with three populations generally delineated—two in the Atlantic, and one in the Pacific ranging from Japan and Korea to the western American coast. In U.S. waters, this latter group travels between Alaska and Mexico. Like many other whale species, the sei divides its time between warmer equatorial climes and the richer regions near the Arctic.

FIN WHALE

Balaenoptera physalus

For centuries, the fin whale (also called the finback or razorback) remained a mystery. Coastal peoples knew the animal by way of occasional carcasses washed up on the beach, but that was about all. Almost never did one pass within sight of shore, and when ships encountered this sea giant, the fin invariably swam off too fast for the vessels to follow. Even whaling ships had little luck catching the speedy fin. Consequently, the fin whale prospered, establishing itself worldwide and building an estimated population approaching half a million.

Fins (named for their somewhat prominent dorsal fin) are immense creatures, second only in the annals of all-time giants to the blue whale, the largest animal ever to exist. Newborn fins weigh two tons and are twenty feet long, but even that seems tiny compared to the seventy-ton, seventy-foot adults. Despite their size, these creatures are sleek in appearance and are sometimes called the greyhounds of the sea. Fins are found throughout the world's offshore waters, with distinct populations scattered around the globe. Like other baleen whales, they generally migrate toward the equator in the fall and toward the poles in spring.

It was only in this century that whalers developed the technological wherewithal (fast ships and explosive harpoons) to go after this species, which they did in a big way. In the 1930s, as the stock of blue whales began to peter out, the fin's commercial value rose considerably. In 1939, 28,000 fins met the harpoon, and hundreds of thousands more did likewise during the following decades. By 1975, the teeming fin whale population had been reduced to 80,000 or so, a number that has since risen to about 120,000. Fewer than

20,000 fin whales likely remain in the eastern Pacific, where they range from Baja California to the Chuckchi Sea in the Arctic.

A rorqual, the fin whale has eighty or so grooves in its throat that expand to accommodate the tremendous volume of water, debris, and food that define mealtime. When thus engorged, the forward portion of the fin's body may nearly double in diameter. Fins feed in great gulps, either on the surface or in the depths. Rarely do they show up in waters less than 650 feet deep, and dives of 1,000 feet have been recorded. One harpooned fin was reported to have bottomed out at 1,640 feet. In addition to plankton and the whale staple krill, fins dine on mackerel, capelin, herring, and other small fish. Like some of their kin, they often scoop up meals while swimming on their sides.

One of the big remaining mysteries about the fin whale concerns its decidedly asymmetrical coloration. Most of the fin's back is dark blue-gray, and its underside is largely white, but the head is a mixture. On the animal's left side, the lower jaw is black, but on the right it is white. Inside the fin's mouth, the contrast is reversed—light on the left and dark on the right. This striking design makes the fin whale the only mammal in the world consistently colored asymmetrically. As an accent, the fin sports a light-colored chevron on its back.

Whale people have long speculated about the purpose of the unusual coloring of the fin's head, but speculation is still all we have. The color contrast may have a place in mating rituals, the way bright plumage does for some birds. Some folks also theorize that the distinct white side might serve to startle and herd prey species into tight groups for easy eating. One observer had it figured out that by circling prey counterclockwise the colors helped camouflage the whale, but another "expert" said there would be more camouflage effect if the fin circled clockwise. All this, of course, leaves people—if not the whales—going in circles and without a clear understanding of nature's purpose in so coloring this great animal.

BLUE WHALE

Balaenoptera musculus

This is it, folks—the largest living creature ever to grace our planet. Larger than thirty elephants. Bigger than any dinosaur. As long as three railroad cars. The great leviathan of the deep. A big blue whale may measure 100 feet from tip to distant tip and weigh up to 150 tons—if you could ever get one on a scale. Its heart alone is nearly the size of a Volkswagen Bug. Its blow rises 30 feet in the air. One testicle weighs 100 pounds. The tongue weighs 4 tons. The stomach holds a ton of food, and the animal eats four times a day. About 2,000 gallons of blood course through its veins. At birth, a blue whale infant weighs 2 or 3 tons and hits the tape at 25 feet, about the size of a school bus. And talk about hungry—the calf consumes 200 gallons of its mother's milk and puts on 200 pounds *every day.*

Blue whales are long and slender, colored bluish gray with mottled lighter blotches. Unlike some of its kin, the blue is not much of a social creature, usually confining its cliques to three or four widely spaced companions. On the high-latitude feeding grounds, however, blues are often seen in pairs (of undetermined gender), suggesting the possibility of monogamy—or perhaps a strong mother-offspring bond. The blue whale is a rather long-lived creature and does not even begin breeding until the age of six. Estimates of its longevity go as high as a century, but most blues probably don't approach that lofty age.

As do many other cetaceans, blue whales conduct great annual migrations, moving into the relatively barren warm equatorial waters during the winter to breed and give birth, then summering in the nutrient-rich polar regions. Incredibly, this massive animal goes without food for the several months of its equatorial stay, living instead off the fat reserves it accumulated in the far north (or far south for southern hemisphere blues). Researchers believe blue whales give birth (to a single calf) every other year, and because gestation lasts nearly a year, both breeding and birthing can be accomplished during their tropical stay, with a female mating during one visit and delivering a calf during the next.

Blue whales are not notoriously deep divers, spending most of their time within a hundred yards of the surface. Following a few short breaths, the blue whale dives and normally remains submerged for ten or fifteen minutes. Despite its gargantuan size, this species is a rapid swimmer, with reported speeds of nearly thirty miles per hour. As might be expected, a harpooned blue whale can be a dynamo of power and energy, and whaling history is full of stories of harpooned blue whales dragging ships about the ocean. One such Japanese vessel found itself moving six knots in one direction while its engines strained to move in the other.

Like a gargantuan vacuum cleaner, the blue whale feeds by swimming along—on its side—with its mammoth mouth open. Into that orifice flow sixty tons or so of water, food, and debris. Soon the whole burden goes out the way it came in, with the bristlelike baleen catching and holding krill and other goodies. Because the blue whale fasts for most of the winter, it must put on large quantities of fat during the summer—a chore it accomplishes by consuming three million calories per day. Ironically, nourishment for this largest of all animals comes mostly in the form of tiny, shrimplike crustaceans weighing a tenth of a gram apiece.

Early whalers mostly avoided this species, since their vessels and equipment were no match for it, but technology eventually overtook the great blue. Gradually, this species became one of the whalers' favorite quarries, and for decades mariners pursued the great blue whale with singular dedication. Once, an estimated 225,000 of these animals roamed the world's seas, but 90 percent of them had vanished by 1900.

Modern advances tipped the balance even further in the whalers' favor, and the rapacious overharvest of this species continued unabated into the 1930s. The several following decades saw various attempts to salvage the blue whale industry, but too much damage had been done, and populations continued to decline. Finally in 1966, the International Whaling Commission granted this species complete protection (but poachers probably killed some blue whales even after that date).

Today, at least some blue whales remain in all oceans. Not long ago, conservationists estimated the global population at about ten thousand, but recent information suggests that only a thousand or so blues remain. In the American West, blue whales sometimes show up along the coasts of Washington, Oregon, and California en route to or from the warm waters off Baja California. Formerly, this Pacific population contained an estimated fifteen hundred blues, but if the above worldwide revision proves correct, this figure must be slashed drastically as well. Although blue whale behemoths are no longer being slaughtered, water pollution and the commercial harvest of krill could cause them problems for years to come.

WOODLAND CARIBOU

Rangifer tarandus caribou
STATUS: ENDANGERED

Most people picture caribou in great teeming, grunting, hoof-clicking throngs on the barren northland tundra. Tens of thousands at a crack, and not a tree in sight. This is accurate as far as it goes, but it leaves out some important members of the caribou clan.

After all the lumping and splitting are done, taxonomists list four subspecies of caribou in North America. Three are indeed tundra animals and generally fit the above description. The fourth is called the woodland caribou and exists mostly in a wide swath across wooded Canada, plus a small contingent in the Selkirk Mountains in northern Idaho and eastern Washington. (In a further differentiation, biologists have divided woodland caribou into a northern ecotype and a mountain ecotype. The former numbers in the hundreds of thousands and exists all across Canada. The mountain ecotype contains only a couple of thousand animals that live almost exclusively in British Columbia and Alberta. The Selkirk caribou in the United States is part of this group.) The woodland caribou are larger, darker, and less gregarious than their tundra-dwelling cousins, but the most striking disparity between the two is the habitat they have chosen.

As their name suggests, woodland caribou are creatures of the forest. They once occupied timbered portions of most northern tier states, including Maine, Vermont, New York, Wisconsin, Minnesota, Montana, and others, and even ranged as far south as Wyoming. Large and unwary, these animals provided easy provender for meat-hungry settlers, and over the last 150 years they vanished from nearly all U.S. territory. A few hung on, however, in the wild mountains where Idaho and Washington meet, and they dwelled there in relative anonymity until about the middle of this century.

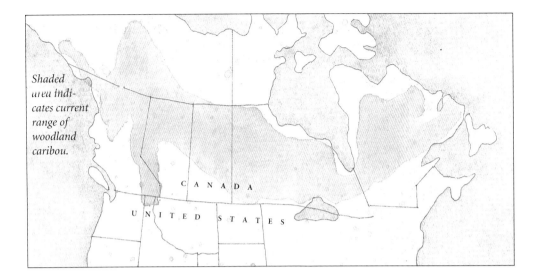

Shaded area indicates current range of woodland caribou.

In 1950, biologists estimated this last U.S. population (which also includes part of British Columbia in its range) at one hundred individuals, but no intensive studies were done until the 1980s. Surveys then indicated a herd size of only twenty-five or thirty animals. Scattered reports—not always substantiated—also suggested the presence of a few caribou in Montana, but these were probably itinerants and not part of a breeding population.

Between 1987 and 1990, authorities released into the Idaho Selkirks an additional sixty woodland caribou captured in Canada. These animals have mixed well with the original herd, but mortality has been high. Currently, the population estimate for the entire·Selkirk herd is just forty-seven caribou. Half of these animals spend most of their time in Idaho, and half generally reside just over the border in British Columbia—although some interchange occurs between the groups. There is now talk of relocating additional Canadian woodland caribou to the Washington portion of the Selkirk Mountains to establish a separate herd.

Woodland caribou are medium-sized members of the deer family, residing between deer and elk on the heft scale. A large male might weigh six hundred pounds and females about half that. Both genders have antlers, although the bull's headgear is more massive than the cow's. Their color ranges from a deep chocolate midsummer brown to a grayish tan in the spring. Bulls develop a white mane in the fall. During the winter, these caribou get nearly all of their nutrition from arboreal lichens, while summer fare expands to include a variety of grasses, sedges, forbs, mushrooms, and herbaceous vegetation—especially huckleberry.

Although woodland caribou do not conduct the extensive mass migrations of their tundra relatives, they are still seasonal travelers—in a more vertical sense. With the coming of winter, they move downslope to modest elevations (4,200 to 6,200 feet), where mature cedar and hemlock forests create a canopy that helps hold snow depths to a minimum. Early soft snow generally makes travel difficult, so the less of it the better. In midwinter, when the snow cover has hardened to the point of supporting a caribou's weight (which, distributed to four massive hooves, amounts to relatively few pounds per square inch), these animals head for the high ridges—generally above 6,000 feet. Here, snow depths of six to twelve feet allow the caribou to reach lichens high in the trees. With the exception of mountain goats, these caribou are the only large animals to tough out winter in the high country.

In the spring, the herd again moves downslope to find the areas of early greenup, and their diet switches from the wispy "old man's beard" lichen to a variety of ground vegetation. In early June, the pregnant cows are ready to give birth, but before doing so they return once more to the high elevations. Here, the snow may still lie three feet deep, but the wolves, grizzlies, cougars, and other predators that might kill a calf are few. When the calves are about a month old, the mothers and their young rejoin the herd. As summer moves up the slopes, the caribou follow. When the snow flies again, the cycle starts anew.

The woodland caribou rut peaks in October, with each dominant male gathering as large a harem as he can control—perhaps six to ten cows. Females don't breed until they are three years old, and twins are rare. Even with just one calf for a cow to care for, mortality among the young is high—from predators, weather, accidents, and abandonment. Nearly half the calves may be lost in their first few months of life. With reproduction barely replacing natural mortality, it is little wonder that this caribou herd has not been growing.

A major problem recently appears to be cougar predation. Logging and other habitat alterations in this region have helped increase the white-tailed deer population. This, in turn, has supported a larger number of cougars, and when cougars are plentiful, some of them are bound to kill caribou. In addition, massive fires in the 1960s destroyed huge habitat tracts that still are of little use to the caribou.

But humans must share some of the blame. Logging—especially of old-growth cedar and hemlock forests (the crucial early winter habitat)—has been a big problem. From a purely economic standpoint, foresters would prefer to replace these decadent stands with other species, but once logged, caribou habitat can be replaced only by 150 years or so of uninterrupted growth. Although the selective removal of trees can actually improve things for the caribou, the prevailing practice is to create clearcuts, which essentially removes the habitat from caribou use.

In addition, poachers take a few of the animals, and hunters (apparently unaware of the existence of caribou in Idaho and Washington) sometimes mistake them for deer or elk. New mountain roads also bring more people and more disturbance into caribou terrain. There are no highways in caribou range in this country, but the presence of a Canadian thoroughfare just a few miles into British Columbia has resulted in several road kills. Conservationists worry that a major accident—a large truck hitting a herd of caribou drawn to the highway to lick de-icing salt, for example—could wipe out a significant portion of this population.

To help protect and preserve this small herd, authorities have altered forest management practices, vigorously prosecuted the people responsible for illegal kills, closed roads, and conducted informational programs to alert hunters (and other forest users) to the caribou presence. Still, the long-term prognosis is not good for the Selkirk caribou. With fewer than fifty individuals, this herd will likely continue to live on the edge of oblivion—if it's lucky.

WESTERN MAMMALS

LISTED AS

THREATENED OR ENDANGERED

BY THE

STATE GOVERNMENTS

Black bear cub.

A R I Z O N A

BLACK-TAILED PRAIRIE DOG

Cynomys ludovicianus
STATE CLASSIFICATION: ENDANGERED

Prairie dogs are simultaneously very easy and very difficult to understand. They move about during the day and don't mind people watching them, but many of their significant activities—mating, giving birth, nursing their young, and sometimes death—occur out of sight underground. Nevertheless, researchers have discovered prairie dogs to possess a rather complex social system, some unique behaviors, and even some seemingly Machiavellian ways of perpetuating their genetic lines.

There are four species of prairie dogs in the United States (plus another in Mexico), all native only to North America. The black-tailed version—so called because of its dark tail tip—is actually the most numerous, with a range stretching across the continent's midsection from Alberta to Mexico. In Arizona, however, the black-tail never spread beyond the southeastern corner of the state, although it was once rather numerous in some localities. As human settlement of the area progressed, prairie dog populations declined—primarily because of the war waged against the animals by ranchers. Then one day several decades ago, agents of the U.S. Fish and Wildlife Service went to the northern foothills of the Chiricahua Mountains and poisoned the last remaining black-tail colony in the state. (Arizona today is not without a prairie dog, however, as the Gunnison's prairie dog still exists here.)

Because many eyes spot danger more quickly than a few, prairie dogs long ago became highly colonial, and the vast grasslands of western America once teemed with billions of the animals. As humans settled the West, however, they shot and poisoned the animals with great dedication, and today the rodents occupy barely 10 percent of their original range. This destruction occurred mostly because conventional wisdom held that prairie dogs hurt ranchers by eating grass destined for bovine bellies. Recent research, however, suggests that while prairie dogs may decrease the quantity of forage available for livestock, they may improve its quality. The prairie dog–livestock interaction is still being investigated.

An adult black-tailed prairie dog weighs about two pounds and is about fourteen inches long, including four inches of tail. With large hindquarters and a waddling gait, this animal resembles nothing so much as a chubby, miniature bear. Its most strenuous activity consists of frequent pell-mell burrow-bound rushes to avoid the real or imagined attack of a predator.

Each black-tailed prairie dog colony—or town—is divided into regions called coteries, not unlike a city composed of neighborhoods. Rocks, vegetation, and scent mark coterie borders. The demarcations often remain invisible to human eyes, but the prairie dogs know precisely where they lie. Each coterie, which may cover about half an acre, contains one adult male, several females, and—after late spring—the young of the year. All residents jealously guard their coterie from intruders, and border disputes (consisting mostly of posturing and ritual attack) are common. Within a coterie, prairie dogs act like a family, frequently greeting each other with what can only be called a kiss. For a gentle second or two, their noses and lips touch in a sort of olfactory identification check that seems to say, "I'm okay and you're okay." Mutual grooming may follow.

Devotion to relatives and the desire to perpetuate one's blood line take some fascinating twists in the highly social prairie dog world. Let's say a prairie dog spots a predator in the colony (coyotes, bobcats, and raptors are some common enemies). If that prairie dog has lots of living kin, it is likely to bark and make a big fuss in order to warn its relatives (along with everyone else) to take to their burrows. But if the sentry has no living kin, it may slip quietly underground, letting the rest of the colony fend for itself.

To avoid breeding with their own daughters (and thereby producing weaker offspring), adult males periodically move to new coteries. Upon arriving at its new neighborhood, however, the male may methodically kill all of that year's young. Since these pups were fathered by some other male, they have no value to the newcomer, and with the young out of the way, the coterie's females will be more likely to breed (with the new boss) the following spring.

When not engaged in social interactions, prairie dogs spend their daylight hours munching on prairie grasses and keeping an eye out for predators. Safety from most enemies is only as far away as the prairie dog's burrow, and a bustling colony of thousands can become deserted in seconds as the predator alarm spreads and everyone dives underground. A few minutes later, heads start popping out of the holes, and soon the residents are again pursuing their normal activities. Around dusk, colony residents begin slipping into their underground chambers for the night.

Prairie dog burrows are marvels of subterranean engineering. Just below the entrance is a shelf—a sort of waiting room—where a prairie dog can listen for footsteps above. From there, a tunnel about seven inches in diameter descends to a depth of several feet. The main part of the burrow often consists of a honeycomb series of rooms with the principal nesting chamber situated well above the lowest part of the tunnel in case of flooding. A burrow may stretch for many yards and be served by two or three entrances.

Invariably, these rodent engineers position one entrance at a slightly higher elevation than the others, either by setting up housekeeping on a slope or by constructing a large mound at one entrance and putting the hole at the very top, like a volcano. This allows them to take advantage of a neat bit of physics called the Bernoulli Principle, which dictates that air will flow into the lower hole and out the upper hole, thereby ventilating the burrow. Not coincidentally, the mounds also make good lookout posts and help prevent flooding.

Although the black-tailed prairie dog has been extirpated from Arizona, the state still lists it as endangered. Three times since 1966, public and private groups have attempted to reintroduce the animal, but those projects all failed—due mostly to local opposition at the release sites. Authorities recently began evaluating the possibility of another introduction, and if all goes well, black-tails could be back in the state in a couple years. And with black-tailed prairie dogs living just twenty miles south of the Arizona border, it would not be impossible for the rodents to establish an Arizona colony on their own.

For more information bout prairie dogs, turn to the section on the federally listed Utah prairie dog, page 63.

CHIHUAHUAN PRONGHORN

Antilocapra americana mexicana
STATE CLASSIFICATION: THREATENED

America is home to three subspecies of pronghorn antelope, those fleet denizens of the prairie West, and at one time it appeared that all three might vanish from the face of the earth. Fortunately, the field of wildlife management was emerging about the time of the pronghorn plight, and the antelope benefited greatly from this new science. The most common subspecies rebounded splendidly, and now nearly a million of them thrive throughout the prairie states. Another race, the Sonoran pronghorn, is federally listed as endangered (see page 55). The third, the Chihuahuan pronghorn, historically existed in southeast Arizona, Mexico, and parts of Texas and New Mexico. It disappeared from Arizona about 1920, primarily due to uncontrolled subsistence hunting and changing land-use patterns. In the 1980s, biologists moved about four hundred Chihuahuan pronghorns from Texas to five sites in Arizona. Two of these populations are doing well, and the remaining three are holding their own. Authorities have even begun to allow a very few hunters to take Chihuahuan pronghorns.

Only very subtle physical distinctions set the Chihuahuan race apart from its "sister" subspecies—color of horn, slightly smaller body size, and skull measurements. As far as habitat is concerned, this animal lies midway between the desert-dwelling Sonoran and the common *americana* subspecies that thrives on the relatively wet prairies of Wyoming, Montana, and several other states. The Chihuahuan seems best adapted to areas where summer monsoons deliver twelve to fifteen inches of rain.

MEADOW JUMPING MOUSE

Zapus hudsonius
STATE CLASSIFICATION: THREATENED

The meadow jumping mouse ranges widely across North America, but in Arizona it is limited to grass and willow meadows in the White Mountains. This species' preferred habitat contains plenty of moisture and diverse vegetation—the kind of setting most often found close to permanent streams. In arid Arizona, areas with plenty of water also attract humans and their animals, and this rodent's threatened status results primarily from overgrazing on and the urbanization of its habitat.

Though the meadow jumping mouse shares many characteristics with other mice, its large hind feet, long tail, and expert jumping ability set it apart. This animal measures about nine inches from stem to stern, but at least half that length is tail. It uses this appendage to help maintain balance during the amazing bong-bong-bong kangaroo-like leaps of up to a yard each that carry it quickly away from predators. The mouse can change direction abruptly with each bounce, and after several leaps it often freezes stock still to avoid detection. Foxes, skunks, weasels, and hawks are a few of the many predators that try to dine on meadow jumping mice.

MEXICAN LONG-TONGUED BAT

Choeronycteris mexicana
STATE CLASSIFICATION: THREATENED

Like other somewhat obscure bat species, the Mexican long-tongued bat is not particularly well known, even by biologists. It is tropical, choosing to spend only the summer in Arizona, where it occurs solely in the southeast part of the state. It also exists in Texas and New Mexico, but most of its range lies farther south. Typically, this species is found in foothills and mountainous settings, provided there are trees present. Roosting areas include caves, old mines, cracks in rocks, and occasionally buildings. These bats are nowhere very numerous, with a local population sometimes consisting of only a dozen or so individuals. Mexican long-tongued bats have a total length of about three and a half inches and come in shades of gray and brown.

As its name suggests, this species is better known in Mexico and features a longer-than-average tongue. Although it may take some insects, the Mexican long-tongued bat feeds primarily on fruit, pollen and nectar. Biologists speculate that the lengthy tongue may allow this bat to retrieve food other bats can't touch, deep inside certain blossoms. The night-blooming agave plant is believed to be a major food source for the bat, and extensive agave harvests in Mexico may be one reason for the animal's recent decline. Human disturbance of roosting sites probably is to blame as well.

For more information about bats, see page 3 in the federal section of this book.

MEXICAN GRAY WOLF

Canis lupus baileyi
STATE CLASSIFICATION: ENDANGERED

This predator is one of the twenty-four subspecies of gray wolf that once roamed the continent. It originally lived—probably in fairly restricted numbers—in much of the American Southwest and, of course, in Mexico. Like its cousins elsewhere in wolfdom, the Mexican subspecies suffered greatly at the arrival of European settlers. In the nineteenth century and the early part of the twentieth, a cloud of hatred hung like a perpetual storm over wolves. Ranchers and hunters shot them on sight, and tremendous effort went into poisoning and trapping them out of existence.

The gray wolf survived by retreating to the wilds of Canada and northern Minnesota, but the Mexican subspecies found no such refuge and so drifted closer and closer to extinction. By the 1920s, most Mexican wolves had disappeared from their range in Texas, New Mexico, and Arizona, although itinerants occasionally wandered north from Mexico—usually to be greeted by a bullet. For a time, the U.S. Fish and Wildlife Service (which already had devoted considerable resources to exterminating wolves) actually maintained a crew of trappers to polish off these immigrants.

Even in Mexico wolves suffered tough times, as ranchers there emulated Americans in perfecting the science of predator persecution. In fairness, it must be pointed out that wolves do kill livestock, but the emotional vendetta carried out against these animals was out of all proportion to real or potential losses of cattle and sheep. Wolf haters stoked the fires of loathing by portraying wolves as great threats to human safety—despite the fact that no wolf on this continent has ever killed a human. Researchers believe wild wolves still exist in Mexico, but there may be as few as ten individuals left.

A few decades ago, the changing public attitude about predators—and endangered species in general—halted the juggernaut of wolf destruction. Early in the 1980s, researchers captured a few wild wolves in Mexico and put them (and their offspring) into several zoos and research centers. These captives (now numbering about forty-four animals) represent the bulk of the Mexican wolf gene pool and the only real hope for this subspecies' eventual recovery.

Biologically and behaviorally, the Mexican wolf differs very little from its gray wolf parent species—except to be somewhat smaller. Since the gray wolf is itself an endangered species on the federal list, it is treated elsewhere in this book (see page 16), and you are invited to turn there for a look at its lifestyle. As a subspecies, the Mexican race is included under that federal protective umbrella and even has a recovery plan of its own. Since it no longer exists in the wild in this country, that recovery centers on the release of captive animals into some portion or portions of its range.

Several locations have been proposed, but the hottest prospect is the 4,000-square-mile White Sands Missile Range in New Mexico, chosen primarily because it is public land with zero cattle. Officials also have identified more than a dozen potential release sites in Arizona, which recently have been narrowed to the one best possibility, the primitive area around the White Mountains near the state's eastern border. The recovery plan for this species calls for a release in the next couple of years, but wolves are an extremely hot political topic, and no one can reliably predict when the Southwest might get its wolves back.

NAVAJO MEXICAN VOLE

Microtus mexicanus navaho
STATE CLASSIFICATION: THREATENED

Voles—sometimes referred to as meadow mice—are small, generally stocky rodents with relatively large heads and short, furry tails (this last characteristic helps distinguish them from mice, with their hairless tails). Their eyes are tiny, black, and beady, and their small ears virtually disappear in their fur. Voles spend their time grooming, constructing mazes of runways both above and below ground, and, of course, eating. Their diet includes seeds, berries, fruit, roots, and other vegetative matter, as well as animal edibles such as insects and snails. In turn, voles provide meals for hawks, weasels, and a host of other predators. For more information about voles, turn to page 1.

The Navajo Mexican vole is known to exist in dry grass, forb, and shrub habitats in low elevation conifer forests in northeastern Arizona. Recently, biologists have determined that additional isolated populations occur elsewhere in the northern part of the state. Mining, recreation development, and overgrazing by livestock jeopardize this species' continued well-being.

NEW MEXICAN BANNER-TAILED KANGAROO RAT

Dipodomys spectabilis baileyi
STATE CLASSIFICATION: ENDANGERED

As this creature's name suggests, its tail is the key to identification. That appendage measures about eight inches, so it's hard to miss in the first place, but a pure white tip (the rest of the animal is pale yellow and brown with a white belly) makes mistaken identity unlikely. Biologists speculate that the distinctive tail tip may help distract attackers the way similar markings do for weasels and other animals. This large rodent inhabits arid grasslands and brush-covered slopes with gravelly soil, where it creates elaborate subterranean burrow systems with up to a dozen escape hatches. A member of this species once created a mound about eighty square feet in area and a foot high with the tailings from its excavations.

Like the twenty other species and subspecies of kangaroo rats, the New Mexican banner-tailed version ventures forth mostly at night to search for seeds, fruit, insects, and leaves. In Arizona, this race once lived in Apache and Coconino counties, but it has not been seen there for several decades. It probably has ceased to exist in the state. For more information about kangaroo rats, please refer to the section of this book covering federally listed species, page 30.

SOUTHWESTERN RIVER OTTER

Lutra canadensis sonora
STATE CLASSIFICATION: ENDANGERED

The river otter's historical range included at least some portion of all Canadian provinces and at least part of every state except Hawaii. Trapping, water pollution, marsh draining, river channelization, and human development around water sources have, however, caused otter territory to shrink considerably over the last couple of centuries. The several subspecies that evolved differ little from the parent form, which is to say a sleek, water-loving, fish-catching, playful, and eminently enjoyable animal.

In Arizona, the *sonora* race existed in the Colorado and Gila rivers and their major tributaries at least until the 1960s and possibly even to the present. Unconfirmed reports say the otter still lives in Arizona, but surveys by biologists in key areas have failed to discover any. Even if the *sonora* subspecies still swims in Arizona waters, its fate may already be sealed. In the early 1980s, authorities released another subspecies *(Lutra canadensis lataxina)* into central Arizona habitats, and it's likely that this immigrant will interbreed with and genetically overpower the native race.

For information about the river otter's biology, ecology and behavior, please refer to the Nebraska section of this book, page 111.

WATER SHREW

Sorex palustris
STATE CLASSIFICATION: ENDANGERED

The water shrew represents the largest of the smallest. Shrews are the tiniest of all mammals, but this species is about as big as shrews get—six inches in total length (half of which is tail) and an adult weight of about half an ounce. If you think that's still on the small side, consider the shrew newborn, which weighs perhaps one one-hundreth of an ounce and is about the size of a peanut (not the shell, just the peanut).

Despite its small stature, this rodent (like most shrews) is a fierce predator of any living thing smaller than itself and many larger creatures as well. Insects, snails, worms, and the like make up most of its diet, and frogs and mice (which are bigger than the shrew) also occasionally end up on the dinner table.

Water shrews are aptly named, never straying far from wet areas. And almost any kind of water habitat will do—rivers, streams, swamps, marshes, or bogs. As a very capable swimmer—both on and below the surface—this species takes to the water without hesitation. It often forages underwater (for invertebrates, tadpoles, and tiny fish), but its greatest aquatic accomplishment occurs topside. The water shrew can—get this—literally walk on water. With a running start and its little legs churning furiously, it can cover considerable distance in the five seconds or so that elapse before the laws of physics reassert themselves and pull it down. Partial webbing on its hind feet and air bubbles clinging to fur on the feet help make this feat possible.

Water shrews sport thick, soft, dark fur with an underside that fades into gray and smoky white. They are rather solitary creatures, coming together briefly to mate, then continuing their frenetic search for sustenance alone (with the female raising the young, of course). Because they are tied inextricably to moist areas, water shrews often maintain elongated home ranges that follow a streambank or lakeshore. In one study, researchers captured more than a hundred water shrews, all of which were found within a foot of water.

Water shrews exist in many parts of North America. In Arizona, however, they are extremely rare and in recent decades were known to occur only in four locations in the White Mountains and the Blue Range in the eastern part of the state. It was news in 1986 when researchers inadvertently captured one of the creatures, but with no sightings for several succeeding years, authorities began to believe the animal was extinct in the state.

In 1992, however, biologists located a bonanza of four individuals, proving that the rodents are still around but extremely scarce. With the nearest other water shrews hundreds of miles away in New Mexico and Utah, the few Arizona animals appear to constitute a totally insular population that will not benefit from immigration. Like most other species living in aquatic areas, this animal has been harmed by the attraction humans and their livestock have for the same habitats.

YUMA PUMA

Felis concolor browni
STATE CLASSIFICATION: ENDANGERED

Felis concolor—it means cat all of one color—is the cougar, mountain lion, and puma (they're all the same animal) that reins as the supreme feline of North America. The *browni* race is a subspecies that exists—or at least is believed to have existed—along the Colorado River and in the desert mountains of extreme western Arizona. Very few specimens found their way into museums, and taxonomists continue to quarrel occasionally over whether this animal ever constituted a separate subspecies. If a population of this race still exists in the Arizona wilds, its status is unknown and its numbers few. Differences between it and the fairly common parent species are probably slight.

In many ways, the cougar is a greatly enlarged version of the house cat. If you want to know how a cougar operates, watch a house cat hunting mice, then imagine a feline fifteen times larger (by weight, not dimensions). Cougars are predators and like all cats hunt primarily by sight and hearing. They eat rabbits and other small animals, but live mostly on deer and elk. Their razor-sharp claws and formidable canine teeth can even bring down moose. It's important to note, however, that cougars pose no threat to healthy ungulate populations, and they only rarely kill livestock (although for some reason, most livestock predation by cougars occurs in Arizona).

For most of the time Europeans have been on this continent, the cougar has been the object of severe persecution. Over the last couple of decades, however, the American public has decided that the cougar is not an animal to be hated and feared. All states have dropped bounties, and cougar hunting is now closely regulated (or forbidden) nearly everywhere. If there is a population of the *browni* subspecies out there, its problems will come largely from habitat loss, not from human hatred. For more information about cougars, please refer to the South Dakota section of this book, page 131.

JAGUAR

Felis onca
STATE CLASSIFICATION: ENDANGERED

In Arizona, the jaguar once existed as a resident in the southeastern part of the state, with occasional records of its presence as far north as the Grand Canyon (probably itinerants). It was long ago wiped out, however, and the sightings that still occur from time to time are almost certainly wanderers from Mexico. Someone reportedly shot one of the cats in Arizona in 1986, but authorities could not confirm that incident. In 1992, another probable jaguar sighting occurred southeast of Tucson, and officials immediately set out baited cameras to capture the cat on film, but it refused to appear. For more information about this great cat, refer to the Texas section of this book, page 136.

Federally listed species classified as threatened or endangered in Arizona are:

BLACK-FOOTED FERRET (page 9)
GRIZZLY BEAR (page 22)
HUALAPAI MEXICAN VOLE (page 27)
LESSER LONG-NOSED BAT (page 7)
MOUNT GRAHAM RED SQUIRREL (page 36)
OCELOT (page 40)
SONORAN PRONGHORN (page 55)

CALIFORNIA

WOLVERINE

Gulo gulo
STATE CLASSIFICATION: THREATENED

With all the bad press the poor wolverine gets, it's no wonder the animal hides out in the wilderness. Few other wild creatures have been so consistently and thoroughly disparaged, reviled, and feared as the wolverine. Devil bear, people sometimes call it. Eskimos christened it *Kee-wa-har-kess*—the evil one. The wolverine, wrote naturalist Ernest Thomas Seton, is a "whirling, shaggy mass with gleaming teeth and eyes, hot-breathed and ferocious." Though Seton probably never got close enough to feel a wolverine's breath, he captured public sentiment about this little animal rather well.

Like most legends, the wolverine reputation has at least a grain of truth at the core. The animal is extremely strong, solitary, persistent, and—when cornered—ferocious. Though it likely cannot back down a grizzly, as some reports would have us believe, it can more than hold its own with creatures anywhere near its size. Though the wolverine probably is not the trapline raider trappers claim, it has likely enjoyed many a meal at their expense.

The wolverine is the second largest member of the weasel family (behind the sea otter). An adult male stands fifteen to eighteen inches tall at the shoulders and tips the scales at forty to sixty pounds. Its legs are short, and its feet feature inch-long claws suitable for climbing and digging. Its powerful jaws are well designed for crushing and tearing frozen meat. Wolverine fur is generally dark brown, with a lighter (off-white to yellow) band running from shoulder to flank on each side. The throat and chest typically show a white blaze. The animal's low posture and somewhat flattened head lend it a badger- or bear-like appearance.

Pound for pound, this is among the strongest animals on earth. More than once, captive wolverines have escaped by ripping chain-link fencing apart with their teeth. In one study, researchers snow-tracked a male wolverine to a rendezvous with a baited steel trap. The wolverine got caught, all right, but then proceeded to separate the jaws of the trap from the frame, leaving the metal pieces lying uselessly in the snow.

Fierce reputation notwithstanding, wolverines are actually rather ineffective predators, due primarily to their short legs and concomitant lack of speed—although they do fairly well in some places and some seasons hunting hares, grouse and other small animals. Insects, berries, fish, eggs, and most anything else edible eventually makes it onto this scavenger's menu, but large prey usually elude the plodding wolverine. An exception is the deer that gets trapped in deep snow in the wolverine's presence. With its large, fully furred feet acting as snowshoes, the wolverine can easily negotiate snow fields that bog hoofed animals down. With a few bounds, the wolverine leaps atop the struggling deer's back, sinks its long canine teeth into the quarry's throat,

94

then holds on until its victim suffocates or bleeds to death.

Mostly, though, wolverines subsist on carrion—often the elk and deer that failed to make it through another winter. To help find these free meals, the wolverine has evolved a nose of the first order, capable of detecting rotting meat literally miles away. Where they coexist with wolves, wolverines often make a decent living by cleaning up after a pack's kill. Leftovers typically are cached against the possibility of poor scavenging tomorrow, and a wolverine rarely leaves an area if there's food still in the larder.

Wolverines are among the continent's most peripatetic creatures, sometimes maintaining home ranges covering hundreds of square miles. When traveling in a straight line, twenty miles or so per day is not unheard of. And there's little that can stop them. They've been known to cross the highest mountain ranges even in the dead of winter. A high metabolism and dense fur make them all but oblivious to winter's cold.

Once, wolverines occupied most of North America, ranging as far south as the Carolinas. Today, they are nowhere abundant but come the closest in Alaska and parts of Canada. In addition to California, the states of Washington, Oregon, Montana, Idaho, Wyoming, Colorado, Minnesota, and Wisconsin have small populations. Versatile in its habitat selection, the animal appears capable of living in alpine, riparian, swampy and even tundra habitats. Its main criterion seems to be isolation from people, making the wolverine a true wilderness species.

In California, a few wolverines still prowl the remote, high-elevation regions of the Cascade and Sierra Nevada mountains. As these formerly inaccessible areas gradually give up their wilderness ambience to timber cutters, miners, and recreationists, the wolverine's foothold on California may be slipping. No one can be sure, but the best estimate is that no more than 100 wolverines inhabit the state.

Since 1991, California wildlife authorities and scientists from the University of California have been attempting to document wolverine presence with photographic self-portraits. At likely spots in potential wolverine territory, they set out cameras rigged to photograph whatever animal takes the bait. A piece of chicken or trout attracts the creature, and when its body breaks an electronic

sensing beam, the shutter trips. So far, several dozen animals have posed for the camera—bears, grey foxes, ringtails, turkey vultures, opossums, skunks, and even one dog. But no wolverines.

That does not mean, however, that the wolverines aren't out there. They are. A few of them, anyway. On lonely, windswept ridges near treeline, they plod along as they have always done, eking a living from the harsh high-country environment.

SAN JOAQUIN ANTELOPE SQUIRREL

Ammospermophilus nelsoni
STATE CLASSIFICATION: THREATENED

Cultivation of native grass and shrublands has eliminated much of this small rodent's habitat and diminished its numbers by perhaps 90 percent. Poisons aimed at the more populous California ground squirrel also take a toll. Once, this diminutive creature ranged over 3.5 million acres in the valley for which it is named, but that territory has shrunk to only 100,000 acres. Many of the existing populations are small and isolated, a situation that can portend inbreeding and the eventual demise of those groups.

The San Joaquin antelope squirrel forages above ground during daylight hours, then retreats to its burrow for the night. This species is grayish brown with one white stripe on each side. Its diet includes a variety of seeds, nuts, fruit, and insects—particularly grasshoppers. The squirrel transports these treasures to its burrow in handy cheek pouches.

The San Joaquin antelope squirrel measures about nine inches, plus a three-inch tail, which it typically arches tightly over its back. Carried this way, the tail may provide some shade in the squirrel's hot, arid habitat. Researchers know that shade is important to the squirrels, because they've found the animals dozing beneath their cars during the heat of the day.

SIERRA NEVADA RED FOX

Vulpes vulpes necator
STATE CLASSIFICATION: THREATENED

The seldom-seen Sierra Nevada red fox lives in the remote high country above 5,000 feet elevation in California's Cascade and Sierra Nevada mountains. Only ten or twenty times each decade does anyone get a glimpse of this recluse, and the population is believed to be quite small. Though probably never very abundant, this species may be in further decline because of human encroachment into its habitat in the form of logging, livestock, and recreational activities.

This animal is California's only native red fox. The much more numerous lowland red fox was actually imported to the state from the Great Plains late in the last century. Aside from their obviously different habitat choices, the two can be distinguished by the Sierra Nevada's smaller size and darker fur. Because of its secretive nature, little is known about the Sierra Nevada subspecies, but its biology and behavior are believed to mimic that of the nation's other red foxes. This animal does appear to prefer sub-alpine fir and lodgepole pine forests, where it probably subsists on ground squirrels, pikas, hares, small birds, and berries.

CALIFORNIA BIGHORN SHEEP

Ovis canadensis californiana
STATE CLASSIFICATION: THREATENED

This sheep is one of three mountain varieties found in California and eight that exist nationwide. Historically ranging along the eastern slopes of the Sierra Nevada Mountains, California bighorns suffered from hunting pressure and habitat loss until in 1972 biologists could find only 195 of them in two separate populations. Trapping and relocation projects have since boosted the census to about 325 animals in six populations.

Despite this improvement, the California bighorn's future remains tenuous, mostly because of its susceptibility to disease. Bighorns are gregarious animals, and it is not uncommon for a lethal contagion to wipe out entire herds. They are especially vulnerable to maladies brought their way by livestock. In 1988, for example, an entire transplanted herd of sixty-five California bighorns perished after contracting pneumonia from a domestic sheep.

California bighorns operate much like mountain sheep everywhere, eking out a living on the meadows of high-country slopes. When confronted by predators, they retreat to nearby precipitous rocks. Males weigh two hundred pounds or so and have thick, magnificent horns that in a mature animal may make a full curl. Females are somewhat smaller and have pointed, goatlike horns. For more information about bighorns, see the New Mexico section of this book, page 115.

MOHAVE GROUND SQUIRREL

Spermophilus mohavensis
STATE CLASSIFICATION: THREATENED

The cinnamon-gray Mohave ground squirrel resides in the western part of the desert that gives the animal its name. The rodent has adapted to life in this harsh climate by remaining underground nearly seven months out of the year (August to February) in a torpid state that conserves energy and reduces the need for food. During this period, it probably munches occasionally on the subterranean parts of plants. There is no estimate of its historic abundance or its current population.

Fruits and seeds of desert plants provide most of this squirrel's diet, and it seems especially fond of territory dominated by the creosote shrub or Joshua tree. Urban and agricultural development are the primary destroyers of the Mohave's habitat. These activities tend to divide the overall population into smaller, isolated groups that then become more susceptible to disease, inbreeding, and eventual elimination.

ISLAND FOX

Urocyon littoralis
STATE CLASSIFICATION: THREATENED

This fox is well named, since it exists only on six of the larger Channel Islands off the southern California coast. Biologists speculate that at some point in the distant past, the fox came to occupy a large island that rising ocean levels have since split into three islands. They further guess that Indians transported the animals to the remaining three islands.

A population estimate—of five or six hundred animals—is available only for San Nicolas Island. Extensive grazing by livestock and other non-native herbivores threatens the fox's well-being, and it appears that feral cats (tame felines gone wild) also cause problems by successfully competing for prey, spreading disease, and perhaps outright domination of the fox (which is itself only about the size of a house cat).

The island fox has a grayish, salt-and-pepper coat with reddish or buff-colored underfur. It is closely related to, but much smaller than, the gray fox that populates the mainland. Like most of its foxy kin, the island species is an opportunistic scavenger, eating everything from crickets to rodents to gull chicks. It also is adept at using virtually all of the available habitat types, from woodlands to beaches to old buildings. After centuries of living on islands devoid of larger predators, the island fox has abandoned the typical fox habit of hunting only at night and is instead active at all hours.

PENINSULAR BIGHORN SHEEP

Ovis canadensis cremnobates
STATE CLASSIFICATION: THREATENED

Although this version of bighorn sheep still occupies most of its historic range, its numbers have been reduced dramatically. Uncontrolled hunting during the last century probably started this species' slide. In 1972, when peninsular bighorns were first deemed to be in trouble, biologists estimated the population at eleven hundred. Today, that figure stands at five to six hundred. Fortunately, several thousand peninsular bighorns also exist in Baja California, Mexico.

This bighorn subspecies prefers to dwell on the lower slopes (generally below 4,000 feet elevation) of the desert mountains in San Diego and Riverside counties. This brings them into at least occasional contact with domestic sheep, which often end up transmitting diseases to the wild herd. Bighorn lambs in particular have a very difficult time surviving.

Federally listed species that exist in California or in the waters off the California coast are:

AMARGOSA VOLE (page 1)
BLUE WHALE (page 78)
FIN WHALE (page 77)
FRESNO KANGAROO RAT (page 32)
GIANT KANGAROO RAT (page 32)
GUADALUPE FUR SEAL (page 25)
HUMPBACK WHALE (page 69)
MORRO BAY KANGAROO RAT (page 32)
POINT ARENA MOUNTAIN BEAVER (page 43)
RIGHT WHALE (page 75)
SALT MARSH HARVEST MOUSE (page 49)
SAN JOAQUIN KIT FOX (page 52)
SEI WHALE (page 76)
SOUTHERN SEA OTTER (page 58)
SPERM WHALE (page 73)
STELLER SEA LION (page 61)
STEPHENS' KANGAROO RAT (page 31)
TIPTON KANGAROO RAT (page 32)

100

COLORADO

LYNX

Felis lynx
STATE CLASSIFICATION: ENDANGERED

The lynx marches to the beat of a different drummer. It has always been at least a little mysterious—a now-you-see-it, now-you-don't phantom. Full of contradictions, plagued with problems and saddled with what appear to be some pretty serious shortcomings, it seems—well—jinxed. Lucky to survive at all. A creature slightly out of step with the rest of nature. At least that's the human perception. And although it's often greatly exaggerated, a fertile germ of truth exists at the heart of every chapter of lynx lore. This is indeed one fascinating animal.

The lynx's "phantom of the North" reputation comes from its quiet, curious ways and its occasional interest in humans. More than one human visitor in lynx country has climaxed that eerie feeling of being watched by spotting a lynx calmly staring from some hidden spot. Biologists who track the cats in the woods (either in the snow or with radio collars) sometimes question just who is following whom. Mostly, though, lynx act like most other shy and reclusive predators. Few people—even those who work or live in lynx land—ever get more than a glimpse of the creature.

The collection of lynx difficulties is real enough, however—starting with its diet. Long ago, the predator lynx took a risky dietary turn by selecting a single prey species, the snowshoe hare, as its primary food source. When hares abound, lynx prosper, with each cat killing perhaps a hare every other day. Bouyed by such good nutrition, virtually every female breeds, litter sizes increase, and lynx numbers rise. When hares become scarce, however, lynx struggle to survive. Some of the cats—usually the young—starve. Others scrape by, but their reproduction declines, and future feline generations suffer. Still others hit the trail looking for food and wander into places where they shouldn't be—like subdivisions and traps. All this happens over and over as hare populations periodically peak and plummet, dragging the poor lynx along behind.

Then there's the lynx's famous curiosity. Dangle a bird wing or strip of tinfoil or any other interesting item above a trap, and if there's a lynx in the neighborhood, it will eventually get caught. Docile to a fault, the trapped lynx often waits calmly until the trapper arrives to provide the coup de grace in the form of a bullet or a clubbing. Though a lynx pelt is no great treasure, lots of these animals have ended up at the furrier just because they're easy to catch—and more recently because many of the world's other cats are now fully protected.

Another problem is the lynx's quarrelsome look-alike cousin, the bobcat. Although the lynx is usually bigger, the bobcat has developed the irascible, mean-spirited personality necessary to make it the boss whenever these two cats meet. As a result, the bobcat fills the medium-sized feline predator niche in most parts of the country. The lynx prevails only in the high-elevation or high-latitude places where deep winter snows make the going impossible for the bobcat. The lynx gets around in these regions on oversized feet (four inches in diameter) that function like snowshoes.

Though an adult lynx weighs only about twenty-two pounds—barely twice the size of a house cat—it is a powerful predatory package of long legs, daggerlike fangs, and sharp claws nearly an inch long. It also has a stubby four-inch tail, a ruff of facial fur, and a grayish brown coat mottled with black. Its most prominent features are feet that appear too large for its body and a long tuft of hair atop each ear.

The lynx depends primarily on its keen vision and hearing to find the snowshoe hares—and occasionally birds, rodents, or other animals—upon which it preys. Like most felines, the lynx is a lone hunter and setter of ambushes. If the cat does not make a meal of its prey in just a few bounds, it calls off the chase to seek another victim. Occasionally, several lynx—probably a female and her kittens—team up to drive hares from the thick brush into one another's jaws.

Lynx exist throughout the northern hemisphere and have lived on every continent except South America and Australia. They came to North America across the frozen Bering Strait during the Pleistocene Era, perhaps 200,000 years ago. These cats once thrived in the continent's boreal forests, but since European settlement, overtrapping and habitat loss have virtually eliminated them from southern Canada and most states. A few northern and Rocky Mountain states still have remnant lynx populations, with Colorado being the southern end of the animal's range. Only in the forested regions of Alaska and Canada do they exist in large numbers. Biologists estimate a continent-wide population in the tens of thousands.

In Colorado, the lynx has always been rare, but its small numbers shrank even further with the coming of European settlers. Tracks spotted in recent years in Eagle, Clear Creek, Lake, and other counties verify the animal's continued presence, however. Most evidence indicates the cat's habitat preference to be spruce-fir forests with rock outcroppings not far away. The few lynx left in the state likely limit their travels to the rugged, remote country above 9,000 feet. State wildlife authorities are currently searching for lynx to capture and equip with radio collars so that more might be learned about their status in Colorado.

RIVER OTTER

Lutra canadensis
STATE CLASSIFICATION: ENDANGERED

Once widely distributed (but never abundant) along Colorado's major rivers, the river otter disappeared from the state during the last century due to trapping, water pollution, and loss of habitat to agriculture. The last documented sighting of native otters in the state occurred along the Yampa River in 1906. Since 1970, however, Colorado authorities have reintroduced river otters to four waterways—the North Fork of the Colorado, the Dolores, the Piedra and the Gunnison, and otter populations are currently doing well in all but the Gunnison. For additional information about the river otter, please refer to the Nebraska section of this book, page 111.

WOLVERINE

Gulo gulo

STATE CLASSIFICATION: ENDANGERED

Though never common in Colorado (or anywhere else for that matter), the wolverine lost ground with the settling of the state. No scientific evidence exists to document a viable population in the state, but recent reported sightings suggest that a few wolverines may still roam the Colorado Rockies. As with the lynx, authorities are actively looking for Colorado wolverines to study. For more information about this species, please refer to the California section of this book, page 94.

Federally listed species that exist or recently existed in Colorado are:

BLACK-FOOTED FERRET (page 9)
GRAY WOLF (page 16)
GRIZZLY BEAR (page 22)

I D A H O

FISHER

Martes pennanti
STATE CLASSIFICATION: SPECIES OF SPECIAL CONCERN*

First there is the matter of this animal's name. You would think, of course, that this very capable predator made a career of eating fish, but that is not the case. Sure, the fisher will not pass up an easy piscatorial snack—such as dying spawned-out salmon—but it rarely goes out of its way to find fish. One theory about the name is that this species earned its fishy reputation long ago by raiding stores of frozen fish laid in by north-country trappers for feeding their dogs through the winter. Another theory is that the word *fisher* is really a bastardization of the French name for a somewhat look-alike polecat in Europe.

Appellative confusion notwithstanding, the fisher remains one of the premier members of the weasel clan and is native only to North America. Before the arrival of European settlers, this animal ranged from British Columbia to Nova Scotia and as far south as California in the West and Illinois in the Midwest. With the exception of a few

In addition to listing three mammals (grizzly, gray wolf, and woodland caribou) as threatened or endangered, Idaho classifies several other animals as "species of special concern."

upper plains regions, most of the northern tier of states had fishers. Idaho was certainly included. There even are reports of fishers existing as far south as Tennessee, Alabama, and the Carolinas.

About a century ago, however, the fisher's stock began to decline, as trappers pursued the animal relentlessly for its thick, rich, very valuable fur. The fisher's innate curiosity helped make it an easy mark. In addition, the crosscut saws of an emerging timber industry eliminated acre after acre of fisher habitat. Never abundant in any area, the fisher began to wink out of region after region, retreating to the more inaccessible terrain of boreal and mountain forests. Today, fishers remain only in northern regions and in those fingers of wooded terrain that reach south into such places as California and Utah. Several other states have, however, instituted reintroduction programs.

The fisher is a minklike terrestrial hunter that preys on hares, squirrels, moles, mice, shrews, and a host of other small creatures. It exists in a variety of habitats, ranging from cedar swamps to alder forests to wooded river bottoms. Its favorite surroundings, however, are coniferous forests or conifer regions mixed with deciduous trees. These places all have one thing in common—overhead cover in the form of a forest canopy, which probably helps protect fishers from raptors.

Fishers are generally dark brown to black, often with a sprinkling of light guard hairs that give their coats a grizzled cast. Their fur is thick and rich and valuable to humans. An adult male weighs about ten pounds, measures two feet from nose to rump and carries a bushy foot-long tail. Females are considerably smaller (sometimes only half that size), but their fur is finer, darker, and less frosted with light hairs.

Actually, the fisher most closely resembles the pine marten (see page 122 in the New Mexico section of this book) in shape, features, lifestyle, and hunting techniques. People have long marveled at the marten's ability to take to the trees and chase down those quintessential arboreal scramblers, the squirrels. Well, the fisher goes one step further, sometimes pursuing the marten into the branches and at least occasionally dispatching it. An experienced fisher plying its predatory trade above ground level is a study in grace, agility, speed, and strength.

Another fisher claim to fame is its expertise in taking porcupines, an animal often granted safe passage by other predators. Once, researchers thought the fisher accomplished this feat by flipping the porcupine over to expose its soft, quill-less belly. Biologists now know that the confrontation actually occurs head-on, with the fisher attacking its opponent's essentially defenseless face. Circling the porcupine, the fisher darts in to bite its quarry's head, then retreats before the porcupine can turn and slap the fisher with its heavily quilled tail. Again and again the fisher attacks and drops back with lightning speed, until eventually—often after thirty minutes or more—the porcupine is worn down and ready for the kill. Cougars, wolves, coyotes, and other predators also take porcupines occasionally, but the fisher is the acknowledged champion. Some states have reintroduced fishers with the expressed hope of reducing the number of tree-killing porcupines. Nature, however, is very good at balances. For one reason or another, most attacks by fishers on porcupines fail, and the quilled creatures remain widely distributed.

Fishers are solitary most of the year, seeking out others of their kind only during the mating season in late winter and early spring. Like many members of the weasel family (and certain other species), they employ the fascinating reproductive device called delayed implantation. Following copulation, embryos form within the female, but after only fifteen days or so they enter a dormant stage. Throughout the summer, autumn, and most of the following winter, they remain in a state of suspended animation. Finally, in the dead of winter, they begin growing again, and a month later the female gives birth to about three young. In just a few days, she breeds again, and the cycle starts anew. Scientists aren't sure why some animals developed delayed implantation, but one theory holds that this technique allows young to be born as early as possible in the spring without subjecting the adults to the stressful practice of mating during extremely cold periods.

Fishers largely disappeared from Idaho several decades ago. In the 1960s, authorities released several of the animals in the Chamberlain Basin area around Elk City, and a small population appears to have taken hold there, since occasional sightings are still being reported. It is possible that fishers exist elsewhere in the state, but given the rugged character of much of Idaho and the fisher's reclusive nature, it's hard to know.

IDAHO GROUND SQUIRREL

Spermophilus brunneus
STATE CLASSIFICATION: SPECIES OF SPECIAL CONCERN

This rodent is the rarest and least known of the eighteen North American members of its genus. Identified only in 1928, the Idaho ground squirrel remained mostly unstudied until recently. Consequently, not much is known about its biology, ecology, or the reason it exists only in a few Idaho counties.

There are really two subspecies of Idaho ground squirrel, separated by thirty miles or so of western terrain and untallied years of evolution. Biologists believe the ancestors of these animals migrated here from the drier South about seven thousand years ago, then became geographically separated. Together, the two races occupy a few dozen sites in only five counties in west-central Idaho. The total population estimate is about thirty thousand animals, with many in the less populous northern race existing in colonies of fewer than three hundred individuals. Thus isolated, these small groups become susceptible to natural disaster, inbreeding, and destruction by humans.

Idaho ground squirrels typically occur in dry meadows in the vicinity of ponderosa pine or Douglas fir forests between 3,750 and 5,100 feet elevation. Usually this habitat also contains reddish rocky soils, plenty of bare ground, and plants such as sage, bunchgrass, wild onions, and wildflowers requiring little water.

One of the mysteries about this species concerns its limited distribution compared to the Columbian ground squirrel, a similar rodent that is capable of thriving in many different types of habitat. Lots of questions remain, but the factor limiting the Idaho ground squirrel's dispersal may be the rockiness of the soil. It's still only a theory, but subterranean rocks may somehow enhance this rodent's chances of surviving hibernation, possibly by retaining heat longer than other soils.

These rodents are about a foot long (nose to tail tip) and live in burrows that are often dug next to a post, rock, log, or clump of sagebrush. They appear to be active only five months out of each year, entering hibernation in August and not emerging until March. Breeding, too, is on a tight schedule, with females receptive to males only one afternoon per year—usually the first or second day after their spring emergence. Females bear but one litter per year.

Although neither subspecies appears to be in imminent danger, there are several threats to their continued existence. In one instance, a golf course was built directly on top of a thriving Idaho ground squirrel colony. Agricultural development occasionally reduces the animal's already limited habitat, and the invasion of exotic plants could alter the food supply. About half the northern population exists on a single private ranch, which could some day cause problems. Another hazard is the shooting of ground squirrels, which has become a springtime recreation in many parts of the West. The most common target is the ubiquitous Columbian ground squirrel, but some of the Idaho species perish as well.

WOLVERINE

Gulo gulo
STATE CLASSIFICATION: SPECIES OF SPECIAL CONCERN

Idaho has a breeding population of wolverines in the rugged Sawtooth region in the south-central part of the state. In addition, wolverines are occasionally sighted in other parts of Idaho, particularly the panhandle area near the Canadian border. Because of the animal's penchant for using only the most inhospitable (to humans) terrain, there is no population estimate for the state. For additional information about the wolverine, refer to the California section of this book, page 94.

Federally listed species that exist in Idaho are:

GRAY WOLF (page 16)
GRIZZLY BEAR (page 22)
WOODLAND CARIBOU (page 80)

K A N S A S

EASTERN SPOTTED SKUNK

Spilogale putorius interrupta
STATE CLASSIFICATION: THREATENED

It is an image that seems more appropriate for cartoons than for the Kansas farmland: Harried by an attacker—perhaps a dog—the small black and white animal stops its retreat and stomps the earth with its paws in a kind of final warning. When the harassment continues, the creature performs a stunning maneuver—rising like a gymnast on its front legs until positioned in a perfect "handstand." With head cocked sideways so it can see what it is doing, the animal contracts muscles near its anus and sends a stream of amber fluid toward the dog. On the way, the solution becomes a mist, hitting the dog full in the face with a powerful, eye-burning stench. As the canine withdraws in stinky ignominy, the spotted skunk returns to all fours and goes about its business. The dog doesn't know what hit it—and most people aren't very familiar with this little acrobat either.

Everyone knows the striped skunk—that attractive, waddling, feared denizen of field and forest that shows up just before dusk and often gets run over by cars on the highway. Flower in the *Bambi* story. Pepe Le Pew in children's movies. The striped skunk is one of America's best-known wildlife species.

Not so the spotted skunk. Although closely related to its striped cousin, the spotted stinker leads a life of relative anonymity. Most people don't even know its name, incorrectly calling it a civet cat, polecat, or even a "phoby" cat (phoby being an abbreviation for hydrophobia or rabies, which the pioneers mistakenly believed every spotted skunk had). Despite the animal's existence throughout much of the country (there are several other subspecies), it remains a virtual unknown.

Compared to the striped skunk, the spotted version is smaller, more nocturnal, not so roly-poly, quicker, and maybe a bit less pungent (although anyone who takes a shot from it would be hard pressed to appreciate the difference). The animal comes in basic black and white, and the so-called spots are really stripes that have had their longitudinal perfection interrupted. Its long, glistening fur is quite attractive and historically has had some value to trappers.

The spotted skunk thrives in all sorts of habitat, including broken woodland, prairie, shrubland, and farming country. Like a good child, it eats whatever Mother Nature puts on the table—mice, birds, eggs, insects, carrion, amphibians, nuts, grain, berries, and a lot more. An adult tips the scales at a pound or so and measures only a foot from nose to nozzle—plus six inches of tail. In good habitat with plenty of food, spotted skunk densities may approach a dozen per square mile.

Behaviorally, the spotted skunk resembles its weasel progenitors, emerging from its den only after dark and foraging busily with an apparently inexhaustible supply of energy. Slender and agile, it sometimes gives up ground pounding in favor of nosing around in trees for songbird nestlings and other arboreal delicacies. Rarely, a spotted skunk might wander into a poultry yard, where its weasel genes may lead it to dispatch several fowl. Because it is alert and moves fast, the spotted skunk does not often end up flattened on some lonely stretch of highway. In Kansas and other northern climes, this animal whiles away the winter with periods of lethargy (but not true hibernation) during which it lives off fat reserves.

Skunks exist only in the Americas, where their overriding claim to fame, of course, is their ability to foul the air—and pets, buildings, clothes, cars, and virtually anything else—with that unmistakable smell. Although spotted skunks do sometimes let fly from their unique handstand position (which they can hold for five seconds or so), most spraying is done on all fours. Fortunately, they use this olfactory attack only as a last resort, usually giving plenty of warning before spraying. What a miserable world it might be if skunks had aggressive, combative personalities that compelled them to shoot first and ask questions later.

Two grape-sized glands imbedded on either side of the anus store the skunk's arsenal of golden fluid. From these sacs, ducts run to a pair of nipples at the lower end of the animal's colon. Normally, these nipple "guns" lie hidden just within the closed anus. When alarmed, however, the skunk raises its tail out of the way and exposes the nipples. The artillery is fully operational at this point, and wise attackers retreat. If they do not, a quick muscle contraction sprays the liquid bullets at the assailant. The skunk can spray from its two nipples singly or together, with the capability of taking several shots (of only a few drops each) before the arsenal is emptied. Recipients may suffer temporary blindness, breathing difficulty, nausea, headaches, and—in the case of a pet—the wrath of their owners.

Spotted skunks of one species or another exist from British Columbia to Pennsylvania to Costa Rica. Human settlement of America probably aided this adaptable omnivore by expanding its menu and creating additional denning sites under farm buildings, in culverts, within woodpiles, and around other accouterments of civilization. Biologically, the *interrupta* race does not differ significantly from other subspecies, but it is rather rare in Kansas. Once, these skunks were quite numerous there, but the advent of clean farming—fewer dilapidated outbuildings, fencerows, brushy areas, and the like—caused their numbers to decline markedly (although the striped skunk continues to prosper). Spotted skunks occasionally turn up in various parts of the state, but the two largest concentrations exist in the urban fringe areas of Wichita and Dodge City.

Federally listed species that exist or recently existed in Kansas are:

BLACK-FOOTED FERRET (page 9)
GRAY BAT (page 5)

MONTANA

Montana does not list any mammals as threatened or endangered other than three that are federally listed. These three are:

BLACK-FOOTED FERRET (page 9)
GRAY WOLF (page 16)
GRIZZLY BEAR (page 22)

NEBRASKA

RIVER OTTER

Lutra canadensis
STATE CLASSIFICATION: ENDANGERED

Over the last few decades, film makers have again and again captured the river otter's essence on celluloid. Even people who have never laid eyes on one of these animals feel they know the otter from its antics on television and movie screens—outswimming a fish, cavorting in pure pleasure down a mud-slick embankment, running and sliding across snow or ice. The otter is well-known as a good-natured clown, capable predator, fun-loving mammal that appears to be part fish. Everybody loves a river otter.

The otter's lustrous chocolate coat ripples over a sleek and slender body. The broad, somewhat flattened head and bulbous nose soften the features of this predator, lending a skilled killer the gentle countenance of a stuffed toy. Comic whiskers protrude from its face. Otter movements seem to vary from pure grace to amusing awkwardness, with little in between. This twenty- to thirty-pound animal is a cartoonist's—and a wildlife watcher's—dream come true.

Above all else, the river otter is aquatic, equally at home in the water and on dry land. It is every inch a wizard in water, outperforming even the fishes in the mortal struggles that constitute life in the wild world. Although the otter often swims with the churning appendage motion typical of mammals, it also is capable of the smooth, sinuous undulations of a fish, its tail acting as a rudder. The strong otter legs are short—perhaps to create less drag—and the toes of its hind feet are webbed—for added propulsion when necessary. This amazing aquabat can swim right side up, upside down, on its side, or any other way it chooses.

Able to remain under water for several minutes and dive to depths of forty feet or more, the river otter is as capable beneath the surface as on it. When submerged, its nostrils and ears close to keep water out. Even when the water temperature lingers just above freezing, the otter gets along fine, kept warm by a dense coat of oily, water-repelling underfur. It even swims beneath the ice provided there are holes enough for an occasional surfacing and breath.

It's no wonder fish constitute most of this animal's diet, meals the otter procures by pursuing prey the same way a northern pike or other piscatorial predator might do. In fact, the otter's main competitors are the fish-eating fish. When crayfish, frogs, turtles, snails, snakes, and other components of the streamside smorgasbord are available, the otter dines on them as well. Although generally crepuscular and nocturnal, otters can be active at any time of day.

On dry land, the river otter is something of a clown, a seemingly clumsy buffoon that appears terribly out of place. Loping along on short legs, it covers ground slowly—unless there's a layer of snow or ice on the land. With a slippery surface under foot, the otter often builds up what momentum it can, then tucks legs against body and throws itself forward to slide along on its chest and belly. Gliding to a stop, it lumbers ahead a short distance, then launches another slide, and in that way travels faster than its legs alone could carry it.

The best-known river otter sliding, however, is that done purely as play. Gathering on a slippery river bank, entire groups of otters may for hours take turns hurling themselves down the muddy slope and into the water like so many children at a playground slide. Other group games include water tag, ducking contests, and wrestling matches. A quiet chatter of chirps and whistles seems to keep everyone apprised of the rules. Solo otters entertain themselves by pushing floating sticks around with their noses or dropping pebbles into pools and retrieving them.

Naturally, river otter habitat is restricted to lakes and riparian zones. The otter does not excavate its own living quarters but readily appropriates the abandoned digs of other animals, including beavers and muskrats. Some otters also construct their own aboveground nests of reeds and rushes. Although tied closely to water features, otters do range widely across North America and historically were absent only from portions of the desert Southwest. This animal can survive just about anywhere—from tundra to mountain slope to marshland—as long as it has clean water and enough prey. Trapping, streamside development, pollution, agriculture, and other characteristics of human civilization have, however, eliminated the river otter from many parts of the country.

Nebraska river otters disappeared early in this century, although a few straggled back (biologists aren't sure from where) during the 1970s and 1980s. At that point, wildlife authorities took over, releasing about 160 otters from other states along several Nebraska rivers between 1986 and 1991. Today, otters frolic in Nebraska on the South Loup, Calamus, North Platte, Platte, Cedar, Elkhorn, and Niobrara rivers. So far, at least two of the transplanted groups have produced young, and biologists are hopeful that otters are back in Nebraska to stay.

SWIFT FOX

Vulpes velox hebes
STATE CLASSIFICATION: ENDANGERED

A few swift foxes remain in Nebraska, but authorities make no population estimate except to say they are very rare. Most of the infrequent sightings (only half a dozen or so confirmed reports each year) come from Box Butte, Dawes, and Sioux counties in the state's northwestern panhandle region. For additional information about the swift fox, please refer to the North Dakota section of this book, page 124.

SOUTHERN FLYING SQUIRREL

Glaucomys volans
STATE CLASSIFICATION: THREATENED

In Nebraska, the southern flying squirrel is found only in the extreme southeastern part of the state where hardwood timber still grows along the Missouri River. State officials have for the past decade been putting out nest boxes as winter denning sites and as a means of measuring the squirrel population, but the news is not good. In recent years, only three locations have produced confirmed sightings of these animals, and they remain very rare in Nebraska. Elsewhere, the southern flying squirrel (and its cousin the northern flying squirrel) are in no danger. The southern version occupies deciduous forests from Minnesota to Maine and south to Mexico and Honduras. Nebraska appears to be the extent of its incursion into the plains states.

This animal's claim to fame, of course, is its ability to fly (actually glide) from tree to tree. The adventure starts high in some oak or other hardwood when the squirrel decides it would rather be in the next tree over. First, the animal leans this way and that to evaluate the distant landing zone it has chosen. Then it throws caution and itself to the wind, exchanging the security of a branch for the uncertainty of free flight. Upon becoming airborne, the squirrel points its limbs toward the four corners of the globe, thereby extending the unique flap of skin that connects its "wrist" and "ankle" on each side. Stretched more or less taut, this portion of pelt acts as an airfoil to turn a quick trip to the ground into an extended lateral glide that may conclude fifty yards from where it started.

By moving its legs on one side or the other, the squirrel can direct the flight and even make relatively sharp turns. Its broad, flat tail trails along behind like a kind of rudder. As the squirrel approaches its landing strip—usually the limbless trunk of a tree—the tail flicks up, which raises the head and forequarters for a vertical touchdown. The legs act as shock absorbers. As soon as it lands, the squirrel scurries around to the opposite side of the tree, probably to foil any avian predators that may have observed its flight. When the need to move on strikes again, the squirrel climbs higher into the tree and repeats the procedure.

It's a pity, really, that this graceful creature has chosen to perform its aerobatics—and everything else—almost exclusively at night. Few people ever have the opportunity to watch a flying squirrel do what it does best. The purpose of all this traveling, of course, is to find a good meal, which in this squirrel's world means hickory nuts, acorns, berries, buds, bark, insects, carrion, and other tasty things.

Except for the wide tail, oversized black eyes, and flight membrane, this animal looks much like other squirrels. Smooth and silky hair covers its nine-inch frame, and the average adult weight is about four ounces. Colors range from grays and browns to pink and buff. When the squirrel is not using it, the flight membrane tucks away against the side of the body.

The southern flying squirrel prefers mature broadleaf forests. Home is generally a cavity abandoned by a woodpecker or some other kind of tree trunk opening, although in very warm climes this arboreal scrambler will use open nests. It also does not hesitate to appropriate unused portions of attics, bird houses, abandoned buildings, or other human edifices. This squirrel does not hibernate, and in cold regions as many as nineteen of the animals have been known to share a single cavity for warmth. Because of their nocturnal nature, flying squirrels often live in close proximity to people without the latter even knowing they are there.

The only federally listed species that recently existed in Nebraska is the BLACK-FOOTED FERRET (page 9).

NEVADA

Nevada does not list any mammals as threatened or endangered, and no federally listed mammals exist in Nevada.

NEW MEXICO

DESERT BIGHORN SHEEP

Ovis canadensis mexicana
STATE CLASSIFICATION: ENDANGERED*

Bighorn sheep are among the continent's most magnificent and most popular wildlife species. Their graceful navigation of rugged terrain, use of open areas where they can easily be seen, and the rams' spectacular horns endear them to wildlife watchers everywhere. A bighorn ram with full-curl headgear posing majestically on a rock outcropping somehow seems to symbolize and summarize all that is grand about the American West.

Historically, seven bighorn subspecies ranged from Alberta to Mexico in a variety of mountainous and desert habitats. No one was counting, but one estimate put the population in 1800 at about two million. By 1960, fewer than twenty thousand bighorn sheep remained—only about eight thousand of which were desert bighorns. "Desert bighorn" is really an unscientific catchall label that includes four subspecies, including the *mexicana* race now endangered in New Mexico. Desert bighorns are typically somewhat smaller than the other races. The precipitous decline had lots of causes—overhunting, competition from livestock, human incursion into sheep habitat, and disease (often delivered to bighorns by a cow or domestic sheep).

No bighorns suffered more than those that chose long ago to make a living in the harsh deserts of the Southwest. Settlers shot the animals for food. Fences, canals, and highways prevented them from moving freely among the separated mountain refuges. Cattle took over prime grazing and watering areas. And humans built their homes and towns near springs and other water features, effectively denying bighorns access to the precious fluid.

Desert bighorns still occupy most of their traditional range—from Baja California to Nevada and Utah, then southeast to New Mexico and west Texas (and into Mexico)—but in far lower numbers than before. Their habitat has been described as mountainous islands in desert seas—very dry seas. Bighorns occupy just the islands, crossing the flatland deserts only to reach other mountains. Wherever they go, water is the factor that limits their range, their movements, and the size of the herds. Fly over desert bighorn territory, and the picture snaps into focus, as bighorn trails emanate like wheel spokes from each watering-hole hub. In the desert, water is everything, and desert bighorns rarely wander farther than a mile or two from the nearest spring or stream.

Desert bighorn rams weigh about 160 pounds (ewes about 110) and stand some 40 inches tall at the shoulder. They are stocky and surefooted, able to negotiate precipitous, rocky slopes with ease. Living where no other native hoofed animals can, they sometimes go three days without drinking (a remarkable feat for a large animal) and tolerate temperatures of up to 120 degrees Fahrenheit. Their diet consists primarily of such delicacies as mountain mahogany, globemallow, and bladderpod—about four pounds of the stuff per sheep per day.

New Mexico classifies its imperiled wildlife either as "endangered (group one)" or "endangered (group two)." Since these rubrics are generally parallel to the more familiar federal terms "threatened" and "endangered," this book uses the latter designations.

The bighorn's most distinctive feature is just that—its big horns (at least in the males—ewes have much shorter horns). The massive, curved, sweeping headgear sets this animal apart from all other horned creatures. During the autumn rut, rams put their adornments to good use in jousting matches designed to grant breeding rights to the eventual winners. At speeds of up to thirty miles per hour, competing rams charge each other head-on, colliding with a resounding smack that sometimes can be heard for a mile. Fortunately, evolution saw fit to outfit these warriors with a unique two-layered skull that effectively cushions the blows. Only rarely do these battles injure a ram.

Other creatures can do damage, however, without ever touching a bighorn. Livestock carry disease to the sheep, consume valuable forage, and drink precious water. So do other non-native species. Burros brought to the Southwest by miners in centuries past now run wild here, as do the aoudads (a sheep from North Africa released in recent years). Because desert bighorns like to keep considerable distance between themselves and other large ungulates, each additional exotic or domestic animal reduces their range.

Living in a closely knit herd makes bighorns susceptible to epizootics of pneumonia, bluetongue, soremouth, and scabies. Significant die-offs can result, and in recent years wildlife managers have gone to great lengths to help prevent the spread of contagions. When scabies caused desert bighorn numbers in one of New Mexico's herds to plummet from about 225 to only 65, authorities launched a rescue operation. First, they set out dozens of salt blocks to lure the bighorns to treatment stations. Above each block of salt hung a bag of pesticide-impregnated dust that would kill the mites that cause the disease. As the sheep licked the salt and bumped against the bag, they'd be getting medical treatment. There was just one problem—bighorns wouldn't come near the things.

So, officials decided to take the medicine to the sheep. Flying low in a helicopter over a running bighorn (or two or three), rescuers dropped a net on the animals. Once the sheep became thoroughly entangled, a biologist jumped from the hovering helicopter and rushed to inject the animal(s) with a tranquilizer. In a sling beneath the chopper, the drugged sheep then got a quick ride to the treatment site. Sick animals received whatever treatment they needed, and workers dipped all arrivals in a pesticide solution. Several days later, they got a second dipping. When the threat of reinfection had passed, the patients were released. Many bighorns that evaded capture were later treated with an injection delivered by a special gun fired from a helicopter.

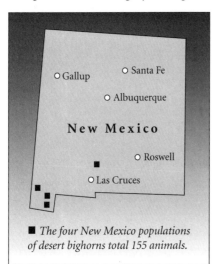

The four New Mexico populations of desert bighorns total 155 animals.

Such tactics notwithstanding, New Mexico's desert bighorn numbers have continued to decline. Currently there are four populations in the state—in the Big Hatchet, San Andres, Peloncillo, and Alamo Hueco mountain ranges—totaling about 155 animals. Another herd of 125 exists in a captive breeding facility at Redrock and will be used to augment the wild populations or perhaps start new ones. Over the breadth of their range, however, the four desert bighorn subspecies are doing much better than these figures might suggest, with a recently estimated population of about 15,000.

ARIZONA SHREW

Sorex arizonae
STATE CLASSIFICATION: ENDANGERED

Shrews are diminutive, hyperactive rodents that usually can be distinguished from mice by their smaller size, more pointed snouts, tiny eyes, and rather inconspicuous ears. Their high metabolism makes them almost perpetually hungry, and it's not unusual for a shrew to consume food equal to its own weight (perhaps half an ounce) every day. Some species could starve to death if they go only several hours without eating, and they often forage around the clock by alternating periods of hunting with short naps. To a shrew, dinner usually comes in the form of animal, not vegetable, matter—insects, worms, spiders, snails, slugs, and the like.

Shrews have a reputation—not totally undeserved—for fierceness, and ounce-for-ounce they may well be among the most capable combatants in the animal world. But they have their homey side, too. At some point, it often becomes necessary for a female shrew to move her young offspring to a new locale. Rather than take a chance on anyone getting lost in the tall vegetation (when you're a shrew, everything is tall), the family travels together. Mother takes the lead, with one youngster holding her tail in its mouth. The second baby grabs the tail of the first, and so on down the line until a living chain of shrews is winding its way to a new home.

The Arizona shrew is extremely rare, existing only in southeastern Arizona and the Animas Mountains of southwest New Mexico (plus the Mexican state of Chihuahua). Fewer than a dozen specimens grace university and museum collections. Lay observers probably could not distinguish between this creature and its close relatives, but scientists have found several diagnostic dental characteristics. This species has short, dense, pale gray, velvety fur. It appears to prefer relatively moist, montane habitats where trees such as Douglas fir, aspen, and netleaf oak predominate. Hawks, owls, weasels, and other small predators are its chief enemies.

WHITE-SIDED JACKRABBIT

Lepus callotis
STATE CLASSIFICATION: ENDANGERED

This prairie bounder has had an on-again, off-again relationship with the biologists who assess its status. When discovered in 1892, the white-sided jackrabbit was thought to be rather common. By 1972, however, only two documented specimens had been procured, and scientists began to disbelieve the previous accounts. During the late 1970s and early 1980s, researchers found a viable—but declining—population. They estimated a species-wide tally of only 340 animals, a figure that likely has been reduced since that time. Overgrazing of grasslands by livestock and the conversion of native prairie to crop land are probably the primary causes of this species' decline.

White-sided jackrabbits look much like their more common black-tailed cousins. Both species exhibit varying degrees of white fur on their sides, making the pattern of black on the ears the most diagnostic distinction. Like most of its kind, this rabbit species can reproduce several times each year, although the litters average only two or three young.

This rare rabbit occurs only in southern Hidalgo County (and across the border in Mexico). It is a pure grassland denizen, and where shrubs begin to invade, the black-tailed species takes over. Since the white-sided jackrabbit is largely nocturnal, people generally get a look at it only when they flush it from its grassy daybed. Interestingly, white-sided jackrabbits may be a faithful lot. They are invariably seen in pairs, and on those occasions when the genders could be determined, the brace consisted of a male and a female. This has led biologists to the unlikely supposition that white-sided jackrabbits may mate for life.

COLORADO CHIPMUNK

Eutamias quadrivittatus australis
STATE CLASSIFICATION: THREATENED

Overall, the Colorado chipmunk is doing fine, but the *australis* subspecies (referred to as the southern race) does not exist in great numbers. While its cousins occur throughout a big chunk of the West, the southern race remains confined to the Oscura and Organ mountains in just three counties in central and southern New Mexico. Authorities estimate a population of one or two thousand individuals in the Organs, but there is no estimate for the Oscuras.

Like other chipmunks, the Colorado version is quick, darting, alert and often vocal. Although some subtle color and shading distinctions set this subspecies apart from other chipmunks, the key to identification lies in looking at a map, not at the animal. The southern race is the only chipmunk in the two mountain ranges it calls home. As with all chipmunks, the Colorado features nine stripes (five dark and four light) running the length of its body. It can be distinguished from similar-appearing ground squirrels by stripes that extend onto the face instead of ending at the neck.

This small rodent is most common in the ponderosa pine, juniper, oak, and sumac habitats found on north-facing slopes in the vicinity of 6,500 feet elevation. Although they climb rather well, Colorado chipmunks spend most of their time on the ground scrounging for the seeds, berries, insects, and leaves that constitute the bulk of their diet. They are active only during the day and often announce their presence with repeated chirps of alarm or indignation at having their territory invaded.

SPOTTED BAT

Euderma maculatum
STATE CLASSIFICATION: THREATENED

Biologists do not know a great deal about this species, one of about one thousand bat varieties worldwide. The spotted bat is fairly large as bats go, measuring four or five inches in total length and weighing about six-tenths of an ounce. It can be identified by its large pinkish red ears (the longest bat ears in North America) and a distinctive series of white spots on its otherwise black shoulders and rump. This color contrast makes it a striking creature. The spotted bat appears to feed primarily on moths.

Discovered only in 1890, spotted bats are believed to live throughout much of the western United States in a variety of habitats ranging from river bottoms to spruce and fir forests. They are abundant almost nowhere. Most of the relatively few spotted bats captured by researchers have been taken near water, indicating a preference for feeding in these areas. They roost in cliff crevices or under rocky overhangs.

In New Mexico, spotted bats occur mostly west of the Rio Grande Valley, primarily in the Jemez, San Mateo and Mogollon mountains. Biologists have captured lactating females in these areas during June and July, indicating early summer births (probably of one young per female, as is typical for bats). Recent surveys in the state indicate fewer spotted bats in places where they previously had been more or less regular visitors. Authorities suspect they could suffer from pesticide poisoning acquired by eating contaminated insects.

For more information on bats, refer to the section of this book covering federally listed species, page 3.

LEAST SHREW

Cryptotis parva
STATE CLASSIFICATION: THREATENED

This quick, darting little animal does not differ significantly from other members of the shrew world. (Dental records are often necessary to distinguish one species from another.) It has beady black eyes, soft gray coat, ears mostly hidden in its fur, and an energetic lifestyle. It seems to be always on the move, nose twitching and tiny lungs working at the rate of one breath per second or faster. It takes grooming seriously, frequently using its feet as a comb.

The least shrew makes its living in New Mexico, as elsewhere, by hunting for insects and other small animals. It also is not above eating carrion, such as a dead mouse—which the shrew must certainly regard as a great feast. Although this animal has only mediocre senses of hearing, sight, and smell, its ability to perceive things tactilely—particularly via sensitive hairs on its head and back—is quite advanced.

Despite shrews' reputation for being aggressive, vicious, self-absorbed little creatures, biologists have found the least shrew to be rather social. In one instance, twenty-five were living in a single nest, and in another case thirty-one dwelled in apparent harmony beneath the same log. Two captive least shrews even exhibited a division of labor. In digging a burrow, one animal performed most of the excavation, while the other spent its time compacting the tunnel walls.

The least shrew is found from South Dakota to Connecticut and south into Mexico. In New Mexico, however, its range appears restricted to just three areas—near the community of Tucumcari and on the La Grulla and Bitter Lake National Wildlife Refuges, all in the eastern part of the state. It prefers areas with a moderate amount of moisture. Because the moist areas that appeal to the shrew also attract livestock and human activities, the animal is likely to continue losing habitat.

SOUTHERN YELLOW BAT

Nycteris ega
STATE CLASSIFICATION: THREATENED

This medium-sized bat (overall length about four or five inches) is actually a neotropical creature that is at the northern end of its range when in the United States. It occurs from southern California to southern Texas and south into Central and South America. In New Mexico, it exists only in Hidalgo County's Guadalupe Canyon and Animas Mountains. New Mexico's southern yellow bats appear to migrate south for the winter, although this is not the case throughout the animal's U.S. range.

As its name suggests, this animal's pelage is a buffy yellow with some darker grizzling in certain individuals. Its ears are short and rounded and its wings relatively long. Biologists know very little about how this bat operates, but it is presumed to feed primarily on medium-sized, night-flying insects. In New Mexico, the southern yellow bat is typically associated with wooded areas (cottonwood, Arizona sycamore, and Arizona white oak, to name a few) near water. In other regions, ornamental palm trees appear to be a favorite. This bat roosts in trees, usually singly or in small family groups. Unlike many others bat, females of the southern yellow species often bear multiple young—up to four in some instances.

More information about bats is available on page 3 in the federal section of this book.

LEAST CHIPMUNK

Eutamias minimus atristriatus
STATE CLASSIFICATION: ENDANGERED

The least chipmunk is just that—the smallest of North America's twenty-three chipmunk species. It stretches all of four and a half inches from head to rear (plus a three-and-a-half-inch tail) and weighs less than two ounces. Like the rest of its clan, this animal has a distinctive series of light and dark stripes running the length of its body. This contrast plus the animal's sometimes orange-red coloration can give it a rather striking appearance.

Spritely and agile, the least chipmunk spends its days (it is diurnal) scouting out the supply of nuts, fruits, grains and other vegetable matter that sustain it. When given reason to do so, it readily climbs trees. Mostly, though, it is a ground dweller, occupying a short burrow that features a resting and storehouse chamber about a foot below the surface. Though there is much variation in its habitats, this species seems to prefer fairly open areas in the vicinity of trees.

Northern populations deal with winter by hibernating, and those in New Mexico probably do so, too, at least at higher elevations. After feasting fully on autumn's bounty (and storing plenty underground), the chipmunk goes through a period of progressively deeper sleeps each night as its biological systems prepare for shutdown. Then, with a plug of dirt and debris in the burrow entrance to keep out the cold and the riffraff, it curls into a tight ball and drifts off into hibernation. Its body temperature remains just above the ambient temperature in the nest, and its heartbeat and respiration also decrease. Occasionally throughout the winter, it may wake up, snack from the pantry, then doze off again.

The parent species *(Eutamias minimus)* boasts the greatest range of any chipmunk, frolicking from the Canadian Yukon east to Quebec and south to New Mexico. The *atristriatus* subspecies, however, is severely restricted, existing only on Sierra Blanca Peak and in the Sacramento Mountains, both in the south-central part of the state.

And maybe not even there. In 1902, researchers considered this subspecies numerous and widespread in the Sacramentos, and as recently as the 1950s and 1960s biologists collected specimens there. An intensive survey in 1982, however, failed to turn up a single individual, and it is now likely that this chipmunk race is extinct in the Sacramentos. Intense human development and competition from the more common gray-footed chipmunk are the likely causes. That leaves the 12,000-foot Sierra Blanca, where the 1982 study found a population of just fifteen to twenty least chipmunks of this race. Nothing has occurred since that time to suggest greater numbers today, making this subspecies—if it still exists at all—perhaps the rarest in the state.

MONTANE VOLE

Microtus montanus arizonensis
STATE CLASSIFICATION: THREATENED

Voles are small, mouselike rodents with relatively large heads, short legs, and short fur-covered tails. The distinctive tail helps distinguish them from similar creatures. They are mostly grassland animals, where they often make their high numbers known by creating a maze of tiny runways in the vegetation (and a parallel system beneath the surface). They get along well with water and have good swimming skills. They are active around the clock. More information about voles can be found on pages 1 and 89.

The montane vole (montane refers to moist, cool slopes dominated by evergreen trees) occurs from British Columbia to California to New Mexico. The *arizonensis* subspecies, however, exists only in east-central Arizona and adjacent New Mexico. Although locally numerous in Arizona, the montane vole in New Mexico is restricted—rather severely—to the Centerfire Bog area of Catron County, where it appears limited to wet sedge and grassy meadows that border marshes and open water at around 7,000 feet elevation. It feeds primarily on grasses and sedges and bears litters of four to six young several times per year.

PINE MARTEN

Martes americana
STATE CLASSIFICATION: THREATENED

This capable predator prowls the boreal portions of the continent from Alaska to New Brunswick, south into California, throughout the Northwest, and along the Rocky Mountains into New Mexico. Nowhere is it particularly abundant, however, thanks in part to the lush fur that long ago made it a target for trappers. In New Mexico, this species' range is confined to the San Juan, Sangre de Cristo, and Jemez mountains in the northern part of the state. Probably never very common here—even before the arrival of Europeans—the marten is now considered rare in New Mexico.

And that's a shame, because this is a fascinating, beautiful animal. The marten's short legs, long and slender body and rounded ears identify it as a member of the weasel family. An adult marten weighs five or six pounds and is perhaps thirty inches long (including nine inches of tail). When adorned with dark fur (marten pelage runs the gamut from nearly blonde to nearly black), it is sometimes mistaken for a mink, although the marten's typically buffy throat and chest clearly set it apart.

And so do its acrobatic skills. Martens regularly pursue sprightly squirrels into the branches, follow their every movement, and in a matter of seconds end up with a squirrel dinner. Fast, bold, and deadly, the marten has been referred to as arboreal lightning.

As a stellar member of the weasel family, this animal's stock in trade is killing. Besides squirrels, the marten menu features mice, voles, grouse, rabbits, frogs, pikas, chipmunks, small birds, and other tasty inhabitants of the woods. Although largely nocturnal, martens do venture forth during the day, as well. They spend most of their hunting time on the ground, taking to the trees only when it appears that dinner may be up there somewhere. Martens prefer to live in high-elevation spruce and fir forests where the trappings of human civilization are few.

Because of its speed, climbing ability, and generally aggressive nature, the marten's natural enemies are probably limited to bobcats, fishers, lynx, great horned owls, and perhaps a few others. Humans are by far the greatest marten predator, killing millions of them for their fur over the years. Curious about everything in its environment, a marten will go out of its way to investigate a bit of dangling tinfoil or a strange new smell, and when these attractions adorn a steel trap, curiosity does indeed become a killer. The loss of spruce-fir habitat to timber harvesting is also a threat to this animal.

SOUTHERN POCKET GOPHER

Thomomys umbrinus
STATE CLASSIFICATION: THREATENED

More than thirty species of this burrowing rodent live out their subterranean lives across North America. In parts of Arizona and Mexico, the southern pocket gopher is rather common, but within the borders of New Mexico it exists primarily above 7,000 feet only in the Animas Mountains in the southwestern corner of the state. Within this severely restricted range, the animal appears to be doing fairly well, with no imminent threats to its existence.

If ever a creature adapted well to its habitat, it is the pocket gopher. Unlike the many burrowing rodents that use tunnels only as a place of refuge, the pocket gopher spends nearly its entire life underground. A special gland washes the ubiquitous dirt from its eyes. A flap of skin keeps debris from its ears. A naked, touch-sensitive tail helps the gopher dissipate body heat and find its way in the subterranean dark. Even the animal's pugnacious, antisocial personality seems well suited to a creature that will spend most of its life alone in a tunnel. Pocket gophers normally encounter others of their kind only during the mating season.

The pocket gopher is well built for a life of tunnel labor. A thick and stocky body, short legs, and the seeming absence of a neck lend it a sort of fullback appearance. Eyes and ears—in an environment where there is little to see or hear—are small. Measuring only five inches or so in length (plus a couple of inches of tail), the southern pocket gopher is indeed a compact digging machine. Long claws on its strong front feet do most of the labor, but truly hard-packed earth calls for the special chiseling skills of large, beaverlike incisors. To keep dirt out of its mouth, the gopher simply closes its lips behind the exposed teeth. Because the claws and incisors get worn down by the work, they grow at an accelerated rate. When a good amount of dirt has been dug loose, the gopher turns around in the tunnel and pushes the load toward the surface the way any good miner might do. As the work continues, these tailings form a mound on the surface, and a series of such piles testifies to pocket gopher industriousness. Each mound harbors a burrow entrance, but the opening is always plugged tightly with earth.

As the gopher creates a network of tunnels several inches below the surface, it eats or stores the tasty roots and tubers it encounters. To supplement this diet, the animal sometimes goes topside—always at night—to harvest the stems and leaves of plants. This booty it stuffs into two external cheek pouches (or pockets) and hauls to its underground larder.

MEADOW JUMPING MOUSE

Zapus hudsonius
STATE CLASSIFICATION: THREATENED

In New Mexico, this species occurs in the San Juan, Jemez, and Sacramento mountains and in parts of the Rio Grande Valley. For details about the meadow jumping mouse, refer to the Arizona section of this book, page 85.

Federally listed species classified as threatened or endangered in New Mexico are:

GRAY WOLF (page 16)
MEXICAN LONG-NOSED BAT (page 8)
LESSER LONG-NOSED BAT (page 7)

NORTH DAKOTA

NORTHERN SWIFT FOX

Vulpes velox hebes
STATE CLASSIFICATION: ENDANGERED

First, let's try to make some sense of foxy nomenclature. Nature originally designed three sizes of canines for life on the western prairies and deserts—the large wolf, the medium-sized coyote, and the little fox. There was no trouble with any of this until Latin-learned biologists ventured onto the scene during the last century. Some of these folks, called lumpers, were satisfied with just three types of wild dogs, naming the wolf *Canis lupus,* the coyote *Canis latrans,* and the diminutive fox *Vulpes macrotis* (which was very different from the common red fox, *Vulpes vulpes).* Since *Vulpes macrotis* is quite a mouthful, people took to calling this smallest of the prairie canines the kit fox.

Then came the splitters, biologists who seek out differences among similar animals and invent new names for the species or subspecies they discover. The splitters found certain variations among kit foxes—ear size, skull measurements and habitat preference—and dutifully divided this clan into two groups, *Vulpes macrotis* and *Vulpes velox.* The common name for the new species became the swift fox.

In later years, there followed a parade of scientists with advanced degrees in taxonomic hair splitting who sought and found enough variations among these two groups to further divide them into ten subspecies—eight kit foxes and two swift foxes. If you're confused, don't feel bad, as biologists still occasionally quarrel among themselves about how to catalog foxes. For most purposes (especially the lay person's appreciation of these animals), swift and kit foxes are virtually identical, except for their range. Kit foxes tend to be desert dwellers, while swift foxes prefer the prairie. (For more information about kit foxes, please refer to the Oregon section of this book, page 128, and to the description of the San Joaquin kit fox in the section covering federally listed species, page 52.)

Since swift foxes have been split into only two subspecies, this distinction is easy to understand, even if not totally justified. One race exists in Texas, New Mexico, Colorado, Oklahoma and additional areas toward the southern end of the Great Plains. The other subspecies, *Vulpes velox hebes,* occupies (or perhaps "occupied" would be more accurate) the northern prairies, and it is this race that has a position on North Dakota's endangered species list. (To further complicate things, Canada has for several years conducted a restoration project to return swift foxes to the prairie provinces, and some seed stock for these releases were Colorado animals from the southern subspecies of swift fox.)

Swift foxes once inhabited most of the plains from Canada to Texas, but with the arrival of white settlers fell victim in large numbers to poisons, bullets, and traps. Although rather timid, these animals typically show little fear of people, which makes them easy marks for trappers and anyone with a rifle. A century ago (and even as recently as the 1950s and 1960s) all predators were considered vermin, and livestock producers conducted great wars to rid the plains of wolves and coyotes. The swift fox suffered as an unintended casualty of that conflict, as it often scavenged for meals at cow carcasses laced with strychnine and other poisons intended for its larger relatives.

Humans also effected a more subtle change in swift fox status. When wolves were the ruling canine on the plains, coyote numbers remained rather low, while foxes generally prospered. Wolves, it seems, tolerated the smaller fox but held coyote prosperity in check. However, as people methodically eliminated the wolf, coyote numbers climbed, and the new king of the canine corps did not look kindly on foxes, probably because coyotes and foxes both prey on small species, while wolves generally attack deer and other large animals. So, by removing the wolf, people made life tough for the fox. Swift fox numbers fell, and despite some increases in recent years, this animal remains rare.

The swift fox once ranged across most of North Dakota, but for nearly all of the last century, reports of its sparse presence have come only from the area south and west of the Missouri River. Few swift foxes—and no breeding population—exist in the state today. Officials still receive occasional reports of swift fox presence in North Dakota, but the last truly reliable sighting occurred in the mid 1980s. Any swift foxes sighted here now are probably itinerants from other areas.

Swift foxes got their name quite legitimately by dashing over the prairie at what seemed to be incredible speed (actual top end about twenty-five miles an hour). Their small size may have added to the illusion of quickness, but there certainly is no question about this animal's adroitness afoot. As the smallest of the wild dogs, the swift fox probably found itself quite frequently on the intended menu of a coyote or wolf. Unable to outrun the longer legs of these enemies over the long haul, the fox opted for maneuverability, a trait that later frustrated many a settler's hound as well.

With an enemy in hot pursuit, the fox deliberately slows its speed and allows its pursuer to narrow the gap, which probably causes the attacker to turn on the afterburners. Just as the jaws of death are closing in, however, the swift fox abruptly changes direction. Cranking along at top speed, the much larger coyote, dog, or wolf can't match the quick turn, and by the time it overcomes its forward momentum, the swift fox has a substantial lead again. After a few of these jerky surprises, the attacker gives up. At least that seems to be the fox's aim, which like most plans doesn't always work. Coyotes probably are still the swift fox's primary enemy—at least now that humans no longer put poison baits on the prairie.

It is surprising how small these animals actually are, standing just a foot tall at the shoulders and weighing only five pounds—considerably less than most house cats. They are beautiful, delicate creatures, cloaked in soft shades of ocher and tan. A black tip at the end of the bushy tail, a splash of black on either side of the muzzle, and a set of extra-large ears complete their identification.

Swift foxes dwell underground throughout the year—another technique for avoiding coyotes and other large predators—and they are among the most nocturnal of all animals, venturing above ground for a nightly rodent search only after dark and returning to their burrows at the first hint of dawn. Consequently, even in the areas where they remain, few people know they exist.

BLACK BEAR

Ursus americanus
STATE CLASSIFICATION: ENDANGERED

Though rather common in many other states, the black bear in North Dakota is definitely an endangered—and probably even an extirpated—species. Once, these animals ranged over most of the state and were especially common in the Turtle Mountains, Red River Valley, and Pembina Hills. As with so many other species, however, black bear numbers declined greatly with the coming of white settlers. Occasionally, a bear still shows up in the Turtle Mountains on the Canadian border, but these are probably wanderers from Riding Mountain National Park in Manitoba. The Pembina Gorge in the northeastern corner of the state also sees a bear now and then, but these are likely Minnesota bears on a pilgrimage. For additional information about the black bear, please refer to the description of the Louisiana black bear in the section covering federally listed species, page 33.

FISHER

Martes pennanti
STATE CLASSIFICATION: ENDANGERED

The tree-loving fisher was originally abundant in certain parts of the state—namely the Turtle Mountains and the wooded valleys of the Souris, Yellowstone, and Missouri rivers. Trapping pressure and habitat loss changed that long ago, making the fisher extremely rare here. The only recent reports of these animals (in 1976, 1985, and 1989) come from the north and northeastern parts of the state, but there almost certainly is no breeding population of fishers in North Dakota. For additional information about this animal, please refer to the Idaho section of this book, page 104.

MOUNTAIN LION

Felis concolor
STATE CLASSIFICATION: THREATENED

Although the mountain lion (also called cougar) has not maintained a resident population in North Dakota for quite some time, occasional itinerants (one or two per year) appear in the Turtle Mountains on the Canadian border and in the badlands in the western part of the state. In 1989, residents of a nursing home in the middle of Bismarck (the second largest city in the state) even spotted one in that institution's parking lot. Since mountain lions are great wanderers, it's difficult to say where these cats come from, but Canada and the Black Hills of South Dakota are good guesses. For additional information about mountain lions, please refer to the South Dakota section of this book, page 131.

RIVER OTTER

Lutra canadensis
STATE CLASSIFICATION: ENDANGERED

Like North Dakota's other endangered mammals, the river otter has gone from relative abundance to severe scarcity. The reasons for these declines don't vary much from species to species: trapping, persecution (in the case of predators), and the appropriation of wildlife habitat for human uses. Over the last several years, about one river otter per year has been documented in North Dakota—in several different regions. Again, these animals are probably wandering immigrants. Currently, the North Dakota Game and Fish Department is considering the reintroduction of river otters to the state. For additional information about these animals, please refer to the Nebraska section of this book, page 111.

The only federally listed species that exists or recently existed in North Dakota is the BLACK-FOOTED FERRET (page 9).

O K L A H O M A

Oklahoma does not list any mammals as threatened or endangered other than three that are federally listed and covered elsewhere in this book. These three are:

GRAY BAT (page 5)
INDIANA BAT (page 6)
OZARK BIG-EARED BAT (page 6)

OREGON

KIT FOX

Vulpes macrotis
STATE CLASSIFICATION: THREATENED

As the lengthening shadows fade away into darkness, the kit fox stirs in its underground abode. Since dawn it has snoozed in this subterranean chamber, and now that great motivator—hunger—causes it to awaken. First, only a tiny fist-sized head with large ears appears in the tunnel entrance, but with no danger in sight, the fox soon emerges into the evening cool. The animal stretches away the kinks of daytime slumber, defecates, urinates, then sets off at a brisk walk. The kit fox's single goal this night is to fill its belly with six ounces or so of rodent fare or other nourishment before the sun breaks the horizon.

The kit fox, smallest of America's wild canines, used to be rather common in desert areas of the West. Eight subspecies (with extremely minor differences) roamed from Oregon and Idaho in the north to New Mexico and Arizona in the south. A close relative, the swift fox, plied its trade on the grassy plain that stretched from Canada to Texas. (For more information about swift foxes and the similarity of the two species, please refer to page 124 in the North Dakota section of this book.)

Then came the white settlers. Trappers took thousands of kit foxes, although furriers did not value the animal's pelage very highly. Because kit foxes often lacked the suspicion and fear of people innate to larger predators, they rarely hesitated to fill their bellies at stations baited with poison-impregnated rotting meat intended for livestock-killing wolves and coyotes. Hunters and most everyone else shot them on sight. Intensive agriculture eliminated their habitat. Farmers poisoned ground squirrels, prairie dogs, and other rodents, and these victims passed their lethal toxins on to the foxes that ate them. Accosted by this colossal, multifaceted change in their environment, kit foxes beat a hasty retreat toward obscurity.

At least one subspecies is already extinct, and another (the San Joaquin kit fox) resides on the federal endangered species list (see page 52). Most other kit fox races also exist in relatively low numbers. As they did elsewhere, kit foxes in Oregon declined rapidly during the early part of this century, becoming extremely rare by the 1980s.

In 1987, when one of the animals was sighted living in a culvert in the southeastern corner of the state, the discovery made news, but when more than two years passed with no additional reports of kit fox presence, biologists began to suspect that the species had been eliminated from the state. In 1990 and 1991, however, Oregon authorities conducted an intensive search for the animals. Biologists drove rural routes at night, shining spotlights into likely foxy places, and they set out fifty cameras, baited and triggered to snap a kit fox portrait. As a result, researchers made seven kit fox sightings and took photos of fourteen others. Two road-killed kit foxes also were discovered during this time. The upshot is that Oregon appears to have a small reproducing kit fox population in three southeastern counties. But because this area represents the northern edge of the kit fox's preferred desert habitat, officials don't expect its range to expand a great deal in the state.

This animal is well suited to life in the desert. Its bushy tail wraps nicely over its nose for warmth on cold desert nights. Kit fox ears may be lined with thick hair to keep out

128

blowing sand, and hair between the toes prevents the animal from sinking in the stuff. Most important of all, kit foxes appear to get by without ever taking a drink. Fluids contained within their prey seem to provide all the moisture these creatures require.

The kit fox gets its name from its small size—five pounds and a shoulder height of barely a foot. (By comparison, a common red fox weighs about twelve pounds). As a predator of mice, kangaroo rats, rabbits, and other small animals, the kit fox competes directly with the much larger coyote for sustenance. This may explain why the fox long ago made an evolutionary decision to dwell underground year round (other wild canines generally do so only while raising pups). Protected by tunnels too small for coyotes to enter, the kit fox need worry about its larger relative only while foraging topside. Recent studies indicate that when given the chance, coyotes will indeed kill kit foxes—although they usually do not make a meal of them.

Although kit foxes often appropriate tunnels originally excavated by a badger or other animal, they also appear to be fairly good diggers in their own right. Outside the pup-rearing season (spring and summer), an adult kit fox may live alone in a fairly simple burrow with only a couple of entrances. Natal dens—which are used year after year—can, however, become elaborate affairs, as the expecting couple annually cleans and remodels the den in preparation for whelping. Often, this preparation includes the addition of a new entrance, and over the years these openings can total twenty or more (but normally far fewer).

Because the kit fox rarely ventures from its den during the day, few people ever get a glimpse of this delicate and beautiful animal. The pleasing shades of grays, browns, buffs, rusts, and yellows that cloak the fox's back and sides are accented by a generally white belly, black tail tip, and a chevron of black on either side of its muzzle. Another defining characteristic is the animal's extra large ears, a feature biologists cannot explain.

Researchers once thought that kit foxes mated for life but more recently have decided that this is probably not the case. The male does, however, play an active role in rearing the young. During the two-month period in which the parents capture solid food for the pups (usually four or five), the adults must bring to their burrow about one hundred pounds of meat—the equivalent of a couple of dozen jackrabbits or eight hundred or so kangaroo rats.

With the first hint of pink streaking the eastern sky, the kit fox heads home. The night's hunting has been good, the kangaroo rats plentiful and easy to catch. Pursued by a coyote for a few minutes around midnight, the fox burned some extra calories, but escaped quickly enough by ducking into an unoccupied burrow. When it emerged an hour later, the coyote had gone. Arriving now at its own burrow, the fox pauses for a moment at the entrance, casting one last look about its territory. Satisfied that all is well, the animal slips beneath the surface, leaving the daylight hours to others.

WOLVERINE

Gulo gulo
STATE CLASSIFICATION: THREATENED.

In Oregon, wolverines remain rather rare, with a small population in the Cascade mountain range and at least a few of the animals in the Wallowa Whitman mountains in the eastern part of the state. On at least three recent occasions, baited cameras have captured wolverines on film in this latter region. For more information about the wolverine, please refer to the California section of this book, page 94.

Federally listed species that exist or recently existed in Oregon or in the waters off the Oregon coast are:

BLUE WHALE (page 78)
COLUMBIAN WHITE-TAILED DEER (page 14)
FIN WHALE (page 77)
GRAY WOLF (page 16)
HUMPBACK WHALE (page 69)
RIGHT WHALE (page 75)
SEI WHALE (page 76)
SOUTHERN SEA OTTER (page 58)
SPERM WHALE (page 73)

S O U T H   D A K O T A

COUGAR

Felis concolor
STATE CLASSIFICATION: THREATENED

Whether you call this animal cougar, mountain lion, puma, or any of the other names coined by European settlers, it remains one of the premier predators on the continent. One-on-one, only the grizzly bear and the jaguar would be its equal, and no prey animal—not even an elk or moose weighing nearly half a ton—is safe from this great feline. As one biologist has said, the cougar represents the "epitome of predatory perfection—raw power perfectly controlled."

Fortunately, the cougar as a species is doing quite well. Though rare in South Dakota, the big cat abounds in Montana, Idaho, Oregon, California, Arizona, and several other western states. In fact, some areas have so many cougars that young cats dispersing from their mothers' territories are bumping into people and getting into trouble. Now and then, one of them attacks a child or chases a jogger up a tree, but for the most part cougars and people live a peaceful coexistence.

As it does elsewhere, the secretive cougar maintains a low profile in South Dakota. There likely have been a few of the cats in the Black Hills and the nearby Badlands since the state became settled a century ago, but sightings were rare prior to 1987. Since then, the pace has picked up, with more than twenty documented cougar reports over the last few years. Apparently the cat uses all of the heavily wooded Black Hills, from Spearfish to Hot Springs and from the Wyoming border to the very edge of Rapid City, the second largest city in the state. The many white-tailed deer in the Black Hills provide an excellent prey base for the big cats. Authorities can't be sure, but they believe a breeding population (not just transients) exists in the state. There is no population estimate, but cougar numbers in South Dakota are certainly quite small.

The cougar is North America's big cat, several times larger than either the bobcat or the lynx. Male cougars weigh about 160 pounds (females about 135) and measure up to 7 feet from nose to the end of their long tail, making them the second largest feline (next to the jaguar) in the Americas. Adults can breed at any time of year, and the female later gives birth to two or three kittens. The young stay with their mother about eighteen months, then move off to establish their own territories. Normal cougar color is a tawny brown, except for the black tip of its thick tail.

Like most felines, cougars rely primarily on sight, hearing, and stealth to get themselves fed; razor-sharp claws, large canine teeth, and incredible strength ensure that the job gets done quickly. They eat rabbits and other small animals but live mostly on deer and elk.

Typically, a cougar stalks to within a few feet of its intended prey, then attacks in a blur of power and coordination. Leaping atop the back of a deer, the cat sinks its teeth into the animal's neck, usually snapping the spinal cord. If the prey is an elk, a single bite will not do. Instead, the cat grasps the elk's head with its paws and in one sudden twist snaps the victim's neck. The bull elk that a cougar dispatches in a few seconds may weigh eight hundred pounds—five times as much as the cat.

131

Originally, cougars thrived from Patagonia to Canada and from the Atlantic to the Pacific. Until just a few decades ago, they were generally treated as vermin by ranchers, sportsmen, and virtually everyone else. In that familiar story, an assortment of bullets, traps, and poisons eliminated them from nearly every chunk of ground where humans wanted to live or run their livestock. Only in the remote and rugged West did the cougar hang on.

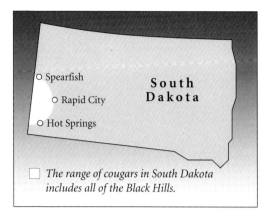

The range of cougars in South Dakota includes all of the Black Hills.

In the 1960s, however, things began to change, as environmental awareness grew and pioneering biologists like Maurice Hornocker lifted the veil of mystery from this great cat. As the public learned more about the animal, the old image of a deer-killing, sheep-eating marauder faded into history. Although the cat certainly takes livestock on occasion (almost exclusively in the Southwest, for some reason), such incidents are rare. Likewise, the cougar kills far fewer deer than previously thought, and often slays the old and the weak anyway, animals with little reproductive value. Today, the public generally considers the cougar a graceful, beautiful and valuable part of the wildlife mosaic, and most people in the West would be thrilled to get just a glimpse of this magnificent creature.

It is interesting to note that both the persecution of this cat and the scientific unlocking of its secrets hinged on a single cougar behavioral idiosyncrasy. Somewhere deep in the cat's evolutionary past, an animal that barked probably preyed on cougars, and the cats learned to escape by climbing trees. That noisy predator has long since passed from the scene, but cougars still take to the trees when pursued by a barking dog—though the big cat could easily kill any canine attacker. Even a tiny poodle—if it makes enough noise—can put a cougar on the run. For centuries hunters have pursued cougars with hounds, then shot them out of the trees. Likewise, biologists use dogs to tree cougars for research, and most of what we know about these animals comes to us by way of cats that have been sent into the branches by hounds.

Cougars are solitary animals, coming together with others of their kind only for brief mating liaisons. The rest of the time, each cat operates alone (except, of course, a female with kittens), patrolling the ridges and ravines of the hundreds of square miles that constitute its territory. Though the cougar guards its home range jealously against other cats, direct confrontations are rare. Instead, the cougar marks its boundaries with urine and feces, and potential competitors generally respect these borders. Right now, somewhere in the Black Hills, one of these great cats is doing just that—leaving telltale signs that say this is cougar country. When it comes to a state's wildlife resources, that's a hard act to follow.

BLACK BEAR

Ursus americanus
STATE CLASSIFICATION: THREATENED

The black bear is another species that is scarce in South Dakota (and some other states) but plentiful overall. Most Americans are familiar with this iron-gutted, woodland denizen from abundant movies and television shows that seem always to highlight the animal's comic qualities. The black bear is perhaps the wildlife species people want to see most when they go to national parks such as Yellowstone and Yosemite. The bears became a virtual institution in Yellowstone years ago as they panhandled for food along roadways, but garbage-handling policies have since put the bruins out of sight.

Black bears are omnivores, which means they'll eat just about anything, and this omnivore takes its title seriously. These hefty bruins (an average adult male may weigh 350 pounds) kill ground squirrels and other small prey, but most of their diet consists of vegetative victuals such as berries, fruit, acorns, and grasses. Also on the menu are carrion, insects, fish, eggs, and almost anything else with calories. They consider human garbage to be fine fare.

The black bear is indeed rare in South Dakota, with reports of its presence coming solely from Custer County at the southern end of the Black Hills. Since sightings are so few, it may be that South Dakota's black bears are occasional wanderers from Wyoming and not part of a breeding population in the state. For additional information about the black bear, please refer to the description of the Louisiana black bear in the section covering federally listed species, page 33.

RIVER OTTER

Lutra canadensis
STATE CLASSIFICATION: THREATENED

Once common across much of the nation, river otters have lost ground to water pollution, trapping and agricultural and residential uses of riparian areas. They still occur in fair numbers in many regions, but the only documented reports (infrequent at best) of their presence in South Dakota come from Hughes County along the Missouri River in the central part of the state. With a recent, but unconfirmed, sighting in the Black Hills, it's possible that a few otters occasionally exist there as well. For additional information about river otters, please refer to the Nebraska section of this book, page 111.

SWIFT FOX

Vulpes velox
STATE CLASSIFICATION: THREATENED

This small predator once ranged across most of South Dakota but became a casualty in the pioneers' war on wolves, coyotes, and most other predators. A few swift foxes remain in the state, although they can be difficult to detect—let alone count—because they spend virtually all their daylight hours in underground burrows. Infrequent reports of swift foxes come from the southwestern part of the state, where a small breeding population likely exists. For additional information about the swift fox, please refer to the North Dakota section of this book, page 124. In addition, the Oregon section depicts a close relative, the kit fox (page 128), and the section covering federally listed species contains a description of the San Joaquin kit fox subspecies (page 52).

The only federally listed species that exists or recently existed in South Dakota is the BLACK-FOOTED FERRET (page 9).

TEXAS

JAGUAR

Felis onca
STATE CLASSIFICATION: ENDANGERED

This is the big one. The one speakers of Spanish in the Americas call *el tigre*. The largest cat in the western hemisphere. With some individuals weighing nearly 350 pounds (the average size is much less, however), the jaguar is the lord of its domain, a predator without predators, a creature at the apex of the food chain. Only humans are its enemies.

Everyone knows the jaguar—brooding, silent, aloof, deadly, and so very beautiful. Take short, stiff fur and color it golden brown. Now add a sprinkling of black spots about the head and shoulders, but farther back tease these blotches into ornate rosettes, many of which enclose one or more smaller dots. Let this animal stand thirty inches tall at the shoulders and give it a short but thick tail. Make its build stocky and solid and its head massive with small ears and eyes. Include large canine teeth and razor sharp claws. Finally, throw in some facial whiskers to make the creature distinctly feline, and—presto—you have a jaguar.

The jaguar is a cat for all seasons, thriving from dense jungle to desert to piney alpine woods—although it seems to prefer habitat with fairly heavy cover. Jaguar tracks have been found at 8,000 feet in Peru and near sea level in other places. Contrary to feline reputation, this cat likes to live near water, and the tropical forest appears to be its favorite haunt. The jaguar's current range includes much of Central and South America.

Fully capable of dispatching any manner of livestock—even a horse—the jaguar has long been one of the predators ranchers hate most. Usually, though, a deer, peccary, tapir, capybara, or other wild creature assuages the cat's considerable hunger. In some regions, the jaguar is reported to be particularly fond of turtles, which it may catch when the female reptile waddles onto a beach to lay her eggs. Sometimes the cat cracks the turtle's shell to get at the meal inside, but in other instances it somehow leaves the carapace intact. Like other cats, the jaguar is a climber (though because of its size and relatively short tail, not a particularly agile one) and occasionally takes to the trees to catch a monkey.

In the feline tradition, the jaguar hunts by stealth and ambush, using its keen sight and hearing to locate prey. Lacking stamina, the cat must catch and kill its quarry in the first burst of pursuit or give up the chase. It dispatches small animals with a single swat of a sharply clawed paw. Larger prey require a spine- or artery-severing bite to the neck or the crunching delivery of jaguar canine teeth to the victim's brain—right through the skull. However it occurs, death comes quickly.

So awesome is the jaguar's power that civilizations long ago worshipped it as a god. They created stone effigies in the cat's honor and sometimes staked goats or other livestock in the forest as a sacrifice to it. The cat's teeth and claws—and even its hair and bones—were considered magical. For hundreds of years, jaguar images found their way into the sculpture, tapestry, and history of America's native peoples.

More modern humans perhaps feared the cat the way their ancestors did, but centuries of respect for the beast turned to hatred in just a few generations. Traps and poisons replaced sacrifices as woodland offerings to jaguars, and that great equalizer—the rifle—made the cat the loser in many encounters with people. Early in this century, furriers and the devotees of high fashion took a liking to jaguar skins, and thousands of the cats ended up as coats. Though jaguars are now legally protected throughout most of their range, South American ranchers—with justification in certain cases—still shoot some cats. A more insidious enemy, however, is the methodical elimination of the cat's tropical forest habitat.

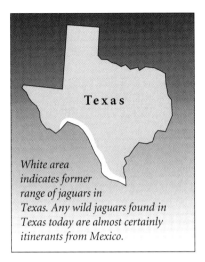

White area indicates former range of jaguars in Texas. Any wild jaguars found in Texas today are almost certainly itinerants from Mexico.

As you read this, it is unlikely that any wild jaguars stand on U.S. soil, although they roamed in prehistoric times as far north as Pennsylvania and Alaska. Recent centuries confined the cats to a swath stretching from California to Texas, but breeding populations died out there long ago. Several dozen times since 1900, however, jaguars from Mexico have found their way back into the American Southwest, probably by following densely vegetated river bottoms and canyons. Invariably, these immigrants have been met with a bullet. It has been several decades since the last confirmed jaguar sighting in Texas, and even unconfirmed (and probably incorrect) reports of the cat are now rather rare. With no resident jaguar population across the border in Mexico, it is doubtful that the Lone Star state will ever again have wild jaguars.

The latest jaguar occurrences in the United States have all been in Arizona, with the last documented sighting in 1971. An unconfirmed shooting of a male jaguar occurred in 1986 in that state's Dragoon Mountains. Severely declining populations in Mexico—and elsewhere—make it increasingly unlikely that this magnificent cat will ever again set foot on American soil. But who knows? When you're a jaguar, you can go pretty much where you want, and the possibility—however remote—exists that now and then one of these great cats still prowls the Southwest.

EASTERN BIG-EARED BAT

Plecotus rafinesquii
STATE CLASSIFICATION: THREATENED

This species—fairly common in other parts of the country—has stretched its range to include a few counties in east Texas, where it occasionally is found in small numbers. Since few, if any, of these bats have ever been seen in the state during late winter, it is possible that they seasonally migrate to other regions. Judging from the documented sightings, eastern big-eared bats inhabit hollow trees, abandoned buildings, and caves. Compared to other bats, they roost in areas that are more open and have greater lighting. Colonies sometimes number up to a hundred individuals. This medium-sized bat puts its name-sake attribute to good use in echolocating the moths and other nocturnal insects that make up the bulk of its diet. For more information about bats, refer to the section of this book covering federally listed species, page 3.

MANATEE

Trichechus manatus
STATE CLASSIFICATION: ENDANGERED

Though we humans should probably try to refrain from passing judgment on the members of nature's family, it is difficult to look at the manatee and not summon words like "strange" and "weird." Often called the sea cow, this gentle behemoth does indeed spend its active time quietly grazing the submerged pastures of America's southeastern coasts and inlets, including—at least historically—the mouth of the Rio Grande River in Texas.

Taxonomically, the manatee is a sirenian, a group of large, aquatic mammals that exist in many tropical and subtropical regions. It is unlike any other creature in this country, more elephant than whale but not really much of either. Although oddness, like beauty, exists only in the eye of the beholder, the manatee does appear to be something of an experiment. For starters, it is built like a gray blimp with flippers and a nose. Its upper lip is split in the center, allowing each half of that body part to operate independently. And the female's mammary glands are located in what essentially is the animal's armpit. Other manatees, of course, find all this quite normal.

The manatee is a shy and gentle creature that quietly prospects the watery depths for tasty vegetation. And a lot of it. An adult manatee can measure ten feet from end to end and tip the scale at about twelve hundred pounds—with an appetite to match. Depending on what's on the menu, a manatee may need to consume one-fourth of its own weight each day. The gas created by all this digestion (plus the air in its large lungs) makes the animal rather buoyant, a condition that is overcome in part by very dense bones, most of which have no marrow cavities. Without this ballast, the manatee would have a tough time diving.

The manatee seems to prefer quiet places where aquatic vegetation abounds and some terrestrial plant life hangs over the water within easy reach. It is usually found in bays, estuaries, and river mouths, not in the open ocean. The manatee passes away much time lounging on the bottom of turbid pools, rising to the surface for air every ten minutes or so. Although it can dive to depths of thirty feet or more, it usually goes no deeper than a few yards. The manatee can survive in salt or fresh water and easily moves from one to the other, although it must return periodically to fresh water.

Because manatees lack the necessary adaptations for dealing with the cold, they are strictly warm-water creatures, migrating to more clement climes when necessary. Despite their large size and apparent lethargy, they do at least occasionally get downright playful. One popular leisure pastime is body surfing in the strong currents below dams, an activity that sometimes involves several of the animals simultaneously "riding the big one" and making turns in near perfect synchrony.

Perhaps a thousand or so manatees remain in Florida. This species actually is listed as endangered by the federal government, but the feds consider its presence limited to the Southeast. Although manatees existed at one time in Texas waters, the state has no population of the animals now. A dead one washed ashore dead near Galveston in 1988, but that individual probably came from Florida or the Caribbean. Humans are this species' greatest enemy. Collisions with power boats do the most damage, but additional manatees die from vandals' bullets, in flood-control structures, and by becoming entangled in nets and ropes.

PALO DURO MOUSE

Peromyscus truei comanche
STATE CLASSIFICATION: THREATENED

This animal inhabits a very narrow range of habitat in the north Texas breaks where the high plains meet the canyonlands. It is probably a relic species, a throwback to the time when pinyon pine and juniper covered much more of this country. Presently, the Palo Duro mouse (named for a canyon where it is found) is most numerous along the escarpment of the Llano Estacado in the Texas panhandle. In addition to junipers, it seems to exist most often amid prickly pear cactus, acacia, and mesquite. Although Texas has protected this rodent since 1977, populations are isolated from one another, making them subject to elimination via natural catastrophe or inbreeding. In addition, this animal's habitat—mostly on private land—is always subject to alteration.

MARGAY

Felis wiedii
STATE CLASSIFICATION: ENDANGERED

This little cat is essentially a downsized ocelot, with the same black spot patterns on a golden brown background. The margay is a forest animal—and for a very good reason. Even in a family of good climbers, this cat's arboreal agility is outstanding. In fact, the margay makes much of its living snatching prey from branches high above the ground. Squirrels and other rodents are its favorite food, but birds, insects, fruit, and even sloths and monkeys also fuel this feline. Contributing to the margay's climbing skill are a long tail for balancing and ankles that rotate 180 degrees outward to provide a solid grip in virtually any situation. The margay can come down a tree trunk head first (like a squirrel), hang from limbs (like a monkey), and execute great leaps (like an Olympian). It has been known to exit trees voluntarily from great heights, apparently without harm.

The margay's preferred habitat is the moist conifer forest of Central and South

Coatimundi

America, where it hunts at night and spends most days lazing high in the branches of a tree. The animal's beautiful fur (and that fur's resemblance to the even more valuable ocelot pelt) makes this cat a prime target for market hunters and trappers. The margay would probably be federally listed as endangered in the United States, except for the fact that it almost certainly does not exist here.

The last confirmed report of margay presence in Texas was nearly 150 years ago, and many observers suspect that that animal was an itinerant from Mexico. It may well be that the United States never did support a breeding margay population. Although it would not be impossible for a wanderer from Mexico to cross the border occasionally, Texas authorities virtually never receive even unsubstantiated reports of this cat.

COATIMUNDI

Nasua nasua
STATE CLASSIFICATION: ENDANGERED

Also referred to by its nickname coati, this south-of-the-border omnivore somewhat resembles a raccoon, although the coati's smaller size, pointed snout, and more slender build make the chances of mistaken identity rather slight. Like raccoons, however, they are good climbers and take readily to the water. Coatis are largely diurnal and often travel in bands of a couple of dozen animals over a home range of several hundred acres.

Weighing in the neighborhood of fifteen or twenty pounds—but with the appetite of a much larger animal—the coati seems perpetually on the prowl for food, poking its inquisitive nose anywhere a meal might be hiding. Gastronomically, almost anything is fair game—lizards, rodents, nuts, berries, insects, worms, carrion, and anything else it can capture or stumble upon. Coati color is usually brownish red, often with a yellow tint to its forequarters. Splashes of off-white are plentiful around its muzzle, throat, chin, ears and eyes. Its eighteen-inch tail sports several muted bands.

Like many other Texas wildlife species, coatis are primarily more southern animals, with a range that extends all the way to Peru. Rather adaptable, they exist in tropical habitats at sea level, in juniper-pine forests at eight thousand feet, and nearly everywhere in between.

In the United States, their range may include a half dozen Texas counties (and some parts of southern Arizona and New Mexico), but Texas authorities have no recent confirmed reports of their presence. However, given the nearby existence of Mexican coatis, this animal's existence in the Lone Star state—even a remote resident population or two—would be no big surprise.

COUE'S RICE RAT

Oryzomys couesi
STATE CLASSIFICATION: THREATENED

This animal is one of fifty rice rat species found from Texas and Louisiana south to Tierra del Fuego. Little is known about this particular species' range, numbers, or threats in Texas. In general, though, rice rats live in a variety of habitats that are wet enough to support the rich herbaceous vegetation they require for nourishment. They get along well in aquatic environments and are capable swimmers both on and below the water's surface. When alarmed while swimming, the rice rat can dive like a muskrat.

Rice rat body length is about six inches, plus three inches of tail. Coloration is grayish brown to ocher with lighter underparts. Like many other rodents, rice rats are extremely prolific. Females are ready to breed at the tender age of seven weeks, gestation is about twenty-five days, and the female is often mating again within ten hours of giving birth. Up to seven litters (of about four young each) per year per female are possible, although five or six are more likely the average. A short lifespan—often less than a year—prevents their populations from exploding, although they can become serious pests under certain conditions.

MEXICAN WOLF

Canis lupus baileyi
STATE CLASSIFICATION: ENDANGERED

The Mexican wolf last trod Texas ground in the 1970s, and it no longer lives in the wild anywhere in the United States. Futhermore, what few wolves there are in Mexico exist far from the Texas border, making a natural reestablishment virtually impossible. A few Mexican wolves do, however, reside in captivity, and Arizona and New Mexico (in cooperation with the federal government) are planning reintroductions. Texas is not currently involved with the Mexican wolf reintroduction effort, primarily because of strong opposition by state livestock interests and a shortage of suitable large tracts of habitat on public lands. For more information about this species, please refer to the Arizona section of this book (page 88). For information about the parent species *(Canis lupus),* please refer to the section covering federally listed animals (page 16).

TEXAS KANGAROO RAT

Dipodomys elator
STATE CLASSIFICATION: THREATENED

So named because of its long hind legs and significant jumping ability, this species is one of several imperiled kangaroo rats. (For additional information about the others, please refer to the section of this book dealing with federally listed species, page 30.) It is five or so inches in length with a tail much longer than that. Its upper parts are buff and black and its underside mostly white. Cheek pouches serve as handy containers for food—

seeds, leaves, and fruit—as this kangaroo rat bounces stiffly from place to place during its nocturnal feeding forays.

Although once present in Oklahoma as well as Texas, this species now appears endemic only to the Lone Star state, where it inhabits the mesquite grasslands on the rolling northwest plains. The Texas kangaroo rat seems to walk a sort of environmental tightrope in its relationship with humans. On one hand, it often prospers in places where livestock grazing has modified—but not radically altered—the habitat. When cropland replaces pasture, however, this species' stock goes down, and that is the case more and more these days on the range of the Texas kangaroo rat.

BLACK BEAR

Ursus americanus
STATE CLASSIFICATION: ENDANGERED

The black bear in Texas has gone from being rather common historically to a point about a decade ago when biologists considered it extirpated from the state. Recently, however, black bears from Mexico have reestablished populations in those parts of west Texas where mountain ranges break up the Chihuahuan deserts. For additional information about the black bear, please refer to the description of the Louisiana black bear in the section of this book covering federally listed species (page 33).

SOUTHERN YELLOW BAT

Lasiurus ega
STATE CLASSIFICATION: THREATENED

This species is known to exist in Texas only in subtropical riparian woodlands—specifically along the lower Rio Grande Valley. For more information about the southern yellow bat, please refer to the New Mexico section of this book (page 120).

SPOTTED BAT

Euderma maculatum
STATE CLASSIFICATION: THREATENED

In Texas, spotted bat presence has been confirmed only in Big Bend National Park, although it also may use canyon and mountain habitat along the Rio Grande River in this region. For more information about this species, please refer to the New Mexico section of this book (page 119).

Note: The following ten species of marine mammals have exhibited some presence—either historic or current—in the waters off the Texas coast. As highly mobile animals, their status (and sometimes even their biology) is difficult to ascertain, and very little is known about many of these species. Consequently, this book makes no attempt to describe their range or quantify their numbers. Texas is currently reevaluating the inclusion of some of these animals on its threatened and endangered lists.

PYGMY SPERM WHALE

Kogia breviceps
STATE CLASSIFICATION: THREATENED

This stocky-bodied cetacean gets its name from several similarities between it and the much larger sperm whale. These include the presence of a spermaceti organ, a small and underslung lower jaw, and a blowhole positioned off center to the left. There's no real possibility of confusing the two species, however, since the pygmy sperm weighs only nine hundred pounds or so and measures barely thirteen feet from end to end. A male sperm whale, on the other hand, might be sixty feet long and weigh more than forty tons. (For more information about sperm whales, please refer to the section of this book covering federally listed species, page 73.)

Pygmy sperm whales ply the ocean depths searching for squid, octopus, crabs, and fish. They are relatively slow swimmers and do not often congregate in large groups. Because these grayish blue denizens of the deep were never on any whaler's hit list and because they normally stay far from land, biologists know little about their lifestyle. Pygmy sperms beach themselves often enough to indicate that they must exist in fairly large numbers, but no one can be sure. They appear to inhabit all but the coldest of waters.

DWARF SPERM WHALE

Kogia simus
STATE CLASSIFICATION: THREATENED

This is another miniature version of the big daddy sperm whale, smaller even than the pygmy sperm (by several feet and a few hundred pounds). Size differences notwithstanding, the two diminutive (by whale standards) sperm look-alikes were once thought to be of the same species, and at sea it is indeed difficult to tell them apart.

Even less is known about this species, which means its behavior and biology are still largely a mystery. Researchers can only assume it to be similar to the pygmy sperm.

GOOSE-BEAKED WHALE

Ziphius cavirostris
STATE CLASSIFICATION: THREATENED

The eighteen species of beaked whales are medium-to-large cetaceans that the world seems to have passed by, making them probably the least understood large animals on earth. In fact, one species of beaked whale has never been seen in the flesh. This group was likely named for their long snouts, but little else is known about them—where they live, where and when they breed, or even what they usually eat.

The goose-beaked whale, however, is the most often sighted of these rare species. It is typically light gray or rusty red on top and dark on its belly. White blotches, probably caused by parasitic bacteria or protozoa, cover much of its body. Goose-beaks may reach a size of nearly thirty feet and five tons. They can dive deep and remain under water for up to thirty minutes.

GERVAIS' BEAKED WHALE

Mesoplodon europaeus
STATE CLASSIFICATION: THREATENED

This is another of the mysterious beaked whales. The little that is known about the Gervais' beaked whale comes from a few dozen individuals unlucky enough to strand themselves on beaches over the years. Biologists put their maximum length at about seventeen feet and say they probably exist mostly—or even solely—in the tropical and temperate waters of the Atlantic.

SHORT-FINNED PILOT WHALE

Globicephala macrorhynchus
STATE CLASSIFICATION: THREATENED

This jet black, twenty-foot, three-ton whale is known for its ability to go deep—very deep. In the 1970s, the U.S. Navy trained a short-finned pilot whale to hit depths of sixteen hundred feet, and officials at that time believed the species capable of an additional four hundred feet. Despite its obvious aquatic expertise, this whale is also a common strander, sometimes beaching in large numbers. Several years ago, forty-four short-finned pilot whales beached themselves on the Florida coast. Although towed out to sea by rescuers, at least thirteen of the animals returned to the beach several days later. They seem to be gregarious in all activities, sometimes forming groups of a hundred or more and occasionally associating with dolphins. The short-finned pilot whale's distinguishing features include a large, rounded head and relatively short flippers that it appears to hold rigid while swimming. They are fairly common in many of the world's waters.

ATLANTIC SPOTTED DOLPHIN

Stenella plagiodon
STATE CLASSIFICATION: THREATENED

There are several spotted dolphins in the world, and taxonomists continue to fuss about the number of species and subspecies that actually exist. Regardless of how the Latin war turns out, this fun-loving animal will remain a favorite of people everywhere. These are very friendly creatures, indeed, often choosing to come within an arm's reach of swimmers and divers. They appear to get a kick out of riding in a boat's bow wave or simply racing alongside under their own power. When in a sporting mood, they may travel for miles to rendezvous with a passing boat. They also seem to enjoy leaping high out of the water and falling back with a resounding splat.

Atlantic spotted dolphins are generally bluish, and as each individual matures, it becomes covered with the light blotches that give the species its name. Scientists speculate that the spots may help dolphins identify one another while also providing some measure of camouflage to help foil predators. They commonly gather in groups, sometimes of a hundred or more (and, rarely, as many as a thousand). They measure about seven feet in length and weigh in the neighborhood of three hundred pounds. Atlantic spotted dolphins are fairly common in tropical and sometimes temperate waters.

ROUGH-TOOTHED DOLPHIN

Steno bredanensis
STATE CLASSIFICATION: THREATENED

This is another of the many marine mammals about which humans know very little. Believed to be widely distributed but rather rare, the rough-toothed dolphin also has a reputation for great intelligence, a belief garnered from the few that have been studied in captivity. Although its color varies, this animal is generally dark gray to purplish with plenty of yellowish white or even pink blotches. Large individuals may reach 9 feet and 350 pounds, but a generally slender body helps the rough-toothed dolphin achieve speeds of up to 15 miles per hour. It is named for the wrinkle-like vertical ridges that distinguish its teeth from those of other dolphins.

KILLER WHALE

Orcinus orca
STATE CLASSIFICATION: THREATENED

Although technically a dolphin (the largest member of that group), the killer whale is among the best-known marine mammals in the world. Its extremely prominent dorsal fin and spectacular black and white coloration make it easy to identify and nearly impossible to confuse with any other species. A few captive killer whales entertain millions of people each year at various sea parks with their amazing leaping skills and other tricks. Sometimes called the supercetacean, the predatory killer whale has a reputation (mostly deserved) for besting its kin at virtually every aspect of life in the sea—from strength to dominance to speed (up to twenty-three knots).

Like their terrestrial counterparts, the wolves, killer whales are extremely social animals. Family groups (called pods) of up to thirty members remain intact for years and sometimes join with other clans to form groups of one hundred or more individuals. When hunting or traveling as a group, these intelligent animals maintain contact via a sophisticated repertoire of whistles, clicks, creaks, whines, tweets, and other sounds. Each pod apparently has its own dialect, which distinguishes it slightly from neighboring pods.

Killer whales are extremely active animals, breaching frequently and often engaging in "spy hopping," a maneuver in which they sort of tread water in a vertical position with their heads above the surface. They also have a playful side and have been observed pulling kelp bulbs deep under water. When released at great depths, the air-filled kelp rockets to the surface and shoots skyward like a missile—apparently to the enjoyment of the whales.

But above all else, the killer whale is a predator—in fact, the supreme predator of the sea. Sometimes alone but often in pods it preys on everything from schools of fish to other whales. There even are accounts of killer whales preying on blue whales, which at one-hundred-plus tons are fully ten times the size of killer whales. Seals, sea lions, dolphins, porpoises, penguins, and a host of other marine life end up in killer whale stomachs, although fish and squid are the most common fare. In short, nothing in the sea is safe when the killer whale is about (except people—no killer whale in the wild has ever been known to kill a human).

Combining their predatory and social natures, killer whales become the unquestioned masters of their environment. Members of a hunting group spread out to attack from several sides, perhaps with one squad to prevent the prey from reaching the surface (in the case of a mammal) and another to keep it from diving. If the prey is too large to be swallowed whole, these sharp-toothed predators simply start ripping off chunks. Eventually, the prey succumbs, and the feasting gets easier.

Minke whales are frequent targets of killer whale pods, and gray whales at least occasionally just roll over and give up when a pod attacks. Sharks sometimes become victims, too, and there have been reports of killer whales—apparently completing an attack from below—shooting out of the water with a shark held crosswise in their jaws. Scientists working in the polar regions even claim to have seen killer whales tilt ice flows with their backs so that seals might slide down the ice and into the jaws of a podmate.

A large killer whale may weigh nine tons and measure thirty feet in length. They are very cosmopolitan, existing in polar seas, tropical oceans, and virtually all the world's waters in between.

FALSE KILLER WHALE

Pseudorca crassidens
STATE CLASSIFICATION: THREATENED

This dark, slender whale features a gray blaze on its chest and sometimes on the side of its head, attributes that have led some observers to mistake this cetacean for its more famous relative. Like the killer whale, however, the false killer is gregarious and predatory, feeding mostly on squid and large fish. Up close, however, the false killer whale is easily distinguished from its namesake by its smaller size, less pronounced color contrasts, and much shorter dorsal fin. Big groups of false killer whales occasionally strand themselves on beaches.

Fishermen sometimes complain about this species stealing fish from their lines. These whales also are fond of riding—apparently for fun—the bow waves of passing boats. Though not particularly numerous anywhere, they are widely distributed.

PYGMY KILLER WHALE

Feresa attenuata
STATE CLASSIFICATION: THREATENED

For reasons that will probably never be known, this animal got named after the killer whale not for any great overall resemblance but for its similar dentition. This 8-foot, 350-pound dolphin does, however, share its namesake's penchant for being aggressive—even to the point of snapping at humans (at least those in captivity occasionally do). Pygmy killer whales sometimes form groups of a hundred or more, with many members rising to the ocean's surface and diving in unison. They are gray and black, feed on squid and small fish, and appear to prefer tropical waters. Little else is known about this species.

Federally listed species that also exist or recently existed in Texas or waters off the Texas coast are:

BLACK-FOOTED FERRET (page 9)
BLUE WHALE (page 78)
FIN WHALE (page 77)
GRAY WOLF (page 16)
JAGUARUNDI (page 28)
LOUISIANA BLACK BEAR (page 33)
MEXICAN LONG-NOSED BAT (page 8)
OCELOT (page 40)
RED WOLF (page 45)
RIGHT WHALE (page 75)
SPERM WHALE (page 73)

U T A H

Utah does not list any mammals as threatened or endangered other than three that are federally listed and covered elsewhere in this book. These three are:

BLACK-FOOTED FERRET (page 9)
GRAY WOLF (page 16)
UTAH PRAIRIE DOG (page 63)

WASHINGTON

PYGMY RABBIT

Brachylagus idahoensis
STATE CLASSIFICATION: THREATENED

This is a bunny's bunny—the smallest member of the rabbit and hare family in North America. It measures only ten inches or so and often weighs considerably less than a pound. The smooth-furred pygmy rabbit looks much like a diminutive cottontail, although usually of a paler hue. It is buffy gray on top and somewhat white on the underside with a gray cotton-ball tail. As one might expect, its feet, ears, and skull are small.

This species is the only one of its kind to actually dig its own burrows (although it will move into vacant apartments created by other creatures, too). A pygmy-planned subterranean home invariably has its entrances (sometimes several of them) at the base of sagebrush plants. The four-inch holes lead to wider tunnels and chambers that may extend a yard beneath the surface. Topside, a labyrinth of runways connects the entrances and provides the rabbit with quick escape routes. A variety of predators—coyotes, foxes, hawks, and weasels, to name a few—prey on these animals, and the rabbits respond (as their kind often does) with prolificacy. In true rabbit fashion, this species may annually produce three litters of six or eight young each. A timid creature, the pygmy rabbit usually stays within a few dozen yards of its burrow and is primarily active at dusk and dawn.

The pygmy rabbit has selected for itself a rather narrow range of suitable habitat, existing almost exclusively on soft-soiled native prairie covered with dense clumps of large sagebrush between 4,500 and 7,000 feet elevation. It uses the sagebrush for cover but also gets plenty of nutritional mileage out of the plant, at least in the winter when good grasses are scarce. The rabbits sometimes even climb into the branches to get the tastiest parts. Soft soils are important because it must dig burrows. Fortunately, a good-sized chunk of territory in the Great Basin and intermountain regions of the West meets this description. In Washington, however, pygmy rabbit territory has dwindled away to nearly nothing.

Pygmy rabbit range covers large portions of Idaho, Oregon, Utah, and Nevada, plus small bits of California and Montana. Although this territory is home to plenty of healthy populations, it also contains large parcels of terrain devoid of pygmy rabbits. Washington's insular population is totally separate, cut off from the rest of pygmy rabbitdom by huge swaths of uninhabitable (from the rabbit's point of view) land. Because pygmy rabbits will not cross even small sections of open terrain, populations become increasingly isolated as agriculture and other human endeavors chip away at the edges of their sagebrush sanctuaries. Biologists call the phenomenon "island biology," in which isolated populations become more and more vulnerable to inbreeding and to catastrophic disasters like fire and flood. One way to mitigate the effects of island biology is to leave a travel corridor—an ungrazed and unplowed ravine for example—that encourages rabbit movement among habitat chunks.

Once found in several parts of the Columbia River basin, the pygmy rabbit in Washington is now confined to just six sites, all in Douglas County in the central part of the state. Some of these sites are on private land and subject to habitat degradation, but the one with the most pygmies is owned by the state Department of Natural Resources,

149

which should grant the resident rabbits some measure of security. Washington authorities estimate the statewide population at about five hundred animals, but even this is an improvement over a decade ago, when the species was thought to be extinct in Washington. State authorities currently are considering upgrading the pygmy's status to endangered.

Most of the pygmy rabbit's problems have come from lost habitat, not predation. Tied inextricably to terrain dominated by large sagebrush, these diminutive animals suffered increasingly as more and more sagebrush went under the plow. Curiously, however, the rabbits actually prosper under a particular regime of human habitat alteration. Heavy grazing sometimes leads to increased sagebrush density, which suits them just fine. If the livestock are then removed from the land, grasses often return to occupy the open spaces between the sagebrush, which pleases the pygmies even more. Left in this condition, the land makes good pygmy rabbit habitat. (Of course, if livestock are later reintroduced to the area, the sagebrush—and the rabbits—suffers.)

This animal's reliance on sagebrush—preferably big plants—is unwavering. Tunnel entrances usually occur at the base of the plant, and above-ground runways weave a maze of escape routes among the bushes. When a predator shows up, a quick duck into the sagebrush labyrinth may give the attacker the slip.

Federally listed species that exist in Washington or the waters off the Washington coast are:

BLUE WHALE (page 78)
COLUMBIAN WHITE-TAILED DEER (page 14)
FIN WHALE (page 77)
GRAY WOLF (page 16)
GRIZZLY BEAR (page 23)
HUMPBACK WHALE (page 69)
RIGHT WHALE (page 75)
SOUTHERN SEA OTTER (page 58)
SEI WHALE (page 76)
SPERM WHALE (page 73)
WOODLAND CARIBOU (page 80)

WYOMING

Wyoming does not maintain a state list of threatened and endangered species. The following federally listed species exist or may exist in Wyoming:

BLACK-FOOTED FERRET (page 9)
GRAY WOLF (page 16)
GRIZZLY BEAR (page 23)

Epilogue

THE GRAY WHALE: ONE THAT CAME BACK

Assignment to the threatened or endangered species list is not forever. The whole point of naming animals to these rosters is to give them the protection they need to prosper and to one day be taken off the list. For the gray whale, that day came in 1993, when its name was officially removed from the inventory of endangered species. It is the first whale to leave the list and the most recent mammal to do so. Species recovery works. Now meet the gray whale *(Eschrichtius robustus)*.

Remember Bonnet and Crossbeak? No? Well, they're the two gray whales that had the considerable misfortune to get trapped in the ice near Point Barrow, Alaska, in the fall of 1988. As the whole world watched, folks from several countries launched a mammoth rescue (called Operation Breakthrough) to return the whales to the open ocean. Chain saws cut holes in the ice. A huge hover barge blasted the frozen surface with compressed air. A skycrane pounded the ice with a five-ton hammer. An Air Force contraption called the Archimedean Screw Tractor cut swaths in the stuff. Schoolchildren sent the whales letters, and every television reporter in the world (or so it seemed) filed a report from the edge of the whales' tiny breathing hole. In the end, it was a pair of Soviet icebreakers that finally sliced a channel to freedom, and on October 28th the gray whales swam free.

In a way, Bonnet (whose name came from the barnacle patch on its head) and Crossbeak (whose mouth wouldn't close) tell the gray whale story in microcosm. While some other leviathans of the deep cling to a tenuous existence, the gray has made real progress. While some whales are almost never seen, the gray actually supports a thriving whale-watching industry on America's West Coast. While authorities scramble to formulate recovery plans for some of its relatives, the gray whale now swims free and officially unendangered.

Like many of its kin, the gray whale suffered much at the hands of humans. Predictable migrations and an attraction for coastlines and shallow waters long ago made the gray a popular quarry for whalers. Native Americans probably killed a few grays for centuries, but it was not until commercial whalers discovered the species' calving and breeding grounds off California and Mexico in the mid-nineteenthth century that gray numbers really began to plummet. Season after season, savvy sea captains roamed the shallow lagoons, killing many pregnant and nursing females. (In hunting other species, whalers sometimes harpooned a calf, not because they wanted it but because the mother would hover nearby and they could kill her, too. Not with gray whales, however. In most cases, whalers took pains to avoid injuring a gray calf, lest the irate mother go on a rampage and destroy their boats.)

Once there were three major populations of these animals. Gray whales in the north Atlantic long ago disappeared into the bowels of whaling ships. The western Pacific grays (around Korea) appear destined for the same fate. And not long ago, the eastern Pacific population along America's West Coast also seemed to be headed for extinction. Thanks, however, to protective agreements signed in the 1930s and 1940s, this third population hung on. In 1970, authorities beefed up gray whale protection by naming the animal to the Endangered Species List. Since then, this whale has staged a steady comeback, and today there are about as many gray whales off the American coast—an estimated 21,000—as before their exploitation began.

The gray is a medium-sized whale, averaging forty feet in length and weighing between sixteen and thirty-five tons. Not surprisingly, it is colored slate gray, with abundant light blotches. Copious patches of barnacles and whale lice (crustaceans an inch or less in length) add to the gray's splotchy appearance. An adult gray whale may actually be toting around several hundred pounds of these parasites. Like the right whale, the gray lacks a dorsal fin but does exhibit an identifying series of bumps—called knuckles—along the spine near the tail.

Aside from its recent prosperity, the gray whale's big claim to fame is its penchant for travel. Annually, these animals migrate ten or twelve thousand miles from northern feeding grounds to wintering waters and back again, which makes them the champion sojourners among mammals. During these voyages, grays average one hundred miles per day, rarely taking time off to feed or sleep. Incredible as it may seem, these huge animals may eat only during the summer months and sleep only in winter waters.

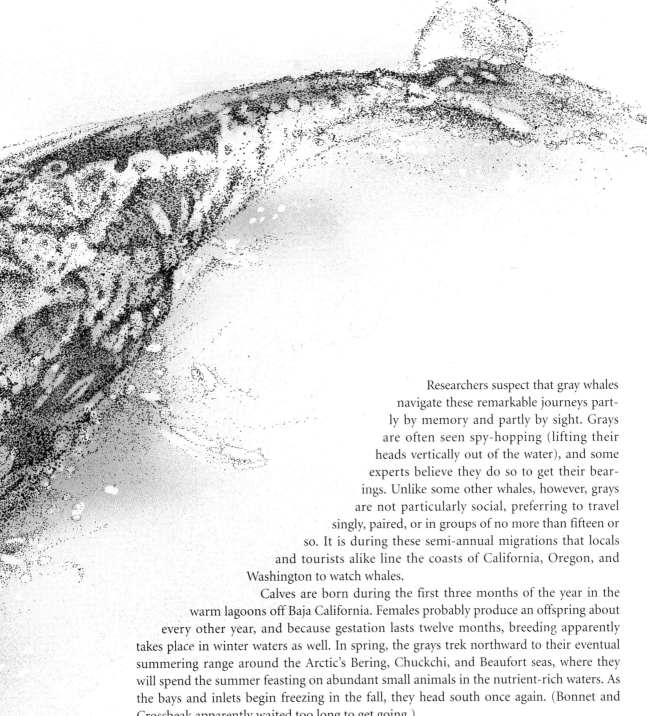

Researchers suspect that gray whales navigate these remarkable journeys partly by memory and partly by sight. Grays are often seen spy-hopping (lifting their heads vertically out of the water), and some experts believe they do so to get their bearings. Unlike some other whales, however, grays are not particularly social, preferring to travel singly, paired, or in groups of no more than fifteen or so. It is during these semi-annual migrations that locals and tourists alike line the coasts of California, Oregon, and Washington to watch whales.

Calves are born during the first three months of the year in the warm lagoons off Baja California. Females probably produce an offspring about every other year, and because gestation lasts twelve months, breeding apparently takes place in winter waters as well. In spring, the grays trek northward to their eventual summering range around the Arctic's Bering, Chuckchi, and Beaufort seas, where they will spend the summer feasting on abundant small animals in the nutrient-rich waters. As the bays and inlets begin freezing in the fall, they head south once again. (Bonnet and Crossbeak apparently waited too long to get going.)

Gray whales are bottom feeders, sucking up huge quantities of food-bearing debris, then spitting out the bad stuff. The good stuff includes mollusks, crustaceans, worms, and a host of other invertebrates. Sometimes, grays feeding in shallow water will surface with detritus still streaming from their mouths, an occasion of great excitement for any hungry sea birds that happen to be nearby. Oddly, most gray whales appear to be right "flippered," choosing to feed by swimming along on the right side rather than in an upright position. Many gray whales exhibit worn baleen plates on the right as well as barnacles scraped from their right sides.

A couple of summers ago, several gray whales made quite an impression on folks around Puget Sound north of Seattle—and on Puget Sound itself. At high tide, the behemoths wallowed in only twelve feet of water, slurping up great quantities of sand from what at low tide became the shoreline. Receding tides revealed shallow pits ten feet across and six inches deep accompanied by mounds of displaced sand. Apparently, the whales were filling their cavernous mouths with sand, straining the material through their baleen plates to extract the numerous ghost shrimp present, then expelling the sand in a heap. Authorities estimated that each mouthful of sand netted a whale eleven pounds of shrimp.

With luck and good management, the gray whale is back to stay. Thousands of visitors to the coasts of Oregon, Washington, and California can count on getting a look at these giants as they ply their trade not far from shore. They are living proof that the road toward extinction is not a one-way street.

CONCLUSION

At the Cincinnati Zoo in Cincinnati, Ohio, there is a sophisticated facility called the Center for Reproduction of Endangered Wildlife. Outside, the building displays a sleek, modern architectural style. Inside, it is a gleaming laboratory full of high-tech equipment and twenty-first-century ideas. CREW, as it is called, has the lofty goal of preserving, through biotechnology, as many endangered species as possible.

The techniques being pioneered here with some of the world's rarest animals come directly from the leading edge of reproductive science: artificial insemination, in vitro fertilization, sperm banks, gene banks, sperm injection, embryo transfer, embryo splitting, cryopreservation, surrogate parenthood, cloning, and others. Their collective purpose is to prevent the extinction of wild creatures through high science. CREW is an ark for endangered species. The work that goes on here is laudable.

And at the same time sad—sad that it must be done at all. So this is what it has come down to. This is the alternative to endangered species protection. Sperm and eggs in a test tube. Embryos bathed in liquid nitrogen instead of growing inside a bestial uterus. How much better to have rare creatures propagating their kind the way nature intended. How much wiser to grant endangered animal species the perpetual right to continued existence. How much greater would our country be with its rich, full wildlife heritage completely intact. How much better it would be if places like CREW were not necessary.

And it can happen. In America, the people still make the choices. If we want protection for our threatened and endangered wild species, all we have to do is say so.

FOR FURTHER READING

America's Neighborhood Bats, by Merlin Tuttle. Austin: University of Texas Press, 1988.

America's Great Cats, by Gary Turbak, Flagstaff, Arizona: Northland Publishing, 1986.

Animals in Peril: A Guide to the Endangered Animals of Canada and the United States, by David Grainger. New York: Pagurian Press, 1978.

The Atlas of Endangered Species, by John Burton. New York: Macmillan, 1991.

California's Wild Heritage, by Peter Steinhart. Sacramento: California Department of Fish and Game, 1990.

Cougar: The American Lion, by Kevin Hansen. Flagstaff, Arizona: Northland Publishing, 1992.

Dolphins, Seals, and Other Sea Mammals, by David Stephen. New York: G. P. Putnam's Sons, 1973.

From the Edge of Extinction: The Fight to Save Endangered Species, by Darryl Stewart. New York: Methuen, 1978.

Gray Wolf, Red Wolf, by Dorothy Hinshaw Patent. New York: Clarion Books, 1990.

The Grizzly Bear, by Thomas McNamee. New York: Knopf, 1984.

Grizzly Years: In Search of the American Wilderness, by Doug Peacock. New York: H. Holt, 1990.

Grzimek's Encyclopedia of Mammals, by Bernhard Grzimek. New York: McGraw-Hill, 1990.

In the Path of the Grizzly, by Alan Carey. Flagstaff, Arizona: Northland Publishing, 1986.

Little Mammals of the Pacific Northwest, by Ellen Kritzman. Seattle: Pacific Search Press, 1977.

Mammals of Arizona, by Donald Hoffmeister. Tucson, Arizona: University of Arizona Press, 1986.

Mammals of the Northern Great Plains, by J. Knox Jones. Lincoln, Nebraska: University of Nebraska Press, 1983.

Manatees and Dugongs, by John Reynolds. New York: Facts on File, 1991.

North American Mammals: Fur-Bearing Animals of the United States and Canada, by Roger Caras. New York: Galahad Books, 1974.

Of Wolves and Men, by Barry Lopez. New York: Scribner, 1978.

The Official World Wildlife Fund Guide to Endangered Species of North America. Washington: Beacham Publishers, 1990.

Seals of the World, by Judith King. Ithaca, New York: British Museum of Natural History, Comstock Publishing Associates, 1983.

The Sierra Club Handbook of Whales and Dolphins, by Stephen Leatherwood et al. San Francisco: Sierra Club Books, 1983.

Continued ➤

Twilight Hunters: Wolves, Coyotes, and Foxes, by Gary Turbak. Flagstaff, Arizona: Northland Publishing, 1987.

Vanishing Wildlife, by Roger Caras. Richmond: Westover Publishing, 1970.

Walker's Mammals of the World, by Ron Nowak. Baltimore: Johns Hopkins University Press, 1991.

The Way of the Wolf, by David Mech. Stillwater, Minnesota: Voyageur Press, 1991.

Wildlife in Peril: The Threatened and Endangered Mammals of Colorado, by John Murray. Niwot, Colorado: Roberts Rinehart, 1987.

The World's Whales: The Complete Illustrated Guide, by Stanley Minasian et al. Washington: Smithsonian Books, 1984.

INDEX

Abalone, 59
Alabama, 5
Alaska, 20, 22, 58, 61, 69, 95
Aleutian Islands, 61, 76
Alligator River National Wildlife Refuge, 46
Amargosa vole, 1-2
Ammospermophilus nelsoni, 96
Antelope, 63. *See also* Chihuahuan pronghorn, Sonoran
    pronghorn
Antilocapra americana mexicana, 87
Antilocapra americana sonoriensis, 55-57
Aplodontia rufa nigra, 43-44
Arctocephalus townsendi, 25-26
Argentina, 41
Arizona shrew, 117
Arizona, 7, 22, 27, 28, 36, 56, 137, 141
    species listed as threatened or endangered,
      85-93
Arkansas, 6
Atlantic spotted dolphin, 146
Auks, vii

Badgers, 65
Baja California, 25, 69, 79, 98, 153
Balaena glacialis, 75-76
Balaenoptera borealis, 76-77
Balaenoptera musculus, 78-79
Balaenoptera physalus, 77-78
Bats. *See also* Eastern big-eared bat, Gray bat,
    Indiana bat, Lesser long-nosed bat, Mexican
    long-nosed bat, Mexican long-tongued bat,
    Ozark big-eared bat, Southern yellow bat,
    Spotted bat
      echolocation, 3-4
      hibernation, 4
      and human intrusion into caves, 4-5
      insectivores, 4
      reproduction, 4
Bears. *See* Black bear, Grizzly bear, Louisiana
    black bear
Beavers. *See* Point Arena mountain beaver
Bering, Vitus, 58, 61
Bering Strait, 102
Bighorn sheep. *See* California bighorn sheep,
    Desert bighorn sheep, Peninsular bighorn sheep
Bison, 16, 17, 55, 63
Black bear, 126, 134, 143. *See also* Louisiana black bear
Black-footed ferret
      breeding cycle, 9-11
      coloring and markings, 9
      decline of, 11
      and prairie dogs, 9, 65
      preservation efforts, 9, 12-13
      reintroduction to wild, 9
Black-tailed prairie dog, 85-86
Blue whale, 78-79
Bobcats, 65, 101

Bonnet and Crossbeak, 151
Brachylagus idahoensis, 149-150
British Columbia, 43

Cabeza Prieta National Wildlife Refuge, 56
California bighorn sheep, 97
California, 1, 22, 25, 30, 31, 32, 43, 49-50, 51,
    52, 58, 67, 76, 79, 149, 153
      species listed as threatened or endangered, 94-98
Canada, 20, 22, 95
Canines. *See* Coyotes, Foxes, Wolves
Canis lupus, 16-21
Canis lupus baileyi, 142
Canis rufus, 45-47
Cape Romain National Wildlife Refuge, 46
Caribou. *See also* Woodland caribou
    types, 80
Cartier, Jacques, vii
Cats. *See* Bobcat, Cougar, Jaguar, Jaguarundi,
    Lynx, Margay, Ocelot, Yuma puma
Center for Reproduction of Endangered Wildlife, 154
Central America, 29, 42, 139-140
Cetaceans. *See* Whales
Chihuahuan pronghorn, 87. *See also* Sonoran
    pronghorn
Chipmunks. *See* Colorado chipmunk, Least chipmunk
Choeronycteris mexicana, 88
Cincinnati (Ohio) Zoo, 154
Clams, 59
Coatimundi, 141
Collins, Judy, 72
Colorado, 22, 95
      species listed as threatened or endangered,
      101-103
Colorado chipmunk, 118
Colorado River, 92
Columbia River, 14, 15, 149
Columbian ground squirrel, 106
Columbian white-tailed deer, 14-15
Conservation ethic
    origins, vii-viii
Coue's rice rat, 142
Cougar, 131-133. *See also* Mountain lion, Yuma
    puma
Coyotes, 45, 46, 47, 52, 54, 57, 65
Crabs, 59
CREW. *See* Center for Reproduction of
    Endangered Wildlife
Crossbeak. *See* Bonnet and Crossbeak
Cryptotis parva, 119-120
Cynomys parvidens, 63-66

Deer. *See* Columbian white-tailed deer
Delayed implantation, 24, 105-106
Desert bighorn sheep, 115-116
Dipodomys elator, 142-143
Dogs. *See also* Canines
    and cougars, 133

Dolphins, 67. *See also* Atlantic spotted dolphin,
        Killer whale, Rough-toothed dolphin
Duck Stamp Act, viii
Dwarf sperm whale, 144

Eagles, 57, 65
Eastern big-eared bat, 138
Eastern spotted skunk, 108-110
Echolocation
        bats, 3-4
        whales, 68
Elk, 63
Endangered species
        reasons for preserving, ix-x
Endangered Species Act, viii-ix
Enhydra lutris nereis, 58-60
Euderma maculatum, 119, 143
Eumetopias jubatus, 61-62
Eutamias minimus atristriatus, 120-121
Eutamias quadrivittatus australis, 118
Extinction of species, vii, x-xi

False killer whale, 147-148
Felines. *See* Cats
Felis concolor, 126, 131-133
Felis concolor browni, 92-93
Felis lynx, 101-102
Felis onca, 93, 136-137
Felis pardalis, 40-42
Felis wiedii, 139-141
Felis yagouaroundi, 28-29
Feresa attenuata, 148
Ferrets. *See* Black-footed ferret
Fin whale, 77-78
Finback whale. *See* Fin whale
Fish and Wildlife Service. *See* U.S. Fish and
        Wildlife Service
Fisher, 126
        breeding cycle, 105-106
        in Idaho, 106
        name history, 104
        and porcupines, 105
        range, 104
Fishing industry
    and sea otters, 59
Florida, 139
Foxes. *See* Island fox, Kit fox, Northern swift fox,
        San Joaquin kit fox, Sierra Nevada red fox,
        Swift fox
            nomenclature of, 124
Fresno kangaroo rat, 32

Gervais' beaked whale, 145
Giant kangaroo rat, 32
Globicephala macrorhynchus, 145
Goose-beaked whale, 145
Gophers. *See* Southern pocket gopher
Gray bat, 5
Gray whales, 147, 151-154
Gray wolf, 16-21. *See also* Mexican gray wolf
Great Smoky Mountains National Park, 46
Grizzly bear, 22-24
Guadalupe fur seal, 25-26
Gulo gulo, 94-96

Hares, 101. *See also* Rabbits
Hawks, 65
Hore, Robert, vii
Hornocker, Maurice, 133
Hualapai Mexican vole, 27
Humpback whale, 69-73

Iceland, 69
Idaho ground squirrel, 106-107
Idaho, 20, 22, 80, 82, 95, 149
            species listed as threatened or endangered,
            104-107
Illinois, 45
Indiana, 6
Indiana bat, 6
International Whaling Commission, 68-69, 72, 76
Island fox, 98

Jaguar, 93, 136-137
Jaguarundi, 28-29
Japan, 58, 68, 69, 77

Kangaroo rats. *See also* Fresno kangaroo rat, Giant
            kangaroo rat, Morro Bay kangaroo rat, New
            Mexican banner-tailed kangaroo rat, Stephens'
            kangaroo rat, Texas kangaroo rat, Tipton kangaroo rat
            ability to live without free water, 31
            burrows, 30-31
            protective physical characteristics, 30
Kansas, 6
        species listed as threatened or endangered,
        108-110
Kentucky, 6
Killer whale, 72, 146-147. *See also* False killer
        whale, Pygmy killer whale
Kit fox, 128-129. *See also* San Joaquin kit fox
Kogia breviceps, 144
Kogia simus, 144
Korea, 77

Lacey Act, viii
Lasiurus ega, 143
Least chipmunk, 120-121
Least shrew, 119-120
Leopold, Aldo, viii, xi
Leptonycteris curasoae yerbabuenae, 7-8
Leptonycteris nivalis, 8
Lepus callotis, 117-118
Lesser long-nosed bat, 7-8
Lewis and Clark, 14, 63
Livestock predation
        by cougars, 133
        by grizzly bears, 23
        by pumas, 93
        by wolves, 17, 47, 88-89
Louisiana, 33, 46
Louisiana black bear, 33-34
Lujan, Manuel, 36
Lutra canadensis, 102, 111-112, 127
Lutra canadensis lataxina, 90
Lutra canadensis sonora, 90
Lynx, 101-102

Manatee, 138-139
Margay, 139-141
Marine mammals. *See* Dolphins, Manatee, Whales
Martens. *See* Pine marten
Martes americana, 122
Martes pennanti, 104-106, 126
Meadow jumping mouse, 87, 123
Meadow mice. *See* Voles
Megaptera novaeangliae, 69-73
Melville, Herman, 73
Mesoplodon europaeus, 145
Mexican gray wolf, 88-89
Mexican long-nosed bat, 8
Mexican long-tongued bat, 88
Mexican wolf, 142. *See also* Mexican gray wolf
Mexico, 7, 8, 25, 26 29, 64, 88, 137, 141
Mice. *See* Meadow jumping mouse, Palo duro
    mouse, Salt marsh harvest mouse
Michigan, 20
Microtus californicus scirpensis, 1-2
Microtus mexicanus hualpaiensis, 27
Microtus mexicanus navaho, 89
Microtus montanus arizonensis, 121
Minke whales, 147
Minnesota, 20, 33, 95
Mississippi, 33
Missouri, 6
Missouri River, 125
Mohave ground squirrel, 97
Montana, 13, 20, 22, 23, 95, 110, 149
Montane vole, 121
Morro Bay kangaroo rat, 32
Mount Graham red squirrel, 36-39
Mountain lion, 126. *See also* Cougar, Yuma puma
Mountain sheep. *See* California bighorn sheep,
    Desert bighorn sheep, Peninsular bighorn sheep
Mt. Graham red squirrel *See* Mount Graham red squirrel
Mussels, 59
Mustela nigripes, 9-13
Myotis grisescens, 5
Myotis sodalis, 6

Nasua nasua, 141
National Marine Fisheries Service, viii
Navajo Mexican vole, 89
Nebraska
    species listed as threatened or endangered,
        111-114
Nevada, 114, 149
New Mexican banner-tailed kangaroo rat, 90
New Mexico, 7, 88, 141
    species listed as threatened or endangered,
        115-123
North Carolina, 46
North Dakota
    species listed as threatened or endangered,
        124-127
Northern swift fox, 124-125
Norway, 69
Nycteris ega, 120

Ocelot, 40-42
Odocoileus virginianus leucurus, 14-15

Oklahoma, 6, 127, 143
Orcinus orca, 146-147
Oregon, 14, 15, 22, 43, 67, 76, 79, 95, 149, 153
    species listed as threatened or endangered,
        128-130
Organ Pipe Cactus National Monument, 56
Oryzomys couesi, 142
Otters. *See* River otter, Southern sea otter, Southwestern
    river otter
Ovis canadensis californiana, 97
Ovis canadensis cremnobates, 98
Ozark big-eared bat, 6-7

Palo duro mouse, 139
Peninsular bighorn sheep, 98
Pennsylvania, 45
Peromyscus truei comanche, 139
Phoenix (Arizona) Zoo, 57
Physeter catodon, 73-75
Pine marten, 122
Pioneers
    and prairie dogs, 11
    and predators, 11
Pittman-Robertson Act, viii
Plecotus rafinesquii, 138
Plecotus townsendii ingens, 6-7
Point Arena mountain beaver, 43-44
Point Defiance Zoo (Tacoma, Washington), 46
Porpoises, 67
Prairie dogs, 9, 11. *See also* Black-tailed prairie dog,
    Utah prairie dog
        and bison, 63
        and black-footed ferrets, 9, 65
        relocation of, 64
Pronghorns. *See* Chihuahuan pronghorn, Sonoran
    pronghorn
Pseudorca crassidens, 147-148
Pt. Arena mountain beaver *See* Point Arena mountain beaver
Puma. *See* Yuma puma
Pygmy rabbit, 149-150
Pygmy sperm whale, 144

Rabbits. *See* Pygmy rabbit, White-sided jackrabbit.
    See also Hares
Race, xi
Rats. *See* Coue's rice rat. *See also* Kangaroo rats
Razorback whale. *See* Fin whale
Red wolf, 45-47
Reithrodontomys raviventris, 49-51
Right whale, 75-76
Rio Grande River, 138
River otter, 102, 111-112, 127, 135
Rodents, 1-2. *See also* Chipmunks, Gophers, Hares,
    Kangaroo rats, Mice, Prairie dogs, Rabbits, Rats,
    Shrews, Squirrels, Voles
Rough-toothed dolphin, 146
Russia, 58

Salt marsh harvest mouse, 49-51
San Diego (California) Zoo, 25
San Joaquin antelope squirrel, 96
San Joaquin kit fox, 52-54
San Nicholas Island, California, 98
Sea cows. *See* Manatee

Seals and sea lions. *See* Guadalupe fur seal, Steller sea lion
Sei whale, 76-77
Selkirk Mountains, 80
Seton, Ernest Thompson, 63, 94
Sharks, 72, 147
Sheep. *See* California bighorn sheep, Desert bighorn sheep, Peninsular bighorn sheep
Short-finned pilot whale, 145
Shrews. *See* Arizona shrew, Least shrew, Water shrew
Sierra Nevada red fox, 96-97
Skunks. *See also* Eastern spotted skunk, Striped Skunk
Snail darter, viii-ix
Sonoran pronghorn, 55-57. *See also* Chihuahuan pronghorn
Sorex arizonae, 117
Sorex palustris, 91
South America, 29, 42, 139-140
South Carolina, 46
South Dakota, 11, 13
    species listed as threatened or endangered, 131-135
Southern flying squirrel, 113-114
Southern pocket gopher, 122-123
Southern sea otter, 58-60
Southern states, 45
Southern yellow bat, 120, 143
Southwestern river otter, 90
Soviet Union, 68, 69
Sperm whale, 73-75. *See also* Dwarf sperm whale, Pygmy sperm whale
Spermophilus brunneus, 106-107
Spermophilus mohavensis, 97
Spilogale putorius interrupta, 108-110
Spotted bat, 119, 143
Squirrels. *See* Idaho ground squirrel, Mohave ground squirrel, Mount Graham red squirrel, San Joaquin antelope squirrel, Southern flying squirrel
Steller, George Wilhelm, 61
Steller sea lion, 61-62
Stenella plagiodon, 146
Steno bredanensis, 146
Stephens' kangaroo rat, 31
Subspecies, xi
Swift fox, 113; 135. *See also* Northern swift fox

Tamiasciurus hudsonicus grahamensis, 36-39
Tellico Dam (Tennessee), viii-ix
Tennessee, viii-ix, 46
Texas kangaroo rat, 142-143
Texas, 8, 22, 28, 29, 33, 41, 42, 45, 46, 88
    species listed as threatened or endangered, 136-148
Thomomys umbrinus, 122-123
Timber wolf. *See* Gray wolf
Tipton kangaroo rat, 32
Trichechus manatus, 138-139

U.S. Fish and Wildlife Service, viii, 12, 47, 88
Ursus americanus, 126, 134, 143
Ursus americanus luteolus, 33
Ursus arctos horribilis, 22-24
Utah, 148, 149
Utah prairie dog, 63-66

Voles. *See* Amargosa vole, Hualapai Mexican vole, Montane vole, Navajo Mexican vole
Vulpes macrotis mutica, 52-54
Vulpes velox hebes, 113
Vulpes vulpes necator, 96-97

Washington, 14, 15, 22, 43, 46, 67, 76, 79, 80, 82, 95, 153
    species listed as threatened or endangered, 149-150
Water shrew, 91
Weasels. *See* Black-footed ferret, Fisher, Pine marten
Whales, 67-69. *See also* Blue whale, Dwarf sperm whale, False killer whale, Fin whale, Gervais' beaked whale, Goose-beaked whale, Gray whales, Humpback whale, Killer whale, Minke whales, Pygmy killer whale, Pygmy sperm whale, Right whale, Sei whale, Short-finned pilot whale, Sperm whale
    baleen, 67
    calorie intake, 68
    clicking of sperms, 73-75
    echolocation, 68
    evolution into sea creatures, 67
    sense of hearing, 68
    singing of humpbacks, 72-73
    spy hopping, 147, 153
    and whaling industry, 68-69, 73-74, 75, 77
White Mountains, 89
White Sands Missile Range, 89
White-sided jackrabbit, 117-118
Wildcats. *See* Bobcat, Cougar, Jaguar, Jaguarundi, Lynx, Ocelot, Yuma puma
Wildlife management, viii
Wisconsin, 20, 95
Wolverine, 103, 107, 130
    carrion eater, 95
    predator, 94-95
    reputation of, 94
    wandering behavior, 95
Wolves, 52. *See also* Gray wolf, Mexican gray wolf, Red wolf
    alpha males, 16
    areas of strong population, 20
    breeding cycle, 16-17
    fear and eradication of, 17-18, 45, 88-89
    mating, 16
    return and reintroduction of, 20-21, 46
Woodland caribou, 80-82
Wyoming, 22, 95, 150
    ferrets in, 9, 12, 13

Yellowstone National Park, 20, 21
Yew trees, x
Yuma puma, 92-93

Zapus hudsonius, 87
Ziphius cavirostris, 145

ABOUT THE AUTHOR

GARY TURBAK, a native of South Dakota, is a full-time freelance writer whose work has appeared in *Equinox, Reader's Digest, Field and Stream, National and International Wildlife, Writer's Digest, Wildlife Conservation,* and many other widely circulated periodicals. This is his fifth non-fiction book. He is a Vietnam veteran, a cat lover, a former teacher, a professional photographer, and a lifelong student of wildlife. Gary and his wife live in Missoula, Montana.

ABOUT THE ILLUSTRATOR

LAWRENCE ORMSBY studied art at the Colorado Institute of Art in Denver. His drawings have appeared in books, posters, limited edition prints, and trail guides for more than twenty-five national parks; have received numerous awards; and have appeared in *Arizona Highways,* Edward Abbey's *Desert Solitaire,* the non-fiction books *Pueblo Birds & Myths* and *RavenSong,* and exhibits at the Smithsonian Institution.

Be on the watch for Northland Publishing's

ANIMALS IN DANGER
A NATURAL HISTORY SERIES FOR CHILDREN

by Gary Turbak, illustrated by Lawrence Ormsby

A terrific way to introduce six- to nine-year-olds to the concept of endangerment, with each book centering on one habitat and ten of the animals that inhabit it. Call **1-800-346-3257** for more information.